THE
SEEKER'S GUIDE
TO
THE SECRET TEACHINGS
OF ALL AGES

THE
SEEKER'S GUIDE
TO
THE SECRET TEACHINGS
OF ALL AGES

THE AUTHORIZED COMPANION TO
MANLY P. HALL'S ESOTERIC LANDMARK

MITCH HOROWITZ

BESTSELLING AUTHOR OF *OCCULT AMERICA*

MEDIA

Published 2020 by Gildan Media LLC
aka G&D Media
www.GandDmedia.com

First Edition: 2020

Cover design by Tom McKeveny

Interior design by Meghan Day Healey of Story Horse, LLC.

Library of Congress Cataloging-in-Publication Data is available
upon request

ISBN: 978-1-7225-0318-5

10   9   8   7   6   5   4   3   2   1

CONTENTS

___ ❦ ___

PREFACE

──── ୭ ୧ ────

BY GREG SALYER, PH.D.,

President/CEO, Philosophical Research Society

A mong the many joys I have in serving as president of the Philosophical Research Society (PRS) is watching Manly P. Hall's foundational work, *The Secret Teachings of All Ages*, fly off of our shelves in our bookstore and warehouse. It is a beautiful and daunting book, and I frequently think of a young Manly Hall in his mid-twenties composing this book in the mid-1920s for publication before the end of the person's and the century's third decade.

What an amazing time it was in Los Angeles and the world. People living in the 1920s were only a few years past the First World War and from their own influenza pandemic. World War I was responsible for the deaths of twenty-million people; the 1918 H1N1 virus killed fifty million people worldwide. White supremacy spit forth its venom thanks in part to D.W. Griffith's *Birth of a Nation*, which prompted a rebirth of the Ku Klux Klan, and by the mid-1920s, the KKK boasted a membership of millions. Women were granted the right to vote, while serving alcohol was prohibited through the Volstead Act, which produced an unprecedented wave of lawlessness and the birth of organized crime. The world and the nation were churning.

Los Angeles in the 1920s also saw the birth of the film industry, and Mr. Hall befriended many of its stars through the years including Boris Karloff, Bela Lugosi, and Burl Ives, among others. Manly also appeared in his own film, the astrologically themed thriller, *When Were You Born*? The city itself doubled in size in the decade of *The Secret Teachings of All Ages*, which no doubt increased Hall's readership, though the book was shipped all over the world.

Along with Hollywood's booming industry, there was oil and railroad money in Southern California. Some of that money may have supported Mr. Hall in the founding of PRS, including his travels and publications, through the munificence of Carolyn Lloyd and her daughter Alma Estelle. More important, perhaps, was that Southern California was emerging as a new Eden, a "west of the west." Crass boosterism, the folklore of therapeutic climatology, and creative mythology caused a great migration to the area for those looking for new beginnings, healing, and wealth.

Carey McWilliams, the venerable historian of Southern California, argues that once these migrants arrived in a region that promised renewed health but had no medical infrastructure, they began seeking alternative methods of well-being. Put another way, Los Angeles was, for a number of reasons, becoming *a city of seekers*. Hall himself, in a 1932 lecture titled "The Horoscope of Los Angeles," proclaimed: "Los Angeles is the greenhouse of America. It is a place of experimentation in which we are combining facts and producing new species. . . . It is primarily fitted to be the greatest cultural center of the world. A city that is sacred in being a nucleus where the finer principles of life can come into expression."

It was into this rich and evocative environment that a young Manly Palmer Hall introduced "the big book," *The Secret Teachings of All Ages*. It was never meant to be an easy book, as the original title expresses: "An Encyclopedic Outline of Masonic, Hermetic, Qabbalistic and Rosicrucian Symbolical Philosophy." In its original dimensions, it is not even easy to hold in one's hands—large, heavy, and laden with wisdom. It is unquestionably a foundational and remarkable text, a wellspring of esoteric knowledge wedded to practical insights for living.

Now, nearly one hundred years later, we are thrilled to have PRS lecturer-in-residence Mitch Horowitz lead readers through Hall's signature work. The big book put Mitch on his path as an esoteric seeker, author, and speaker, and it is fitting that he would write this companion text. *The Seeker's Guide* is no line-by-line interpretation of *The Secret Teachings of All Ages*. After all, Hall's work is not a Bible that produces exponentially more text about it; rather, it is an encyclopedic reference work for those who seek wisdom that is not usually found in the standard venues, such as university curricula and mainstream publishing. *The Seeker's Guide to the Secret Teachings of All Ages* is a dialogue with the big book's history and significance as "practical and profound wisdom for the twenty-first century." May it guide you through our current struggles and your own search for meaning.

INTRODUCTION

———— ๑ ๑ ————

The Secret Teachings and You

Welcome to a twelve-chapter guidebook to *The Secret Teachings of All Ages*. It is a special privilege to join you in embarking on this new exploration of Manly P. Hall's "Great Book." For us at the Philosophical Research Society (PRS), the learning center founded by Hall in 1934, this practical guide represents a new chapter in the long and still-developing life of Hall's extraordinary work.

Readers can sometimes feel lost before the vastness of Manly P. Hall's legendary compendium. In response, this guidebook introduces, surveys, and expands upon the core subjects in Manly's unparalleled and now hugely popular opus of esoteric, occult, and symbolic philosophy. My hope is that this companion volume helps you encounter *The Secret Teach-*

ings of All Ages in a wholly new and revealing way. The *Seeker's Guide* accessibly explores Manly's historical analyses and philosophical ideas, and also considers recent developments in the fields that Manly studied and the insights he presaged. For both first-time students and longtime readers, *The Seeker's Guide to The Secret Teachings of All Ages* provides fresh inroads into the esoteric splendor of Manly's work.

The Secret Teachings of All Ages is one of the most significant esoteric wisdom books of modern life. In 1928, Manly P. Hall originally published his book in a sumptuous, table-sized edition. In 2003, PRS and I reissued a popular "reader's edition" as an adjunct to facilitate a readier, more accessible reading experience. As I am writing these words in 2020, *The Secret Teachings of All Ages* has sold well over one million copies in aggregate in various editions. As such, it has proven one of the most popular "underground" books in history—so much so that it is now emerging aboveground—and it holds legendary status among its generations of students. We hope that this *Seeker's Guide* itself proves a worthy stage in the work's still-developing history.

The first chapter of the *Seeker's Guide* began as a 2019 lecture I delivered in the auditorium of PRS. It explores some of the circumstances that allowed Manly Hall, as a 27-year-old author and seeker, to complete his epic work in 1928. I try to get to the heart of some of the historical and biographical aspects of Manly's life, and some of the building blocks that contributed to his wonderful, perennial achievement. The ensuing eleven chapters are oriented toward elucidating the core subjects that populate *The Secret Teachings of All Ages*, and highlighting how they relate to our lives and search today. Each of these chapters began as lectures that I delivered in 2019 in the library of PRS, steps away from the office that Manly P. Hall occupied until his death in 1990.* Here is a summary of what you will be encountering:

I. Discovering *The Secret Teachings of All Ages*
How did a 27-year-old independent scholar with little formal education come to write the most significant codex of mythical, symbolic, and occult philosophies of the modern era? We explore the life and background of Manly P. Hall, the extraordinary breadth and significance of his Great Book, and the teacher's career beyond it.

II. The Meaning of Philosophy
Manly P. Hall believed that philosophy must be a living and relevant guide to life. In this section, we survey his view of figures ranging from Plato to Francis Bacon, and his perspective on the ideals of the Ancient Egyptians, Vedic scholars, Zoroastrian mystics, the Jewish,

---

* Special thanks go to Devon Deimler, Ph.D., a scholar of spirituality whose impeccable transcriptions facilitated the adaptation of this series into a book.

Muslim, and Christian masters, and the clandestine thought movements of Rosicrucianism, Illuminism, and Freemasonry, among others. To Hall, the inner meaning and authentic purpose of philosophy is self-refinement. This section provides a broad overview of his perspective.

III. Ancient Egypt and the Question of Primeval Civilizations

The section explores Manly P. Hall's esoteric interpretation of the Great Pyramid and his theories about the existence and meaning of Atlantis and other lost or mythical civilizations. Virtually every culture, from Mayan to Hebraic to Vedic, has a central flood myth—these will be explored for both parabolic meaning and as alternate history, including contemporary theories that would predate the Great Sphinx at Giza.

IV. Science of the Stars

In this section we explore the joint development of astrology and astronomy in Persia, Babylon, Egypt, and the Hellenic world, as well as the cosmically aligned monoliths and calendar systems of the ancient Mayan, Celtic, and Vedic cultures. Special attention is paid to the earliest developments of astrology; how the field branched off into Hellenic and modern Western astrology, and how Western (tropical) and Eastern (sidereal) forms of astrology developed along differing tracks and coexist today.

V. The Hermetic World

Manly P. Hall placed special emphasis on the ancient Greek-Egyptian thought movement called Hermeticism. This esoteric philosophy, which grew from an amalgam of Egypt's mystery traditions, alchemy, and Neo-Platonism, is an invaluable retention of primeval spirituality. It gave birth to the occult revival of the Renaissance, and continues to reverberate in our world. This section surveys the history, retentions, and practical meaning of Hermeticism.

VI. Hellenic Mysteries

Inheritor of the mystery traditions of Egypt, the Hellenic world codified vast amounts of esoteric philosophy and symbolism. This section considers the mathematics of Pythagoras and the meaning of the sacred numerals (e.g., the number 10), shapes (e.g., the triangle), symbols (e.g., the pentagram), and musical theories (e.g., the music of the spheres) that the primeval philosopher introduced to Western life. We also explore the Oracle at Delphi, which Manly P. Hall described in a manner once dismissed by mainstream academia and later validated by contemporary archeological findings.

VII. The Role of Secret Societies

Manly P. Hall theorized that secret fraternities—especially Freemasonry and the thought movement called Rosicrucianism—vouchsafed esoteric and symbolic teachings. In Hall's view, this secrecy served both to protect such teachings from inquisitors and the profane, and to allow their dissemination at propitious moments in history. In Hall's historicism, clandestine brotherhoods represent a hidden thought school extending back to the Pharaonic Age.

VIII. The Secret History of America

Pursuant to the previous section, Manly P. Hall believed that America itself was a product of ideals and principles closely held by secret societies, which sought to imbue the new republic with principles of liberty, religious toleration, and protection of the individual search for meaning. In this section we survey where Hall's ideas converge with and depart from mainstream historicism, and what truths—both parabolic and factual—they contain. We also consider how outsider spiritual movements and reformist politics traditionally intersect and build on one another.

IX. Mysterious Beasts and Natural Wonders

Fairies, wood sprites, dragons, mermaids, man-bats, and "conventional gnomes"—fantastical creatures and mythical monsters also make an appearance in *The Secret Teachings of All Ages*. In this lively and adventurous section we consider ancient (and not-so-ancient) humanity's fascination with the odd, outlandish, and anomalous—and ask whether, just maybe, they knew something we don't (or don't yet).

Special attention is paid to the allegorical meanings of chimerical beasts.

X. Mystic Christianity

Christianity itself harbors profound and multi-layered sub-meanings, symbolism, and mystical traditions. In this section we explore Manly P. Hall's analysis of the message of Christ; the mysteries and legends of Christendom, including the Arthurian tales, the Holy Grail, and alchemical symbolism; and the meaning and endurance of Gnostic Christianity. We look, too, at saint veneration and various modern mystical expressions of Christianity.

XI. Kabbalah and the Hebrew Masters

In this section we examine the myriad strands of Kabbalistic philosophy, including those that reflect recognized Jewish tradition and those that branch off into broader occult dimensions. We explore the world of the ancient Hebrews and how it informed their religious and ethical codes. We consider key tenets of Kabbalah and how esoteric seekers and movements, both ancient and modern, adopt the tradition.

XII. The Tarot and Magick

It is not always easy—or accurate—to draw ready connections between ancient and modern esoteric practices. In this final section, we consider the authentic connections and divergences between antique and modern occultism. We attempt to demarcate where tradition ends and modern innovation begins, noting that the modern is a meaningful expression of its own. Particular attention is paid to Tarot and its archetypal images, as well as ceremonial magick and its attachments to the ancient past.

My deepest wish is that these twelve chapters give you a fuller, richer picture of some of the themes, ideas, and analyses that weave in and out of Manly's encyclopedia arcana. The book is rounded out with two appendices in which I explore the making of the 2003 "reader's edition" and provide a brief biography of the author.

The Secret Teachings of All Ages is more than a great codex of esoteric wisdom, although that would be sufficient to justify its reputation. It is also a book that can alter the lives of those who encounter it. It certainly did mine, as I note in the first chapter. Hence, I feel that this learning program represents a great adventure for us both. It is not only about the accumulation of knowledge—but also about the accumulation of experience of *oneself*. And, very possibly, an altered and expanded self-conception.

—Mitch Horowitz
New York City
Summer 2020

Discovering *The Secret Teachings of All Ages*

I feel personally moved by everything that's happening around the work of Manly P. Hall today, because when Manly died in 1990, he was very concerned in the closing years of his life that his work would be overlooked, that it would be forgotten, and that it might end up sitting in massive storage lockers somewhere. He was unsure about the physical future of his Los Angeles campus, the Philosophical Research Society (PRS). He felt uneasy about the question of whether his work and his lectures would be embraced in the dawning digital age, which he witnessed the opening embers of in the closing years of his life.

Yet I think it can be said without any hyperbole that there are probably more people reading Manly P. Hall's work today, in the opening decades of the twenty-first century, than did over the course of his entire life. He has not been forgotten. And thanks to efforts like the digitization of his library catalogue, republications of his work, and efforts like this guidebook, a new generation—in a very measurable sense—is coming to Manly P. Hall's work. This is an extraordinary tribute to the man and I wish so deeply that he were here to see it. In any case, this posterity opens a fitting *second chapter* to the life of someone who dedicated himself to cataloging and documenting mystical, occult, and eso-teric wisdom. And his achievement is being embraced in a new range of ways across our culture today and around the world.

Personally, I would not have found my own way as a writer, speaker, and historian of alternative spir-ituality if it weren't for Manly. I never knew him, but I have a tendency—as I'm sure many of you reading this do—to enter into a person's body of work, to enter someone's teachings, initially based on his or her per-sona. I grow very attached to individuals and figures, and if I find something constructively magnetic and encouraging about that person's presence and life, then I tend to find my way very deeply into their work. And I fell *all* the way into Manly's work.

It started in New York City, about twenty-five years before this writing. I was at lunch with a couple of friends, one of whom was named Pythia. That was an initiate name she received from the twentieth century Sufi teacher Pir Vilayat Inayat Khan (1916–2004). And

Pythia, I later learned, was the same name given to the great oracle of Delphi in Hellenic antiquity. I later looked up this name in *The Secret Teachings of All Ages* to find its etymology. Manly wrote: "The name Pythoness, or Pythia, given to the female hierophant of the oracle, means literally one who has been thrown into a religious frenzy by inhaling fumes rising from decomposing matter."

As I sat with these two friends, I asked, "Who should I be reading in the occult and the esoteric? Who should I be reading to further my studies?" I remember the response as though it was moments ago. Pythia sat across the table from me and she said, "Manly P. Hall," lingering over every syllable. I immediately wanted to know who *was* behind this stately name, a name that didn't even sound like it belonged to the twentieth century. Who was this man?

After lunch, I immediately went online and got a copy of a hardback edition of *The Secret Teachings of All Ages*. And I just *fell* completely into it. I stayed up through the night reading it. I studied every minutely rendered caption, chart, and arcane diagram. I was overwhelmed with the experience. And it filled me with a kind of joy. Finding the book was, in a way, like finding myself.

But I also realized that the size and expense of the book, as well as the jarring and complex nature of how it was laid out, could serve as a deterrent to some readers. I was concerned that, after all these years, it was a book that people *owned* but were not necessarily reading.

So, as I was then working in publishing, I mapped out the idea of taking the full, unabridged text and turning it into a "reader's edition," which could be held in the hand and read like any traditional book. I brought this idea to Obadiah Harris, the president of PRS at the time and the man who took over operations and restored them to financial health after Hall's death. Obadiah and I spoke in Manly's office for about forty-five minutes, and he gave me his complete blessing to take this wonderful, massive work—which had existed unchanged since 1928—and reprocess it into the size and dimensions and layout of a traditional trade paperback.* This was done not to *replace* the original, which nothing can do, but to better facilitate the reading experience. And what people discovered, and what I discovered, is that when you have the text of this book laid out in front of you—a book that can seem so intimidating and even impenetrable in its magisterial original edition, so that you're not even sure where to enter—it turns out, in fact, to be an immensely readable and accessible work. Once you get into the flow of it, the text of *The Secret Teachings of All Ages* goes down rather easily and even infectiously.

---

* I tell the full story behind the making of this 2003 edition in Appendix A: "Bringing the 'Secret Teachings' Into the Twenty-First Century."

I often encourage people to take an undaunted approach to works of esoteric or occult wisdom, works that too often develop a reputation for being "unreadable." Some people say that Madame H.P. Blavatsky's two-volume cosmological epic *The Secret Doctrine* (1888) is unreadable. It is not unreadable. If you can turn the pages, or press an arrow button on a screen, you can read it. Just keep doing that. G.I. Gurdjieff's magisterial allegory, *Beelzebub's Tales to His Grandson* (1950) is complex and jarringly—as well as *intentionally*—unfamiliar. It is intended to disrupt rote thought. But, again, it is *not* unreadable. It's like a journey; you put one foot in front of the other and you keep turning the pages. When people claim that these books are unreadable—or that they conceal themselves from the reader—it is often a tipoff that they haven't attempted to read them.

I feel that Manly's book can be grouped with those volumes as three of the most important compendiums of esoteric wisdom that have reached us in the modern age. All three are very different kinds of books with different purposes and personas behind them. But they are foundational works, each one in its own right, by which no reader should feel intimidated. I feel strongly about this. Mozart always made the point that he wrote his operas for people to enjoy. Ralph Waldo Emerson delivered his essays and lectures with the intention of reaching a broad general public. These artists, like all artists, wanted *constituencies*. All you need is to find that one entry point and you can enter into what feels like an extraordinary relationship with these figures, who are *not so far away* and whose work should be understood as accessible to every motivated person.

None of the figures I have just mentioned, Manly P. Hall included, had anything like a traditional education by today's standards. None of them had higher degrees, except Emerson. Manly himself had spent very little time in any kind of conventional classroom. Hence, their intention was certainly not to put their work out of reach to the everyday person, but rather to catalogue it in such a way that any sensitive person could enter.

The wonderful thing about *The Secret Teachings of All Ages* is that when you enter it, it's almost like stepping into an enchanting maze or aviary. You simply don't know where you're going to come out. And you might come out, as I did, finding yourself changed from who you were when you entered. This is because Manly's book seems to interact with the individual in such a way that it may awaken things in you, things that you might have felt when you were very young—an interest perhaps in reincarnation or the extra-physical properties of the mind or the interior meaning of myth and parable. His book can reawaken things in you that may have lain dormant and that you may never have rediscovered until you took that step of going into it. In that sense, *The Secret Teachings of All Ages* is an intimate adventure.

* * *

It is impossible to separate *The Secret Teachings of All Ages* as a book from Manly P. Hall himself. There's an authentic mystery in how Manly at a very young age produced such a vast and masterful work. It's worth taking a moment to look briefly at his biography. He was born in 1901 in Peterborough, Canada, outside Toronto. His mother, Louise Palmer Hall, was a chiropractor and a remarkably progressive woman for her era. She played the violin, wore a wristwatch, which was uncommon among late-Victorian women, and took pride in being independently educated. Louise wanted to raise her child with a sense of the esoteric possibilities and the different religious ideas and myths that populated the world. But things were profoundly difficult for this family. His father, who was kind of a knockabout, disappeared very shortly after he was born and his mother felt somewhat overwhelmed by the circumstances of raising him. So, as it happened, Manly was raised by his maternal grandmother, who was a woman of independent means; her husband had been a fire insurance executive. One time a reporter from the *Los Angeles Times* asked Manly later in life what he would have done for a living if he hadn't become an esoteric philosopher. The mystic replied that he probably would have sold fire insurance. The reporter couldn't figure out what he was referencing, but that was the job held by his grandfather—and his supposition was probably correct.

Manly's grandmother raised him in the American West. They lived in the Dakotas and the Midwest, and as a result of moving around he had very little formal schooling. It was a lonely upbringing; he was isolated and not infrequently sick; he spent most of his time one-on-one with his grandmother; although he also got a great deal of reading done while recovering in bed. It was, in many respects, a lonely childhood, and one marked by little contact with others his age. (One of Manly's first books in 1925 was called, *The Ways of the Lonely Ones*.) To relieve routine and foster a kind of well-roundedness, Manly's grandmother would take him on trips to museums in Chicago, Philadelphia, and New York City, and he started to assemble a self-taught education.

When Manly was about fifteen, his grandmother, perhaps feeling that he finally needed some formal schooling, enrolled him in a military academy in New York City. This period lasted only about nine months, for which I'm sure he was grateful. Manly didn't take well to regimental life. In a photograph from around 1916, the teen appears stiffly with his grandmother dressed in formal military regalia and carrying a ceremonial sword; it's all very Edwardian-looking and today seems like it belongs to another world.

When Manly was about sixteen, his grandmother died and he knocked about trying to figure out what to do with his life. He worked as a clerk at banks and brokerage houses in New York City and then he started to make his way out to Southern California to reunite with his mother who was living there at the time. Looking for personal guidance and direction, Manly also began to develop an interest in religion and esoteric philosophy. When he reached California, it was undergoing a post-war population and economic boom, and this included the proliferation of esoteric organizations, through which he began to study.

Manly was very involved with the work of the Theosophical Society and Theosophical libraries became a favorite haunt of his. There existed a variety of self-styled Rosicrucian fellowships, including Max Heindel's Rosicrucian Order, and those places, too, provided Manly with reading opportunities and possibilities for growth. Early in adulthood, probably when he was nineteen, Manly began to discover his fluency in public speaking. The teen delivered his first public talk on the topic of reincarnation in a rented room above a bank in Santa Monica. There were a handful of listeners from whom he and a friend took a public collection at the door, which amounted to about thirty-five cents. After speaking, Manly and his companion went across the street and got ice cream sundaes. It was a very happy memory for him, and it established him for the first time—and with quick momentum—as a public speaker on esoterica. It didn't hurt matters that he was strikingly handsome, large-framed, broad-shouldered, and angular. He looked like a silent-screen movie star and he wore his hair attractively though unfashionably long for that day. The heavy-lidded teen began to attract attention as a kind of local boy wonder on the Southern California spiritual scene.

When Manly was about twenty, he became a pastor at a liberal evangelical congregation in Los Angeles called the Church of the People. He delivered sermons on reviving ancient wisdom and on how ethical philosophy and training could solve the problems of the current day, including crime, delinquency, abuse of alcohol, and the sense of ennui, purposelessness, and depression felt by many people. He began to attract attention from different reporters in town. One journalist, a woman from the *Los Angeles Times*, seemed almost to fall in love with him at one of his Church of the People services. "He is tall," the *Times* reported in 1923, "with unusually broad shoulders—football shoulders—but he wears his curly, dark brown hair bobbed like a girl's, and even his face and eyes convey an almost feminine impression."

His youth, physical appearance, speaking prowess, and easy command of different esoteric subjects also drew financial backers. This was a wonderful facet of Los Angeles life at the time: because LA was still very much an agricultural town, and the movie industry was in relative infancy, there were people of means, including oil and railroad magnates, who proved eager to support writers, artists, and spiritual or arts groups who were building up the cultural character of the town. Families who had made fortunes in railroads, oil fields, and banking wanted to become benefactors of Manly.

Through his supporters, he was able, in his early twenties, to begin traveling the world. He traveled to Japan, Egypt, India, Sri Lanka, and different nations of the East. And he wrote letters back home to friends and distant family members about his travels, which are collected in volumes in the PRS library. But there is an interesting quality to the letters, which almost deepens the mystery of the man and of when he turned a corner to become the brilliant figure we recall him as. The letters themselves often have a kind of *ordinary* quality to them; nothing in his letters is particularly quotable or memorable. In many regards, his letters home read like standard, if literate, travelogues of the era. He describes, in a linear fashion, sites seen and locations logged. Nothing in them breathes life into the experiences and, curiously, there's not much of a clue of the greatness that was soon to come.

But something transformed within the man around 1922, which saw the publication of Manly's first book, *Initiates of the Flame*. *Initiates of the Flame*, although it's a very short work, is almost like *The Secret Teachings of All Ages* in germination. It's a wonderful, living book in which Manly explores the meaning behind ancient symbols: the pentagram, the crucifix, the star of David, the all-seeing eye, the obelisk, the pyramid—all of these objects, albeit in a short space, seem to start coming to life for him, and for the reader. His abilities seem nascently within reach. And he hadn't written widely before. He produced articles here and there, delivered sermons at the Church of the People, and produced his travelogue letters, but nothing really suggested what was to come, until *Initiates of the Flame*. The book totals about 40,000 words with symbolic illustrations. A later edition in 1932 was more lavishly illustrated by Manly's friend and collaborator J. Augustus Knapp, who illustrated *The Secret Teachings of All Ages*. Yet even if you read the first edition today, nearly a century later, it just pulses in your hands. There's something *on fire* in that book, and it marks a turning point in Manly's life where he seems fully in command of his material. Almost immediately after, the 21-year-old writer began laying plans for his great book, *The Secret Teachings of All Ages*.

But what was extraordinary and what was really mysterious is that there was only a span of six years between the publication of the slender *Initiates of the Flame* and *The Secret Teachings of All Ages*, which came out when he was 27. Again, there was no formal education and there existed few guideposts or road signs, beyond those I've mentioned, of what was to come. And, truthfully, although I can trace out some of the forensics, there was no *evident ability* to gain ready mastery of the vast reference material that appears in the book. The bibliography alone contains about a thousand books. The bibliography could be a book in itself. The scale of what he produced, the quality, beauty, ease, and facility of his writing, and the range of his subjects is justly considered astounding. It was not an ordinary accomplishment. If I were to tell you that *Initiates of the Flame* marked a turning point in Manly's life and that decades rather than a few years later he published *The Secret Teachings of All Ages*, it would still be a remarkable story. It would reflect a lifetime well spent. But the period of gestation is only *six years*, with none of the technology that is available today, or even a hint of it.

Now, for source material, Manly did use some of the great libraries that were opening to public use at the time, including the British Library and the New York Public Library. Manly spent hour after hour in the reading room of the New York Public Library and he later remarked that he had no problem checking out the rarest books in their collection, because no one else seemed interested in them. Librarians got to know him as this strange long-haired kid who would come in and request books on Pythagorean mathematics, Egyptian symbolism, sacred geometry, things that few visitors were requesting at the time. And in this hulking form, Manly would sit at the big, beautiful oak tables in the cathedral-sized reading room in the New York Public Library and pour over book after book after book. I have the privilege today to be a writer-in-residence at the New York Public Library and I often sit in that same room and imagine what it must have been like to see him planted behind these massive volumes that few others were interested in.

As Manly observed at the time, a tendency toward philosophical materialism was asserting itself with great vigor and influence within academia—so much so that in the 1920s, unlike the close of the previous century, there wasn't much really significant scholarly work being done on primeval religions, esoteric traditions, and the Eastern traditions. Such work had been done in the late-Victorian era and early twentieth century but had, by that time, petered out; and when contemporary scholars turned their attention to the wisdom traditions they often regarded them in a manner that conscripted their insights and practices to museum cases. Primeval and esoteric thought systems were considered anthropologically significant, they were considered part of social history, but very few scholars at the time would imagine that these teachings had any relevance for the modern individual. Esoterica, initiatory traditions, and symbolism were seen as relics belonging to past cultures, which had themselves been superseded and overshadowed by the march of material progress.

The idea of writing about African ceremonial dances, for example, from the perspective of these practices containing meaning, myth, parable, and lessons, was almost unthinkable to most scholars at the time. The idea of peering into Native American mysticism and asking what it had in common with other religious traditions across the world was a question that almost no one asked. The idea that the religious experiences of seekers in the mystery traditions of ancient Greece, Rome, Egypt, and Persia, might harbor lessons for modern people was almost an unthinkable venture in the mainstream. Authorities could agree to document the timeline and catalogue certain practices for the sake of historical record, but the notion that this material could *impact* the life of the contemporary person was almost never considered—until Manly entered the scene.

Manly believed that primeval wisdom *had* to be rescued because modern scholarship was, in effect, relegating its surviving works to glass museum cases and not treating them as things that had a universal and vital message. And so he toiled *laboriously*, not only at the New York Public Library, but at the British Library and other mass libraries that were just opening to the public at the time. He enlisted the help of a small handful of benefactors and collaborators. He worked closely with a master printer in Los Angeles. He worked with artist J. Augustus Knapp, who had, with the exception of illustrations for an 1895 fantasy novel called *Etidorhpa*, previously worked in advertising and yearned to expand into esoterica. Manly designed every aspect of the book, oversaw its layout, and just kept building and building it.

In terms of subject matter, I've touched only on a sliver of the span and breadth of what he covered. The "Great Book" included Pythagorean mathematics; the mystery traditions of the Egyptian religions; the meaning and significance of hieroglyphs and pyramids; psychological alchemy; the Hermetic-influenced images that appear in the Tarot deck; the esoteric backstory, as he saw it, of the Shakespearean dramas; cryptograms; mystical Christianity; Kabbalah; Native American rites; and myths and traditions and symbols from different lands and civilizations.

I think it's fair to say that he had fun, too. He wrote about mythical beasts, dragons, and serpents. My favorite caption in the book is "Conventional Gnomes" (not the exceptional kind, just the garden variety). Nothing was off limits to Manly. I'll never forget—and this was a turning point in my life, it was an illuminating point in my own life—that when I started reading *The Secret Teachings of All Ages* it occurred to me that seriousness is derived not from your choice of subject. Seriousness is derived from your *treatment* of subject. It freed me to understand that immersing yourself in occult and esoteric subjects, even if nobody else around you is interested in such things—as could seem the case in Manly's day—meant that you didn't derive a sense of seriousness or mission from your topics alone, but rather from how you treated them. This turned on a light for me. It made me realize that I didn't need to conceal or make excuses for the occult subject matter that I was so personally invested in. I didn't need to alter my vocabulary or use respectable or obfuscating terms. As anybody who knows me is aware, I have a real attachment to some of the original terms. I don't run away from terms like occult, ESP, mediumship, or New Age for that matter, because I think all these terms possess historical integrity, and I won't allow them to be defined by scholastic critics for whom they often serve as epithets. Those and other terms meant something to a chain of seekers across many ages—or more recently—and I think they should be retained as they were originally minted. Manly showed me how subjects didn't require altering or disguising so long as one approached them with maturity and seriousness.

And why shouldn't there be a space in our culture today, at the opening of the twenty-first century, for people to explore and take these subjects just as seriously as we take any range of subjects, whether politics or current events (not that we take those very seriously today), or mathematics, geology, archeology, and engineering? Why couldn't you apply the same degree of standards, effort, sweat equity, and intellectual acumen to esoteric and spiritual topics—topics that captured the ideals and imaginations and hopes and strivings of vast numbers of people across centuries? Why not simply ask: What do they hold for us? And come to responses that aren't preconceived or rote, but just address the pure question. Along with that question, Manly exposed me to the idea that pursuing occult and esoteric studies can be a vocation in itself.

Now, I started out by saying that when you enter into *The Secret Teachings of All Ages* or other books I've mentioned, you don't know where you're going to come out. They personally affect you. I've just described how the experience personally affected me, but that question remains one for each individual to discover for him or herself. You don't know what you're going to find. You could find the direction of your life. You could discover that *before* you felt scattered and *after* you experience a sense of mission, purpose—and self. That's what *The Secret Teachings of All Ages* as a book can give you, in addition to the vast compendium of wisdom that it organizes.

Manly didn't have a traditional publisher. He published the book by subscription, on his own. He started by soliciting orders from Masonic temples and different donors and benefactors that he knew. He planned a first printing of 1,200 copies (to cover almost 1,000 subscriptions), which he later had to bump up to 2,500 copies. And when the book came out, it greeted the reader as something *unprecedented*: for those of you who have ever held it in your hands, it's this enormous, tabletop-sized book in a beautiful slipcase. It teems with images, symbols, and passages on a range of occult and mythical topics that could involve you for a lifetime. And yet the *Secret Teachings* was greeted with very little public notice or acclaim. It was an underground book. Although interestingly enough, in New York City, the Crown Prince of Sweden held a book reception for Manly and invited different luminaries; one of the people who signed the guest book that day was General John Pershing, the head of U.S. forces in World War I. So, it was interesting to see the kinds of people that Manly's book could find its way to, and this remained true in later years. Manly personalized a copy to Elvis Presley in the early 1970s.

But, still, it was never a widely known book. It was a hugely expensive book. It was a cumbersome book in terms of physical dimensions. It was not easy to find. It was an object that you had to gravitate towards. And eventually, in the years that immediately followed publication, Manly decided that he wanted to found an academy that could house his book, and different kinds of books, and that could serve as a meeting place where people could discuss esoteric ideas, and where the author could continue his publication efforts. Manly was able to raise enough money—a considerable ability for a teacher—so that in 1934 ground was broken on the Philosophical Research Society (PRS). Manly closely supervised the architecture. He wanted to create it as a kind of mystery school in the ancient Pythagorean tradition; that was his ideal, at least. He succeeded, gloriously, in creating a wholly distinctive and beautiful Mayan-Egyptian-Art Deco campus, and he spent the rest of his life there, writing, speaking, and publishing. He produced literally hundreds of books, thousands of articles, tens of thousands of lectures. You could start reading Manly's lectures and it could occupy literally your entire life.

And again the mystery reasserts itself over and over: how did he accomplish what he did? Where did his prodigiousness come from? People have all kinds of theories involving reincarnation, karma, and recurrently accumulated knowledge, but that is, of course, speculative lore. We really have no way of knowing. There is, however, one thing I'm absolutely certain about—and this is a personal lesson to take away from the life of Manly P. Hall: part his achievement came from *certainty of purpose*.

I'm always encouraging people when they're searching for a way in life, when they're trying to figure out what to do with their existence, or what to do next, that they be *very intimately honest with themselves about what they truly want out of life*. We think that we ask ourselves the question, *what do I want?*—but I believe that we often *deceive* ourselves, and that we actually fail to ask that question in as deep or as penetrating a way as we ought to. That question also gets stolen from us because we are all conditioned by peer pressure, by things that we grew up with, by notions that we inherited from who knows where. And sometimes, even in our most private recesses, we feel *inhibited or embarrassed*, and unable to really ask and probe that question seriously.

Sometimes, frankly, we're afraid of what we're going to find. We slide into these roles in life and we think we have to occupy them and that we owe some sort of loyalty to these roles that we find ourselves in. But if we are willing to suspend fealty to these roles, new possibilities can appear. Someone who considers him or herself "spiritual" might discover that actually what they really want is to be greatly successful in the world and perhaps be immersed in finance or something like that. But often they don't want to acknowledge that to themselves; that kind of path is supposed to be superficial, or it's supposed to be somehow a manifestation of attachment or identification, or someone *told them* that's not the direction in which life lies.

The direction in which life lies is your own greatest self-expression. I believe very strongly that self-expression is sacred. And I believe that when you discover, as Manly did, that *key thing* in life, whatever it is, that *really speaks to you*, I believe in my heart that energies and capacities and abilities you never knew you possessed will begin to unfold before you and from within you. It's absolutely extraordinary. And I've seen it—though too rarely.

As I alluded, our society *takes* from the individual his or her sense of a core, primary purpose in life. We're conditioned and we're dangerously apt to repeat things to ourselves by rote. No sooner do we start to think, "Well, this might be what I really want . . ." than there's another voice saying, "Oh, but that's selfish or that's problematic or that's impossible," or whatever. Just as an internal exercise, I ask everyone reading these words, in your own time and in your own individual manner and with total privacy, to ask yourself with real, unembarrassed candor: *What do I really want from life?* And don't fear the answer. This is what Manly did. This is what fueled his achievement.

I cautioned you not to fear the answer. We get hung up on the possibility that the answer is going to cut in a radically different direction from the persona or the self that we *perceive* we belong to. To use a converse example from the one above, a corporate go-getter might discover that she doesn't really want to be in the corporate world. Maybe she just wants to be at home under the covers, reading, and enjoying solitude. Whatever your answer, and whether you want to follow it, I can only tell you that the best reckoning I can possibly reach about *how* Manly was able to achieve what he did, is that he was able to find that absolutely vital, impassioned, motivating *thing* that he wanted in life, which in his case was to curate and preserve esoteric wisdom, not as a museum piece but as a living, pulsing philosophy with meaning for contemporary men and women. When he found that *thing*, it unlocked uncanny abilities. It may for you, too.

And, believe me, I know all the occult speculations: Manly was the reincarnate of Plato; Manly somehow was the recipient of twelve different lifetimes; Manly had a photographic memory; and so on. I haven't been able to verify any of that—how would I? But what I certainly have been able to verify in my own experience— and, after all, what's more empirical than your own experience on the path?—is that when you discover that one thing that is *vital* to your existence, as Manly did, it will unlock possibilities and intellectual strength and physical stamina and all kinds of qualities in you that you never knew you possessed. It's the closest thing that life grants you to a magic elixir. It's absolutely remarkable. Yet we run from it. Because, again, what we find sometimes contradicts our perceptions of who we're supposed to be or what we're supposed to be doing in the world.

The Secret Teachings of All Ages is, ultimately, a book of practical philosophy. This book dedicated to exploring it should have a practical dimension, as well. Hence, I invite you to take the first step. Take the *first* step. In probing what you want, you don't have to burn the fleet; you simply have to ask the question, in the private recesses of your own life, and with complete, unembarrassed intimacy: "What do I really want from life?" I believe it will unlock—or it can unlock—extraordinary energies. And it's the best explanation—maybe not the only but the best that I've been able to personally arrive at—for how Manly was able to accomplish what he did. He was a living example of the esoteric proportions and inner possibilities of the individual—an actual living example—and we have evidence of it in the form of *The Secret Teachings of All Ages*.

Manly, of course, produced many other books after *The Secret Teachings of All Ages*, some of which were surprisingly influential. Perhaps the best-known was a work that Manly published from his campus in 1944, called *The Secret Destiny of America*. That book was Manly's take on the internal story or the back-story of the founding of the United States. In short, he believed that there were certain enlightened intellects like Francis Bacon and Sir Walter Raleigh and certain so-called secret societies or esoteric fraternities, Freemasonry in particular, that had vouchsafed esoteric wisdom and ideals, and that these things took root and were given birth in the founding of the new republic, which had as one of its central aims—albeit a contradictory one given everything else that was going on—the protection of the individual search for meaning. And this was true a hundred years before the framing of the Constitution.

Manly's perspective was that the ancient ideals of an unadorned, boundaryless spiritual search had gotten vouchsafed in the principles of movements like Freemasonry or intellectual thought movements like Rosicrucianism, and he was intelligently and mea-suredly aware that many of the founders were them-selves Freemasons: George Washington, Benjamin Franklin, Paul Revere, John Hancock, an outsized number of people who signed the Declaration, an out-sized number of people who were framers of the Con-stitution, and an outsized number who ranked among Washington's generals and officers. Esoteric thought was in the air.

What I've described is real history, and *The Secret Destiny of America* itself traveled an extraordinary course. I discovered its influence in a strange way. In 2010, I was on a radio show in New Orleans and after the show the host remarked to me, kind of offhand-edly, "Hey, did you know that Ronald Reagan believed in secret masters of wisdom who were directing American history?" I said no, I hadn't heard that. He sent me the newsletter of California Republican con-gressman which reprinted an essay that Reagan had written in 1981 about what Independence Day meant to him. It contained some oddly tantalizing references along the lines the host had described. I tracked down its original source, which was the July 4th, 1981, issue of *Parade* magazine, not exactly an esoteric journal. The magazine had asked Reagan in his first term as president to write an essay for them on what the Fourth of July personally meant to him. So, at Camp David, Reagan handwrote an essay on a yellow legal pad and he submitted it through his aide Michael Deaver to *Parade* magazine and they published it on Independence Day of 1981. As I read this essay, I grew absolutely astonished to encounter not only ideas but actual *phraseology* that came from the writings of

Manly P. Hall, and specifically from *The Secret Destiny of America*.

In short, Reagan told a fanciful story that Manly had begun recounting in *The Secret Teachings of All Ages*. It involves America being the product of a "Great Plan" for religious liberty and self-governance launched by an ancient order of arcane philosophers and secret societies. In Hall's 1943 essay "The Secret Destiny of America," which formed the nucleus of his later book, he recounts a rousing speech delivered by an "unknown speaker" before the signers of the Declaration of Independence. The "mysterious man," Hall wrote, invisibly entered and exited the locked doors of the Philadelphia statehouse on July 4th, 1776, delivering an oration that bolstered the wavering spirits of the delegates. "God has given America to be free!" commanded the stranger, urging the men to overcome their fears of the noose, axe, or gibbet, and to seal destiny by signing the great document. Newly emboldened, Hall wrote, the delegates rushed forward to add their names. They looked to thank the stranger only to discover that he had vanished from the locked room. Was this, Hall wondered in 1944, "one of the agents of the secret Order, guarding and directing the destiny of America?"

At a 1957 commencement address in Illinois at his alma mater Eureka College, Reagan, then a corporate spokesman for GE, sought to inspire students with this leaf from occult history. "This is a land of destiny,"

Reagan said, "and our forefathers found their way here by some Divine system of selective service gathered here to fulfill a mission to advance man a further step in his climb from the swamps." Reagan then retold, without attribution, the tale of Hall's unknown speaker. "When they turned to thank the speaker for his timely words," Reagan concluded, "he couldn't be found and to this day no one knows who he was or how he entered or left the guarded room."

Reagan revived the story several times, including in *Parade* where he used language very close to Hall's own: "When they turned to thank him for his timely oratory, he was not to be found, nor could any be found who knew who he was or how had come in or gone out through the locked and guarded doors."

Riffing on Hall's theme, Reagan spoke elsewhere of America's divine purpose and of a mysterious plan behind the nation's founding. "You can call it mysticism if you want to," he told the Conservative Political Action Conference (CPAC) in Washington, D.C., in 1974, "but I have always believed that there was some divine plan that placed this great continent between two oceans to be sought out by those who were possessed of an abiding love of freedom and a special kind of courage." Reagan repeated these words almost verbatim before a television audience of millions for the Statue of Liberty centenary on July 4th, 1986.

Where did Manly uncover the tale that made such an impact on a president and his view of American purpose and destiny? In actuality, the episode originated as "The Speech of the Unknown" in a collection of folkloric stories about America's founding, published in 1847 under the title *Washington and his Generals, or Legends of the Revolution* by American social reformer and muckraker George Lippard. Lippard, a friend of Edgar Allan Poe, had a strong taste for the gothic—he cloaked his mystery man in a "dark robe." He also tacitly acknowledged inventing the story: "The name of the Orator . . . is not definitely known. In this speech, it is my wish to compress some portion of the fiery eloquence of the time."

Regardless, the parable took on its own life and came to occupy the same shadowland between fact and fiction as the parables of George Washington chopping down a cherry tree, or young Abe Lincoln walking miles to return a bit of change to a country-store customer. As with most myths, the story assumed different attributes over time. By 1911, the speech resurfaced in a collection of American political oratory, with the robed speaker fancifully identified as Patrick Henry.

For his part, Manly seemed to know little about the story's point of origin. He had been given a copy of the "Speech of the Unknown" by a since-deceased secretary of the Theosophical Society, but with no bibliographical information other than it being from a "rare old volume of early American political speeches." The speech appeared in 1938 in the Society's journal, *The*

Theosophist, with the sole note that it was "published in a rare volume of addresses, and known probably to only one in a million, even of American citizens."

In any case, it is Manly's language that unmistakably marks the Reagan telling. Indeed, there are indications that the two men met to exchange ideas. In an element unique to Manly's version, the mystic-writer attributed the tale of the unknown speaker to the writings of Thomas Jefferson. When Reagan addressed CPAC he added an attribution—of sorts: Reagan said that the tale was told to him "some years ago" by "a writer, who happened to be an avid student of history . . . I was told by this man that the story could be found in the writings of Jefferson. I confess, I never researched or made an effort to verify it."

Gnostic scholar Stephan A. Hoeller, for many years a close associate and friend of Hall's, and a frequent teacher at PRS, affirmed the likelihood of a Reagan and Hall meeting. Hoeller told me that while he was on the Griffith Park campus one day in 1971, early in Reagan's second term as governor, he spotted a black limousine with a uniformed chauffeur standing outside it. Curious, he approached the man and asked, "Who owns this beautiful car?"

"At first," Hoeller recalled, the driver "hemmed and hawed and then said, 'Oh, it's Governor Reagan—he is in meeting with Mr. Hall.'"

Hall's longtime librarian, Pearl M. Thomas, confirmed the account to Hoeller. "They know each other quite well," he recalled Thomas saying. She further told him that Reagan had "called him here at the office several times. But we are not supposed to talk about this."

Hall was known for discretion and avoidance of Hollywood chatter and social climbing; there is no record of his speaking directly about the governor. But when Reagan began his ascent to the White House and his name arose in conversation, Hoeller recalled, the mystic smiled and said, "Yes, yes, we know him." Hoeller, a distinguished man of old-world bearing, eschews hyperbole. He concluded: "There are definitely several indications that there was contact and influence there." The scholar's recollections square with the timing of Reagan's 1974 remarks before CPAC.

Given the fanciful origins of the "unknown speaker," one may wonder what worth, if any, the tale has as history. It is important to remember that myths, ancient and modern, reflect psychological truth and the teller's self-perception, sometimes more so than events themselves. Myths reveal who we aspire to be, and warn us against what we may become. Those on which we dwell reveal character.

In his work, Hall captured an element of what philosopher Jacob Needleman calls "the American soul." Reagan certainly thought so. And, whatever one thinks of the politician, the codes and stories in which Reagan spoke form the skeleton key to the inner man—a fact intuited by President Gerald Ford, who called Reagan "one of the few political leaders I have ever met whose public speeches revealed more than his private conversations."

In light of what I've written, it is also important to understand Manly's "secret society" thesis, in which he describes how esoteric ideals were preserved within the vessel of clandestine fraternities and societies, and later put into governance in the new republic. Aspects of his thesis are over-dramatized. Yet, in the broadest strokes, Manly's outlook provides a vital and not wholly inaccurate insight into an element of American history that most mainstream historians and scholars overlook. Key facets of Manly's "secret society" vision can be seen in the influence of Freemasonic ideals on America's founders.

Indeed, Manly was among the first modern historians to grasp Freemasonry's impact on early America—and the facts are richer and more significant than anything that entertainment or conspiracy would hold. As the most radical thought movement to emerge from the Reformation, Freemasonry was one of the first widespread and well-connected organizations in modern life to espouse religious toleration, ecumenism, internal democracy, and personal liberty—principles that the fraternity helped spread among key American colonists.

It may seem anomalous for liberal principles to arise from within a "secret society," but skullduggery was never Masonry's primary aim. In an age of religious conflict in seventeenth-century Europe—when an individual running afoul of church strictures could suffer persecution or worse—Freemasons maintained secrecy less out of esoteric drama than political expedience. Many Masons believed in a search for religious truth as it existed in all civilizations, including those of a pre-Christian past, and they drew upon occult symbols, from pentagrams to luminescent eyeballs, as codes for ethical development and progress. Reactions from church authorities ranged from suspicion to hostility. European Masons had good reason to be discrete.

Whatever its airs of mystery and all-seeing eyes, Freemasonry's most radical, even dangerous, idea was the encouragement of different faiths within a single nation. As Manly noted, when few other historians did, Washington and other early-American Freemasons rejected a European past in which one overarching authority regulated the exchange of ideas.

Historically, Masonry's voice and principles contributed to America's founding commitment to the individual pursuit of meaning, as Manly also understood. It is critical to realize how deeply a fraternal tie was felt in an agrarian society like the colonies. And taking a leaf from Manly's thesis, it is not going too far to suggest that some key Masons foresaw the nascent republic as a place destined to protect the individual search—from majority rule, from foreign meddling, and from sectarian restriction. That ideal represents

Freemasonry's highest contribution to our national life. This noble, meaningful aspect of Masonic philosophy runs throughout Manly's writing.

I've given you a sense of how Manly's work continued well beyond *The Secret Teachings of All Ages*. But I also believe that his writing and curation never again reached that pinnacle or anywhere near. I say that with deepest love and veneration for the man; I think I've made clear the tremendous respect and admiration I feel for him. I also believe, however, that within the spiritual culture and other reaches of our culture, we must love those whom we admire as one adult loves another. That is, not to put somebody up on a pedestal but to love or admire that person in full light of their greatness along with their faults and failures. There's nothing offkey or disrespectful about exploring the life of someone you love in its totality. Quite the opposite. Sycophancy is often an act of unacknowledged vanity: the true believer *wants* to elevate the teacher because it turns the acolyte into an apostle, of sorts. It also harms the teacher because good students and capable people—people whom the teacher may someday need—are rarely found among sycophants. And I believe this dynamic contributed to grave difficulties that Manly experienced late in life.

The later decades of Manly's life could, I think, be difficult for him because he settled into a routine of delivering another lecture, writing another pamphlet, putting out another book, and there was a detectably uneven quality to his output. In some of his later historical works, there appear inconsistencies and sometimes the weakness of relying or over-relying on a single-source or on folkloric accounts.

In my estimation, Manly peaked when he was very young. You must remember that *The Secret Teachings of All Ages* came out when he was just 27 years old; and although he certainly did other things, *significant* things, well into middle age, there could be—and I think he felt this occasionally—a quality of *sameness*, of routine, and I think it could be depleting for him at times. He had come into so much in the way of resources and benefactors when he was young. He was able to construct his magnificent campus. He was able to create a library and collection filled with rarities and treasures, some of which have been retained to this day and exist in his private vault, others of which were later sold off to pay bills. He had attained a kind of underground fame as America's preeminent philosopher of the esoteric. He would pack the campus auditorium unfailingly on Sunday mornings. He had attained so much, and much of it so young, that I think it was difficult at times for him to determine what was next, what would be his second act, so to speak.

I surmise that this weighed heavily on him as he aged, because, as I was saying when I started, Manly in his final years seemed very concerned that his work was somehow going to be forgotten. He witnessed the early rise of the digital era and I think he was concerned that he would get left behind as this era got underway. And it made him vulnerable. His vulnerability expressed itself in a particularly tragic set of circumstances.

In the late 1980s, there appeared in Manly's orbit a father-son team of con artists, who managed to ingratiate themselves into his life and who whispered in his ear all kinds of promises and possibilities: they were going to broadcast his lectures by satellite around the world, and they were going to ensure that his books and talks got exposed to people everywhere, perennially. Manly was in poor health at the time—he was extremely overweight and he was suffering from a variety of heart and weight-related issues. He handed over the day-to-day functioning of his life too completely and too quickly to this father-son team who were telling him all these wonderful things that they were going to do for him. It seemed that having accomplished so much in life, and having peaked early, Manly felt somewhat lost or distraught in his later years, and he was too ready to believe the promises of people who did not warrant his trust.

This created a string of tragic circumstances, which eventually placed a crushing legal burden on PRS, from which it took the organization years to recover. About two days before Manly's death in 1990, he signed over his will, his collection of antiquities, and all of his properties to one of these figures who had entered his life. He gave these people power of attorney, he gave them the ability to cash checks from his personal account. And two days later, Manly was dead. The cause was pronounced heart failure. Many of his intimates, including his eccentric widow and others around him, felt that the circumstances of his death didn't pass any reasonable person's sniff test; they suspected foul play. His widow in particular—and in fairness she wasn't the only one—felt that these figures who had entered Manly's life had bilked him out of his will, had gotten him to sign over power of attorney with ill intent, had gained control over his bank accounts—and then Manly experienced his demise. There were inconsistencies in the manner in which his death was reported, so went the coroner's report. The L.A. County coroner found that his body had been moved; there were signs of bruises, including unhealed leg wounds. There were definite indications that the body had at one time been outside and was moved inside. There was, finally, a strange passage of time before the death was reported.

The circumstances were sufficiently suspicious so that for about five years the LAPD actually kept the file open; they were considering investigating the death as a homicide. Manly's widow, about two years after his death, had his body exhumed, but that proved inconclusive. Eventually the LAPD did close the file, and Manly's death was attributed to heart failure. The two men who had gotten their claws in him actually died soon after; one passed away of cancer and another of complications related to HIV.

In the end, I don't think there was foul play involved in Manly's death, upon which I expand in my *Occult America*. But I do think that he was the victim of what we today might call elder abuse. He was taken advantage of. So much so that a civil court judge in Los Angeles actually overturned Manly's will and stripped these two figures of executor status, which ignited a huge and very expensive court battle. The legal situation devolved into a dynamic of each against all. Manly's widow, who has since passed on, sued PRS over material there that she felt was her property. The former executors sued all the parties involved. The legal bills just mounted and mounted.

With the great man gone, how would any of this be settled? A new president, Obadiah Harris, came on the scene in 1993. He was a meaningful figure in my life because he gave me some of my earliest opportunities to speak publicly and he authorized the "reader's edition" of the book. Obadiah was finally able to settle all the lawsuits and financial improprieties. It was not easy; legal bills literally ran into the millions, and Obadiah was compelled to sell off more than four hundred antiquities from Manly's library. Fortunately, most of these went to the Getty Museum, which today has a Manly P. Hall collection, so they're properly archived and researchers can view them. I wish that it hadn't been necessary for the organization to sell off any of its holdings, but it's better that they went to museum rather than a private collector, in whose hands they might not be seen again. With that and the passage of time, the organization returned to some degree of financial health.

Manly's life is bookended by two mysteries. The first mystery is: Where did his virtuosity *come from*? And the second is: Where did his wisdom, insight, virtuosity, and ethical prowess *go to* when he proved able to be isolated and taken advantage of? Even in the end, he was possessed of his mental faculties. Manly delivered a lecture from the auditorium stage about one week before his death—and it was classic Manly P. Hall. He sounded resonant. He spoke effortlessly for about two hours without notes. There was no sign of intellectual deterioration. So what *was it* that led him to be taken advantage of by these wolves at his door? I try, at least as best as I'm able, to draw personal lessons from his coda, because I think we should be able to draw personal lessons from the full breadth of people whom we love and admire.

In a sense, I think toward the very end Manly's isolation was a consequence of his success. He had demonstrated such virtuosity and such capacity to attract support and benefactors—and also to know productively what to do with that support when he was a young man—that it freed him of many of life's outer burdens. That's the dream isn't it? Everybody wants to quit his or her day job. But the friction of a day job, as much of a burden as it might sometimes seem, can also be extremely grounding and helpful. The continual need to struggle for what's coming to you can sharpen your mind, tone your acumen, and hone your critical faculties. I also think that late in life Manly was probably surrounded by people who weren't sufficiently formidable to protect him. I think that among some of the people gravitating around Manly at that time there was a bit of a "yes-man" quality. It actually can be extremely helpful to have people around you who occasionally poke thorns in your side, who tell you no, who push back at you. As much as we might want to get rid of such people, and we may sometimes harbor very hard feelings toward those who struggle with us and those with whom we experience some tension, they also serve a protective function. They test us. They tell us what we don't want to hear. This is among the meanings of William Blake's aphorism, "Opposition is true Friendship."

The personal lesson that I take from the closing bookend of his life is: *don't wish too hard for things to be easy.* Don't wish too fondly for favorable circumstances. Because friction, financial demands, and being told *no* by people when you feel that you deserve a *yes* can serve to protect you and keep you sharp and focused. Hunger is important. It is functional. I wish success for everybody reading these words, as I do for myself; but staying hungry can be the best thing that happens to you. Yet when circumstances are such that the road completely opens up before you, it's not always easy to remain hungry, even as that hunger can serve a deeply valuable function. I told you earlier the lesson I take from Manly's younger life. This is the lesson that I take from his older life.

Above all else, the wonderful thing about Manly's life is that he left us with this extraordinary codex, this extraordinary road map to esoteric wisdom, *The Secret Teachings of All Ages*. I know that many people reading these words have already read *The Secret Teachings of All Ages*. But I say to those of you who haven't: I envy you. Because you are about to embark on a wonderful adventure. It is impossible to say, as I alluded, where you are going to end up after entering the book. You will encounter ideas, possibilities, and thought systems that may alter and change—or reveal—who you are. That was Manly's deepest wish. He wrote his "Great Book" to function as a kind of blueprint, road map, and point of embarkation for the seeker. Its doors are open to *anybody*. You do not need to place any label on yourself. If this companion guide keeps you company on the journey, then it has found its mark. So, let us begin entering the great monument that this man left for us—with hopes that his monument is one in which you discover your deepest self.

LESSON II

——— ๑ ๐ ———

The Meaning
of Philosophy

This marks a special point in the *Seeker's Guide* because we now start to explore the specific content of *The Secret Teachings of All Ages*. The theme of this segment is the meaning of philosophy. What did Manly P. Hall wish to accomplish with his writing and publication of *The Secret Teachings of All Ages*? What ideas did Manly hope the book would ignite in the lives of its readers and students?

I mentioned in the previous chapter that *The Secret Teachings of All Ages* is a kind of magical book, insofar as it *works an effect* on the individual; but the effect is *yours* to discover. The effect is going to differ for every reader and student of its pages, and I believe that Manly structured it that way.

I described the book in the opening chapter as a labyrinth: you enter it, it's filled with discoveries, you must traverse through it on your own, and you don't know where it's going to lead you, you don't know where you are going to exit. I can promise you, as a longtime student and lover of the book, that you will exit at a point different from the one in which you entered. And you may emerge as a different person from who you were when you entered. But, again—and this is a principle that I'll return to throughout this guidebook—the point of entry, exit, and reentry are, in meaning and content, yours alone to discover.

As I write this chapter, I am inspired by the magnificent Vedic god Ganesha, the elephant-headed deity about whom Manly wrote with veneration. Traditionally, Ganesha is understood as the remover of barriers. The entire aim of this *Seeker's Guide* hinges on that principle: that barriers be lowered so that you can freely enter and discover your own particular meaning and purpose, both in the book and in life.

In the opening of *The Secret Teachings of All Ages*, Manly notes that his core purpose is to resurrect the true meaning of philosophy. To Manly, philosophy, above all else, must *practical*; it must demonstrate an actual effect in the life of the individual. Like American philosopher William James (1842–1910), Manly did not believe in scholastic philosophy, in philosophical models based strictly on logic, argument, proofs, and assemblage of concentric theories. He wouldn't have dismissed any of that out hand, of course; but, rather, he believed that the *purpose* of philosophy is refinement of the individual. And when the individual encounters the initiatory and self-developmental ideas of esoteric antiquity—as expressed by the progenitors of philosophy and re-expressed by students and seekers across time—these ideas, if authentic, must wield a measurable effect on the seeker and student.

One of Manly's central principles, which you'll find enunciated throughout this guidebook, is that there's no division between the individual and the surrounding cosmos; it's all one whole. When you see or respond to an ancient symbol, the magnetism that you feel in response to that symbol is a *natural* response to your instinct of being unified with the surrounding world, of being unified with the all. "As above, so below" went the great Hermetic dictum, something that we're going to be considering further. (Hermetic philosophy is the subject of lesson V.) That principle—*as above, so below*—can be understood as the heart of Manly Hall's philosophy.

Manly found that principle in the work of the esoteric and utopian philosopher, Francis Bacon (1561–1626). He quotes Bacon early in the book from his essay "Of Atheism" published in 1625: "A little philosophy inclineth man's mind to atheism; but depth in philosophy bringeth men's minds about to religion."

Bacon, too, had an image of the individual—of *you*, the individual—as intimately connected to everything around you; more than connected, but part of one continuum. One of Bacon's core works is the unfinished utopian novel *New Atlantis*, published posthumously in 1626, in which he foresaw an ideal society where men and women are free to pursue learning and refinement. Self-discovery and the search for meaning are at the center of existence in *New Atlantis*. In Bacon's utopian vision, school kids have their lessons projected onto the walls of the city, so that whatever they are engaged in—play or commerce, chores or rest—the lessons of truth are always present. In this sense, all of life is sacred because self-development is at its center. Hence, if we take seriously the dictum "as above, so below"—or, as it's been restated in Western Scripture, "God created man in his own image"—it stands to reason that the central purpose of your life is generativity, creativity, and productivity. That is your birthright. What will you direct it towards?

Arriving at that sense of purpose, arriving at that ideal, entering your own *New Atlantis* is the central task you face. It's the key task that Manly ascribed to seekers of all eras. In that vein, the first principle of philosophy, as Manly enunciates in *The Secret Teachings of All Ages*, is the age-old dictum: *know thyself*. This principle animated Socrates, Plato, Hermes Trismegistus, Buddha, and other figures, both real and mythical, throughout the history of the human search. How do you go about knowing yourself? What is the task of knowing yourself?

Too often in today's world, the quest to *know thyself*, is, I think, misdirected into a kind of morbid self-reflection. Ours is a therapeutic culture, populated with all kinds of spiritual and self-toning options. But I think the possibilities intrinsic to *know thyself* have been narrowed to the point where that expression is poorly understood in many reaches of our culture, because we are conditioned to believe that there is *one answer* to everything; and that at the back of all your motivations, all your problems, all your complexities— at the back of all your possibilities—must lie *one* answer. And I think that's a grave mistake. I think that assumption can lead men and women into *years* of fruitlessly searching for that one answer. What's the one turnkey? What's the one thing that has produced problematic behaviors in me, that has produced addictions in me, that has limited my relationships, that has resulted in problematic repeat behaviors?

The fact is, life is a great complexity, and for that reason a complex of causes are behind every expression in your life. It is not always possible to decipher a single answer. But that shouldn't be seen as something that puts you in front of some impossible task regarding self-knowledge. It may lead you simply to acknowledge and to understand that we are subject to many laws and forces. Again: *as above, so below.* So many things run throughout our lives, so many things play out within our struggles. But given the connectedness of life, a change in one element—even a small element, such as the picking up of a book—can reverberate in unseen and even seismic ways.

Certain causes may be karmic in nature, although I caution not to engage in too quick or easy a reading of just what *karma is*. Karma, as Manly alludes in the *Secret Teachings*, is a vast concept. It's one that you almost need to fall to your knees in front of. It's not easy to gain perspective, even across the span of an entire life, on precisely what karma means, either on a macro or intimate scale. Of course, we view karma colloquially in the West today as a law of cause and effect; but a law may play out across a span of eternal recurrence or multiple lifetimes, as is sometimes taught in the Vedic tradition.

The Vedic tradition—the great philosophy of the East that is in many regards as old as any form of recorded history—did not offer a neat entry point or single perspective on karma or the question of eternal recurrence. We tend to casually understand eternal recurrence or reincarnation as meaning that your individual personality is reborn again and again over the ages, and that you can perhaps pinpoint different lives or different entities through which you as an individual have been expressed. I'm not going to deny that possibility, and I expand on it shortly. I'm not going to deny the great question that may place the individual before. But within the Vedic tradition, the concept of karma or eternal recurrence was not *necessarily personified.* Rather, there exists a great life force from which everything emerges, and upon physical death or bodily death, we re-enter this timeless life force. We re-emerge as products of this life force, perhaps reappearing in physical forms, but not necessarily retaining any kind of individual or antecedent persona or character from the past.

We must not speak of Vedic tradition in too narrow a way; there exist many different schools, streams, schisms, and channels of thought. And, to be sure, some of those schools and channels, both ancient and modern, *do* see the individual as reproducing across different lifetimes in a *distinct* way—including lifetimes that might be non-human, possibly animal life forms. But at the core of Vedic philosophy is the principle that *life is indestructible*, because it is part of the great whole, just as in Hermetic philosophy. Hence, it stands to reason that you, the individual, will, of course, experience bodily decline and demise, will re-enter this life force, and then will enter *again* into a term of physicality on earth. There may be some accumulated debt or benefit that comes with that. But there is not necessarily a traceable cause-and-effect on the individual scale; we lack the perspective to make a determination as to precisely what's occurring karmically—it is playing out on a vast scale—or to treat karma as some sort of pet law that can be used to explain or to determine, for example, the nature of someone's suffering or one's own. The instant that an onlooker announces "karma" as the reason for someone's suffering (and it is usually someone else's) all that person is doing is throwing a stone.

I think we often misuse karma as an escape hatch when we can't explain what's going on, when we experience pain, when we witness suffering, or even witness catastrophes on a national or global scale. I believe that we are too easily tempted to resort to karma as a quick-and-ready philosophical glue, which will bind opposites and explain away complexities and apparent injustices. I think karma can be understood—and must be understood—as one of the many vast laws under which we live and by which we are impacted; its effects are mitigated by the impacts of still other laws.

Within this sphere of existence, for example, we live under multiple physical laws and limits. Mortality alone tells us that. Yet laws can also bend in unexpected ways. A law, in order to be a law, must be universal, it must be ever-operative. However, circumstances of life can alter the manner in which we experience an ever-operative law. For example, we recognize gravity as a universal law, but you're going to experience gravity much differently here on earth than you would experience it on the moon, where you could jump ten feet in the air, or on Jupiter, where its pressure would crush you.

This is because gravity responds to mass. In a certain sense, gravity can be seen as a law of mass being attracted to itself. It elicits a pull on us regardless of what's going on, even if we do not feel it. If you're in the vacuum of space, for example, gravity's impact is not entirely absent, otherwise the cosmos would just drift apart. Even within a vacuum matter is still attracted to itself; it is the maintenance of life. And you're going to experience that law of maintenance differently based on the presence or absence of mass, even though it's always happening.

So, let's say that you've identified a law. Perhaps it is a law of thought causation, which we will be considering later. I take the concept of thought causation very seriously—I believe in a law of thought causation; I write about it quite a bit and it's the subject of the deepest part of my spiritual search, in many regards. But, again, thought causation is going to function very differently, I believe, based upon mitigating circumstances, just as gravity does based on mass.

What I am describing is popularly called the Law of Attraction. But terms like Law of Attraction, and many other phrases, come to our lips too easily. Because if one really honors the idea of a Law of Attraction, then it stands to reason that, like a law of motion or a law of concentration or a law of entropy, it is going to be felt and experienced differently based on circumstances. We live within a concentric circle of existence in which material life, physical life elicits reactions from us, places laws upon us, places limitations on us—maybe not ultimately, but certainly in terms of what we experience. Again, physical mortality alone dictates that.

So, when you begin to ask the question, as I hope you will, *who am I?*, a variant of *know thyself*, you should experience that as a *continual* question, as a question that doesn't demand an answer, which is actually an end to a question, so much as it does a *response*. The deepening of a question is, as Manly understood, one of the great missions of philosophy. A question is not intended to provide you or me or anyone with solutions, with catechism, with ready-made responses— but your question, I believe, will bring you rewards if it is ever-deepening, if it is continually operating. That could almost be seen as the *law of questioning*; questioning is indestructible.

I think that's why true human progress, including inner progress, can never really be stifled or limited. We may lose time, or even generations, to fruitless argumentation or imposed limitations. I certainly think that within our contemporary world we have probably lost a generation of progress, for example, in ESP research or psychical research, because of very partisan and poorly thought-through objections that have limited its funding and resources, particularly on college campuses. But the question involved is indestructible. The question of whether the mind possesses *extra-physical properties*, or in what way these properties appear in our lives and can be felt on us and through us—that question is indestructible. It will *never* be extinguished. It also may never be fully answered. Hence, questioning itself can be understood as a kind of natural law or a metaphysical law.

In that vein, let's return to the question of reincarnation. This is something that Manly writes about early and frequently in the *Secret Teachings* and elsewhere. Reincarnation could be seen as a *subset* of the question of eternal recurrence. Reincarnation remains, for me, a deep question in itself. I have always been intrigued by something that was said on the subject by the writer and paranormal explorer Hans Holzer (1920–2009). Holzer observed that if you submit reincarnation to the general principle that the simplest answer that covers the greatest number of bases is probably the correct one—a variant of what is sometimes called Occam's razor—chances are you'll come to see reincarnation as a likely, and possibly comprehensive, solution to the problems and frustrations of human nature. Holzer observed that many of us experience the peculiar situation of discovering that certain intimate patterns or behaviors in life seem absolutely unchanging or intractable; certain characterological crises or traits are *always* with us, no matter what we do. We can spend years and years talking to a therapist, friends, family members about these repeat patterns within ourselves. We can come to whatever conclusions we may be able to venture about the meaning or causes behind these complexes, whether nature, nurture, or some combination—but they prove intractable. Holzer said that this phenomena could be an argument in favor of the validity of reincarnation and of the importation of traits from other existences, which we have accumulated and carried into our present experience. It is arguably the simplest answer that covers the greatest number of bases. And does it seem so strange or exotic? Consider that belief in reincarnation is globally diverse and literally as old as most recorded history. The concept appears in religions from Hinduism to Judaism. It is an ur-belief of humanity. Holzer posits that reincarnation, this widely embraced concept, covers more bases in character development than either biological determinism or conditioning. It covers the confoundingly dogged nature of our deepest behavioral patterns. I've always liked his observation. I don't see it as fatalistic but as tantalizingly practical.

Speaking personally as the father of two sons, I have observed—as I'm sure many of you reading these words have also noticed—that children seem to enter the world with pronounced and fixed temperaments from the earliest age, even just emergent from the womb. I detected traits in my own newborn sons that distinctly followed them into adolescence, where they are today. And I was fascinated by this, because throughout part of the twentieth century, and certainly into the twenty-first century, there played out a largescale debate in psychological circles about the question of nature versus nurture: are we born with temperamental traits or are they cultivated? Are we just products of conditioning or is something else going on? Are there biological reasons for why we act as we do? And what is the *interplay* between biological factors and early environment? To some therapists, that interplay makes the question of conditioning all the more important, because conditioning and early environment weigh decisively on how temperamental traits play out over the course of a person's life.

Clearly there exist innate temperamental traits in the individual. I think we've seen too much in terms of clinical observation, individual testimony, and personal experience to deny that very young children enter life with a pronounced character or temperament, whether shyness or ebullience, or any number of other proclivities. Later on in this book, we will explore astrology and whether that ancient system can provide insights into character based on the positioning of the cosmos at the time of one's first breath. I personally believe there's value there, as Manly did. Again: *as above, so below.*

All of what we're reviewing presents a wonderful series of scent trails, of hints as to the makeup the individual being, at least from an esoteric perspective. And all of this continues to heighten and expand the first principle of philosophy: *know oneself.* Yet I also believe—and I want to say this with great care, because it can be very easily misunderstood—that philosophy *should be simple*. We speak of the esoteric, we speak of the symbolic, and I've spoken of vast laws and forces that men and women live under. But, in the ultimate sense, I believe that philosophical questions should be something that every individual can get his or her arms around. I believe there's too much scholasticism in our era, in which, for example, the introduction to a classic book—whether the *Tao Te Ching,* the *Bhagavad Gita*, or any of the works of Shakespeare or Ralph Waldo Emerson—is often too long, too encumbered by theory, and too verbose to gainfully get through. I don't believe, frankly, that anybody should be required to read a forty-page introduction before getting down to business in the *Tao Te Ching* or the *Gita* or Emerson.

One time I heard from an academic who wrote to me after I had published a collection of Ralph Waldo Emerson's essays with a very short, gem-like introduction by the philosopher Jacob Needleman. This academic complained that there wasn't enough expository material in the book; there weren't sufficient historical or analytic notes. I pointed out to him that there were some notes, mostly bibliographical, but that wasn't enough to suit him. He wrote the following words to me, and I will never forget them: "It is impossible to understand Emerson without historical notes and analysis." He actually wrote that. It is *impossible* to understand Emerson without expository material. I asked myself, what would Emerson have said about that statement? Emerson wrote his essays, Plato constructed his dialogues, the great unknown author of the *Tao Te Ching* set down the ideas that have formed the heart of our ethics, in order for men and women to experience these things, to freely approach these things.

This returns us to where I began, which is the *practicality of philosophy*. I do not believe any great artistic, ethical, or philosophical work has been created—whether Scripture, operas, or poetry—that the individual, *plain and simple*, cannot approach. Sometimes a taste must be acquired. Sometimes critical analysis supports one's effort. But if an ethical work proves *impenetrable* to the everyday individual, that would give me questions about the nature and the quality of that work itself.

As alluded, I question the need for laborious, expository introductions to some of our classics; I am speaking of introductions that don't necessarily lower barriers—I made earlier reference to Ganesha, our patron deity—but rather introductions that offer analyses that themselves supersede or subtly dictate, suggest, or cordon the reader's personal experience. An introduction, in my view, can and ought to provide some historical notes; can and ought to provide some insight or highlighting of key themes and ideas. The person doing the introducing may want to offer some of his or her own ideas about the material being considered, as I'm attempting to here. But, above all, the purpose of an introduction, with honor to Ganesha, is the *lowering of barriers.* Because I really do believe that all the great esoteric works, in fact, are readable.

As I previously noted, *The Secret Teachings of All Ages* is *readable.* You will discover this when you delve into its pages or return to them. You may find it easier to begin with the "reader's edition." It is not a replacement for the original—nothing can replace the original—but it is a good supplement, and it makes the reading experience more open and approachable. As alluded, you will find when you begin to read the pages of *The Secret Teachings of All Ages* that it's a wonderfully accessible work; there really are no barriers. The writing is simple, clear, smooth, and even conversational. This is true of many great esoteric works by which people feel unnecessarily intimidated.

If, also as mentioned, you want to read Madame Blavatsky's great two-part cosmological work, *The Secret Doctrine,* just approach it. Manly Hall venerated Madame Blavatsky; he spoke of her and wrote of her with the deepest admiration. You can likewise read the magnificent allegorical epic by G.I. Gurdjieff, *Beelzebub's Tales to His Grandson.* Yes, the writing style is difficult, and intentionally so, because Gurdjieff was pushing back at the habitual thought patterns in the individual. He wanted to make the road a little rocky, but, nonetheless, he wrote the book *to be read.* A teacher of mine once told me that the author's wish was for the first edition of the massive book to appear in a pocket-sized dimension, so that you could carry it around with you. (He also joked, "They must have had bigger pockets then"). In reading that book, you'll find that the road may be filled with switchbacks, the road may disrupt some of your habituated behavior, but there are no barriers to entry. All of the great works—Plato, the Vedas, the Upanishads, the Beatitudes—they're all readable, they're all there for you, and they are all in the service of your probing this wonderful question: *Who am I*?

This question forms a kind of organic continuum with another question, to which I alluded earlier: *What am I here to do*? *What am I supposed to be expressing in life?* You may find a very helpful response to that question, a response that belongs to you alone, within the pages of *The Secret Teachings of All Ages*. Who's to say there won't be some symbol, paragraph, chapter, caption, image that won't make you say: "*This* is what I'm looking for; *this* is what I'm going to dedicate my life to." The book helped me understand what I wanted to dedicate my life to, which is documenting metaphysical experience in history and practice. When I read *The Secret Teachings of All Ages* for the first time, going back about 25 years from this writing, I understood that documenting the esoteric could be a vocation in itself, which is what Manly Hall exemplified in his pages.

As I considered in our first chapter, Manly completed the book at the extraordinarily young age of 27. And he wrote it specifically because he feared that the materialist thought taking hold throughout Western culture in the 1920s, both within general society and within academia, was going to lay waste, in a certain sense, to the great esoteric traditions. To many scholars and academics, the esoteric traditions were considered interesting to look at, possessed of anthropological significance, but the idea *would not be broached* that these things could hold relevancy and meaning for the modern person. Manly's pushback against that tendency is what drove him to write *The Secret Teachings of All Ages*.

I hope you won't mind my briefly restating something that I believe is vital to your experience and possibilities. In the first lesson, I approached the question of *how* at such an extraordinarily young age he produced a work of such virtuosity, range, depth, and breadth. I believe part of the answer is found when you meaningfully approach the questions: *What am I here for? What am I supposed to be pursuing?* When those questions bear some kind of fruit for you—as I believe they will—incredible energies and capacities will be unlocked in you: intellectually, physically, creatively, artistically, and intuitively. Different faculties will, I believe, grow sharper and more focused. I have witnessed this in myself and others.

Concentration brings power; that is another natural law. Photons of light elude the natural senses, but when extremely concentrated they form a laser.

You can push air or water out of the way with your hand; but when concentrated either becomes a *force* of irresistible magnitude. Again, this is a natural law: *as above, so below.* We can learn so many things about ourselves by observing the laws of nature. This was a central principle in the work of Ralph Waldo Emerson and the Transcendentalists. It's a central principle in the work of Manly. Hence, the *law of concentration* as observed in nature also plays out within your psyche. That's among the reasons why it is so lifesaving, and why it can bring such an added dimension to your existence, to honestly and intimately approach the questions: *Who am I? What am I here to be doing? Where am I going?* These are often seen as the three central questions of philosophy. They focus your energies.

Many people feel a sense of ennui in life, a sense of directionlessness, a sense of low-grade depression or anxiety. These things often follow us throughout life, like some kind of unwanted creature on our trail. And, again, we search, we go to therapy, we do all kinds of things to try to find out: *Why am I always dogged by this? Why am I always followed by this sense of unease?* Experience has taught me that a lot of what lies behind much of our low-grade depressions or anxieties, or even things that express themselves as neuroses or pathologies, is a sense of frustration in living out your individual potential, a sense of frustration in *exercising your individual power.* When you reach a place of understanding what you're intended to do in life—

and I've verified this in my own experience—some of these difficulties will fall away, like crumpled leaves dropping from a tree that's undergoing some kind of rebirth.

When you find—as you will—a sense of what you're supposed to be doing in life, whatever that may be and whatever line or channel of expression that takes you down, you will discover solutions, possibilities, and *relaxation* where none previously existed. I cannot begin to tell you the therapeutic value in the deepest sense of that word—*therapeia*, the Greeks called it—of meaningfully approaching the question of self-purpose. But in order to approach that question, you must approach it with a *complete lack of embarrassment.* You must approach it with a lack of inhibition. You must approach it individually, but also in light of your surroundings. You require a field that's fertile, where you are among useful, generative people, devices, and schools that don't place limitations on what you're going to discover, and that trust you to verify everything for yourself. Not to verify things in a way that matches whatever somebody else already believes. We're sometimes told to verify things, but the person who's saying so means, "Go and search and when you come to believe what *I* already do—come back to me."

The lowest form of engagement with an idea is agreement or disagreement. What does it matter whether I agree or disagree with what my neighbor thinks? Is it that important? I want the search for meaning to be *protected*; protected from my neighbor and for my neighbor and protected for myself. Agreement or disagreement is unimportant in self-development. What matters is that you be free to approach an idea, such as your self-purpose, with independence, absence of embarrassment, and absence of encumbrance by what other people tell you you're going to find. Or by the conditions, peer pressure, and limits that you have internalized. Once again, the purpose of this *Seeker's Guide* is to lower barriers so you can learn what is absolutely fortifying and true for you as an individual, which in itself will help you see and understand the nature of your connection to everything. *Above, so below.*

In short, Manly opens the book by talking about how the purpose of philosophy is the awakening of the individual to a greater awareness of self. He calls this the central purpose harbored by all of the seminal ethical thinkers: Plato, Socrates, Aristotle, the Vedic sages, the sages of the East; and in the work of all traditions, including Buddhism, Taoism, the Persian faiths, the faith of Mithraism, the Judeo-Christian faith, all the faiths that sprung from the Indus Valley and the Mediterranean Basin, spreading throughout the Eastern and Western worlds, and that also speak to us today. Manly surveys the thought of illumined modern intellects like Francis Bacon, William James, and Ralph Waldo Emerson; and he alludes to ideas that reach us through contemporary religions, like the work of Mary Baker Eddy, the founder of the Christian Science movement, who had wonderful and extraordinary insights of her own. And the list goes on and on. There's such a wonderful plethora of figures who have sought to drink from the wells of ancient wisdom and have come back with their own ideas. Their ideas may not always suit your needs at given points, their ideas may not open a particular path for you, but *some of them will*. Follow the scent trail of personal relevance.

Manly discovered his purpose as a very young man by reading vastly across all these schools, by experiencing as much as he could of the *content* of hallowed philosophy—hallowed not because it is old but because it has posterity. Hallowed because it underscores some of the first principles of life. Primeval ideas resound throughout different cultures and expressions. First principles of human nature are strikingly congruent to the ideas that we have about ourselves today. And in that vein, humanity is vastly older than I think we sometimes appreciate. This is something we explore in the next chapter, which is on the question of primeval civilizations.

I remember once falling to my knees and weeping when I discovered that there exist the remnants of an altar in the Negev desert that was produced about 25,000 years ago by hunter-gatherers on the desert plain. They wanted to erect an altar venerating and worshiping the moon. I think their connection to nature was vastly deeper and more profound than what we experience today. They understood certain things about nature that have been lost to us. This is true of the Native American cultures, as well, about which Manly wrote with veneration not only in *The Secret Teachings of All Ages* but also in a more recent collection of his work that I edited, *The Secret History of America.*

Ancient—truly ancient—people, from the Mediterranean Basin to the continent of North America, possessed a vaster and more profound understanding of nature and our place in it than we do today. The illustrations of *The Secret Teachings of All Ages* reproduce some of the great monuments that the ancients erected in different parts of the world, which are some of the most beautiful primeval touchstones of the human wish to know. Again, just think of it: these ancient beings in the Negev desert some 25,000 years ago looked up at the cosmos and asked, *Who am I?* They didn't experience a sense of separation between above and below. They saw in the moon an object of veneration: it not only governed the seasons, it not only governed planting cycles, it not only marked off the passage of time and the revolutions and movements of the cosmos, but I believe they saw it as an expression of some great higher intellect—a *common* intellect—of which we are all a part. The ancient Greeks and Hermeticists called it *Nous*, or an over-mind. Ralph Waldo Emerson called it the Over-Soul. Emanuel Swedenborg referred to a kind of "divine influx" emanating from a cosmic psyche. Some contemporary people refer to it as Infinite Mind. It is a near-universal principle.

I think all of these instincts approach truth. I think they are in the right direction because they are in the same direction. I always look for parallel insights among people separated by vast amounts of time and geography. This common insight, extending across ages, *connects us* to our primeval ancestors. Every time you embark on these questions—*Who am I? What am I here to do? Where am I going?*—you effectively join a chain of seeking individuals, which extends to antiquity. And the signs and symbols left for us by our ancient ancestors help communicate to us—even today—some of the concerns that they had about the nature of our existence.

Just by *asking a question*, just by entering Manly's great book, you are *innately* joining that chain of human intellects, which, again, throughout history have asked those three vital questions: *Who am I? What am I supposed to be doing? Where am I headed?* The pages of the *Secret Teachings* represent to you an open door. But the byways that you follow and the conclusions you reach are exquisitely your own. In joining together to experience this great book, we help one another find something.

_____ ෨ ෧ _____

Ancient Egypt and the Question of Primeval Civilizations

I n this chapter we explore Ancient Egypt and the question of primeval civilizations. When I say primeval, I mean those civilizations that are of such extreme antiquity that they form the foundation of human civilization; they form the first principles of human life and the earliest abilities of humanity to assemble into a community or polity. Inevitably, when talking about primeval civilizations, one not only encounters Ancient Egypt, but also the question of "Atlantis" or other theorized ancient orders, as Manly explores in the *Secret Teachings*.

Was Atlantis a real place? Was there some lost civilization in human history, as myth holds, that was perhaps greatly advanced, and whose rise and fall is filled with crucial, even existential, questions for humanity? Manly Hall thought so. He wrote with historical interest about the theorized continent of Atlantis, and he drew upon many sources, including, of course, the dialogues of Plato. Plato's dialogues, *Critias* and *Timaeus,* expound upon a civilization called Atlantis; Plato's speakers record a beautiful, greatly advanced civilization. This testimony draws upon the recollections of the great statesman, Solon, who was said to have visited Ancient Egypt, and who possessed an understanding of humanity's deepest, most primeval origins. Plato's record says that this great seafaring civilization grew so mighty and so powerful that it committed, in a sense, the ultimate trespass, which was to attack Athens itself. The Athenians successfully repelled the attack of the Atlanteans, and this ushered in the ultimate fall and disappearance of this hallowed, antique civilization.

Is this a true story? Will we ever know for certain? Will we ever have actual, tactile, evidence of the existence of an Atlantis? I don't think it's a question that humanity will ever answer definitively, certainly not within our generation. But, in a way, I rather like that fact, because I feel that mysteries draw us forward in life, and that with the absence of mysteries we would stagnate. So long as mysteries do not harden into dogma—which can come in the form of certainties, unshakable reference points, and preconceptions that are supposed to be taken as givens—they beckon us, they summon us forward. Mysteries are almost like the call of coyotes in the wilderness, reminding us that there's a world out there that we don't fully know—a world sometimes shrouded in shadow and containing features that we cannot always be certain of, but that we can nonetheless develop deepened questions toward and perhaps derive lessons from. In that sense, the question of Atlantis will always be with us.

In *The Secret Teachings of All Ages*, Manly writes rather extensively about Atlantis, and he takes very literally the presence of an advanced lost civilization. For that reason, it's important, I think, for me to say something about the historicism of this question. I do not believe that individuals in the early twenty-first century—just as when Manly produced *The Secret Teachings of All* Ages in the early twentieth—have a clear idea of the true antiquity of the human story. I do not think we have a comprehensive sense of just how ancient humanity actually is. We certainly have our guideposts; we have crucially important archaeological finds and historical touchstones, in some cases literally. But I think the timeline of human history remains an unsettled question. There are theories, which I think bear some airing, that predate the dawn of Ancient Egyptian civilization, as we know it through its monuments and great works, thousands of years earlier than the traditional timeline of, say, 3,500 B.C. There are defensible archaeological theories that predate Ancient Egypt to 7,500 B.C., or *possibly* as old as

10,000 B.C. Some of these theories, in their most compelling form, postdate the career of Manly P. Hall; but I think he would have wanted them included in any consideration of primeval antiquity, because some of these theories comport well with certain things that he wrote about; indeed, there are several instances in this book where we'll be considering controversial touchstones that Manly wrote about which were later validated by academic archaeology or other sciences. Certain historical episodes that had once been considered mythical or fanciful were later borne out in their validity, more or less as Manly wrote them. Hence, I encourage anyone who wants to remain relevant in his or her field not to say "impossible" too quickly.

This brings me to a contemporary theory about the Great Sphinx on the Giza Plateau. Several years ago, two archaeologists, Robert M. Schoch, a Yale-trained geologist, and the late John Anthony West, an independent archeologist, ventured a compelling and important theory about the timeline of the Sphinx. West and Schoch determined that water damage appears on the oldest portions of the Great Sphinx, and that this water damage suggests the building of the Sphinx at an earlier time in Ancient Egypt's environmental history. The water damage that they detected on the earliest portions of the Sphinx would, as alluded, predate the dawn of Egyptian civilization to possibly 7,500 B.C. or as old as 10,000 B.C. Their theory is not accepted within academic archaeology. In fact, it is violently and sometimes angrily disputed. However, no archaeologist has actually contradicted it. No archaeologist has actually done investigatory work on the monument itself that would overturn the Schoch-West thesis and the implications of the water damage that they documented.

The critics offer *tangential arguments* intended to overturn the thesis. One of the most compelling tangential arguments was promulgated by an archaeologist at the Brooklyn Museum; he observed that there isn't a single shard of pottery, there isn't a single piece of material evidence yet discovered that *corroborates* the Schoch-West timeline. He made his point compellingly, saying in effect: "Show me one piece of pottery, show me one shard; show me one monument of any sort that would line up with the Schoch-West theory." I brought this to the attention of John Anthony West, when he was living not far from me in the Hudson Valley region of New York, and he and I talked this over. His contention to me, and I think he was right, is simply that further investigation is required; he and Schoch pinpointed a vital piece of empirical evidence, which no one in the field has *directly* responded to or has overturned. There are counter theories, of course, which reference various environmental impacts and factors. I don't find that any of the counter theories definitively address the Schoch-West findings. They raise important questions, but they sidestep the full nature of Schoch-West findings. Indeed, they do not rule out the Schoch-West thesis; rather, they provide further circumstantial questions, which are somewhat polemically used to discredit the Schoch-West thesis without directly addressing it.

The question of a primeval civilization has animated the thought of spiritual geniuses and literary giants. The twentieth century spiritual philosopher G.I. Gurdjieff (c.1866–1949) talks about the existence of an ancient civilization, which bears the same timeline as the Schoch-West thesis, in his allegory *Beelzebub's Tales to his Grandson*, which I have mentioned. The Schoch-West thesis also comports with the timeline that Manly P. Hall posits in *The Secret Teachings of All Ages*. It likewise comports with some of what Plato recorded in his dialogues. So, I believe there is a tantalizing question there—and it's a question that has been left largely unaddressed in our time.

You might wonder, as I have: shouldn't there be professors, grad students, and archeologists who want to go back over the Schoch-West research and directly check it out, get right to the heart of things? And that brings us to a thorny question about the politics of academia and archaeology in the late twentieth and early twenty-first centuries. For one thing, it is extremely difficult to gain any kind of exploratory access to the Giza Plateau. These things are very tightly controlled by the ministry of antiquities and various authorities within the Egyptian government, about

which more will be said, and access is closely pro-
scribed. Access is also extremely expensive. Recent to
this writing, I returned from shooting a documentary
in Egypt about the occult book *The Kybalion*, and our
director, Ronni Thomas, discovered how difficult it is
and how *expensive* it is just to shoot documentary foot-
age from a remove at the Egyptian monuments. It's
a licensing and budgetary challenge in itself. Vastly
more so is the task of getting the appropriate licen-
sure and funding to actually gain *up-close* access in an
exploratory manner to study the great monuments,
Giza most especially.

Even getting a greenlight for such a study from an
American university is near-impossible. I was speaking about this with Robert Schoch who holds a faculty
position at Boston University, and he made the point
to me, which is very important, that if a graduate student or anybody in the field of archaeology expresses
interest in exploring this thesis, he or she will almost
immediately be labeled a kind of crank or eccentric.
Academics within that field are intrinsically dismis-
sive of this thesis because, for one thing, it undercuts
the timeline on which many of them have based their
own scholarly work and research. It undercuts the
foundation of some of what they've built their careers
on. The timeline of the Great Sphinx and the pyramids is considered settled, and if you even raise the
question of wanting to study the Sphinx or the great
pyramids in a general manner—much less investigate

the timeline—you are looked at a little funny. You are considered somewhat off-center or eccentric, because, again, that work is considered completed. There is, in effect, no need to peer through Galileo's telescope. So the same faculty advisors and department heads who control your funding, advancement, and tenure when you are enter the field as a graduate student or faculty member, the very people who control the reins of your academic career, are often closed off, if not hostile, toward the question of revisiting any facet of the timeline. Even raising the question itself is sometimes regarded with umbrage, because it implicitly undermines the prevailing research on which many of the senior figures in the field built their reputations. Hence, funding is absent, approbation is absent, and licensing is absent.

For many years, until the deposing of the government of Hosni Mubarak in 2011, the minister of antiquities in Egypt was a figure named Zahi Hawass—a larger-than-life figure and a very powerful man, politically and personally. Understanding the priorities of such a figure, and how they impact archeology, is not always easy; but it is vital to grasping what does and does not get greenlit for study. There was and there remains a political dimension to the job that Hawass and others have occupied as the ministers of antiquity. The political dimension is this: the contemporary nation of Egypt very rightly and justly takes national pride in its place as the cradle of civilization, in its place as the land in which the pyramid builders dwelt. There are probably no monuments of the ancient world that are better known, more inspiring, and more magnificent than the monuments of Ancient Egypt, and, to some degree, this plays a nationalistic role in Egyptian life, as ancient monuments play in the existence of nations all over the world. And there exists a conviction among government figures that any attempt to predate the traditional timeline of Ancient Egypt strikes at the heart of the nation's sense of lineage and custodianship over these monuments. The conclusion is rather hastily jumped to that any attempt to predate or question the timeline of the monuments would strip Egypt of its own sense of lineage, of its own sense of family tree, of national purpose. I don't think that should be the case at all, although I realize the delicateness of the situation and I share the honor and the veneration that many contemporary Egyptians hold for these monuments. I bow my knee to the antiquity of Egyptian civilization. And if we were to discover that Egypt possesses an antiquity that's even *deeper* than what the current time line posits, to me that would only enrich and fortify the lineage of that great civilization; not challenge it, but deepen it. Yet for various reasons the governmental structure within Egypt has for years come to feel that such efforts would serve to defraud the nation of its lineage. (This is exacerbated by the so-called "ancient alien" thesis, of which I am not a partisan, and which some Egyptians, includ-

ing Hawass, feel deprives the nation of its primacy.)
Again, I understand the sensitivity to these questions,
and I share the sensitivity; but in this particular case,
I think a reconsideration of the Schoch-West thesis
would *deepen* our sense of Egyptian antiquity, not dis-
place it.

Of course, this admixture of politics and science
plays out all around the world, within every nation;
because most archeological sites are under some kind
of governmental control, there is always some political
dimension to how they're managed. I must underscore
that this conundrum is reflected in archaeological
research everywhere: in South America, in other parts
of the Mediterranean Basin, in Persia. But because of
the perennial interest in the Sphinx, and the controversies involved, some valid, some not, these questions
persist especially on the Giza Plateau. Now, I haven't
personally researched the "ancient astronaut" theory
or things of that nature. In specifics, I am referencing only the Schoch-West thesis, the possibility that it
raises, and the difficulty in studying it.

There were of course pyramid builders all over the
world. One finds pyramids in the civilizations of Asia.
One finds great burial mounds on the American continent. There are magnificent pyramids and temples
of the Mayan civilization found within Central America, within Mexico, within the civilization of the Aztecs
and other early cultures. There are monuments

throughout the Celtic world, some of which are built up in the form of a mound or a natural pyramid-like structure. There are monuments of this kind within the early Buddhist and Hindu worlds in the form of stupas. It seems to me that a pyramid was one of the central early expressions of humanity's aspiration to *know itself* and to understand how it related to the surrounding cosmos.

Some of these pyramids and some of the related monuments I describe show markings of extraordinary astronomical sophistication. They are keyed to stars and objects in the sky, which ancient people, I think very rightly, understood as part of the arc of nature to which they were intimately connected. This is true within Egypt, the Celtic world, the Mayan world, and other civilizations.

Now returning to the Atlantean thesis, there are, to be sure, explorers who fund independent missions to different parts of the world—coastal waters off Turkey, the Caribbean, the Mediterranean—some of whom have cited evidence of untracked civilizations which they feel are concealed beneath the ocean's tides. So, it's not as if people haven't raised money and made independent efforts (sometimes heroic efforts) to pursue this question by their own lights.

I was referring in our previous lesson to the fact that questions, while indestructible, can be stifled for a period of time, either because funding isn't available or because the prevailing academic or critical or journalistic structure discredits them. So, unfortunately, for many years, we haven't made academic progress on this question. Maybe that will change in future generations. My wish is that there will be a rising crop of students in archaeology who one day rediscover the Schoch-West thesis and dedicate themselves, in one way or another, to exploring it and helping to pursue it, wherever it leads. It's certainly a wonderful question for idealistic students and it's a question that I hope some of them will find a way to take up. It may fall to future generations. Those are the circumstances that we live in. The question itself is indestructible.

But why is it important? Why should we care whether or not these great ancient civilizations existed or existed earlier than we believe? Why should we study the things that they left behind: the pyramids, Stonehenge, stupas, and other monuments from Druidic, Celtic, Vedic, Mayan, and Egyptian traditions? Well, first and foremost, history is a mirror; we cannot know ourselves without being able to gaze into an unclouded mirror. History teaches us things about human nature that we could never know otherwise. *As above, so below*: the earliest impulses that animated our ancestors are the same impulses that exist within us. We help ourselves refine and gain a better understanding of our own pursuit of self-knowledge—*know thyself*—when we understand the commonalities we share with the ancients.

But to understand some of these commonalities requires, at the very outset, knowing that they were *there* and then trying to grapple with some idea of what our ancestors were thinking about. As I mentioned, recent to this writing I returned from filming in Egypt, and the continuum with the ancient past is a question of deep personal importance to me. Another of the controversies that surrounds the monuments of Ancient Egypt is their *purpose*; specifically what was the *function* of the great pyramids?

Now, within traditional archaeology, you'll hear— and again, I think this is part of our human habit—the tendency to seek and seize upon *one answer*, whereas there may be multiple answers. In that vein, we are often taught that the pyramids on the Giza Plateau were crypts, were burial structures, and nothing more. We are told that the pharaohs, possessed of this outsized egotism, built vast monuments to their own lives, to their own temporal power, and placed sarcophagi within these chambers, in which they could be encrypted, so that their greatness would always be looked upon and never be forgotten. In a sense, the pyramids are sometimes described as an ancient symptom of megalomania; they may be engineering marvels, we hear, but the purpose behind them was mere vanity.

Now, while it is true that sarcophagi *are* found in some of the great pyramids, including the central Great Pyramid on the Giza Plateau, it's not at all clear that interment was *the only or exclusive purpose* for which they had been built. It is very important to come back again to this fissure in human nature: that once we determine or locate *one thing*—which may be altogether correct in itself—we conclude that that's all *that was going on*. We're conditioned to believe that there's one motive behind everything, one antecedent behind everything, and once you unlock it, that issue is settled. Hence, some archaeologists perpetuate the belief that these monuments were just great crypts and nothing more, as if one piece of the puzzle is the puzzle itself.

That "nothing more" thesis is not at all clear to me in terms of history or philosophy. For one thing, ancient people viewed and understood death in a very different way than we do. They did not see the dead as forgotten, finished, and gone, just to be burned, buried, or encrypted. Rather, they saw the dead as part of a chain of eternal existence and recurrence; and they often placed the dead within structures or buildings that were actually continually visited and used for a multitude of purposes, including worship, ancestor veneration, prayer, respite, music, calendrics, ceremonial meals, and initiatory rites—all things that populated the minds and energies of the people who crafted the ancient mystery traditions of Egypt, Greece, Rome, Persia, and other parts of the world.

An interesting case appears in England at Avebury, one of the cavern-like monuments located nearby Stonehenge, itself a beautiful sight of calendrics and worship that was built by ancient druids maybe as late as 4,500 B.C. There exist a series of caverns at Avebury that were used as crypts, as a place where the dead are interred—but these chambers clearly functioned as more than that. The chambers were built inside magnificent mounds, which would serve as a marker, not only of calendrics and of the movement of the cosmos, but as a means of venerating the natural world. And we know for a fact that family members would visit these mounds and the caverns within them because they left behind offerings of food and drink. They saw the dead as a continual part of natural world. They saw the dead as palpably present. Ancient people didn't just inter the dead and forget about them; they communed with them, they returned to these sites, they spent time at them, they marked the seasons by them, they constructed and held bonfires and seasonal dances and ceremonies around them. This still goes on in certain parts of the world today, including the African continent.

I mentioned that death was a palpable presence for ancient people; life was precarious; and when they committed themselves to the incredibly arduous task of constructing these monuments, they weren't necessarily building them for a sole purpose. Everything in the ancient world needed to serve the fullest purpose, whether animal carcasses, tools, or monuments. It is difficult to imagine the effort expended in building these structures. We still do not know with any definitiveness, for example, how the vast stones of Stonehenge were transported from their original locations. We don't know for certain how they were uplifted and moved. There are theories, of course, but this engineering question remains. We don't know how the vast heads that populate Easter Island were firmly planted into the ground and uplifted. Again, there are theories. Every few years there'll be a special on cable television or an article upending an old theory and proffering a new one. But it is important to remember that reference is being made to theories, not to solutions.

We still don't fully know or understand how the ancient engineers accomplished much of what they did, sometimes down to the very *basics* of not even knowing how they were able to move their building materials from their original sites. We shouldn't be afraid of the word, "mystery." A mystery is what propels us toward a question and toward thought. A mystery is what keeps life from stagnating. Unanswered questions, as with unmet needs, propel us toward necessity. A question keeps us hungry as individuals and as civilizations. And I think we should always be acknowledging that we approach Giza, Stonehenge, and other such sites *knowing that we don't know* and refusing to regard prevailing theories as settled knowledge no more to be questioned than the rising and setting of the sun.

But that's the corner into which we sometimes paint ourselves. Manly Hall believed, I think with great justice, that the world *does* stand on the shoulders of Ancient Egypt, that the ancients possessed traits, ways of life, and secrets that we haven't even begun to consider. Even according to the traditional timeline, it is difficult for us to understand the depth of Egypt's antiquity. When the Greek philosopher and historian Herodotus (c. 484–c. 425 B.C.) encountered the great pyramids, they were as ancient to him as he is to us. Even according to the most traditional timeline, Egyptian civilization existed for more than 3,500 years. That's far longer than any modern civilization. We have difficulty getting our arms around that. We like to draw conclusions about the rise and fall of civilizations in ways that come too readily to the lips, that spring too readily to mind, without taking account that Ancient Egypt, even according to the traditional timeline, underwent a vast number of changes during its existence. Modes and styles of worship came and went. Methods and styles of buildings came and went. Means and priorities of governance came and went. Ideas were embraced, used, and discarded—and new ones found.

The same is true of Mayan civilization. One cannot talk about Mayan civilization, the ancient civilization that populated the central Americas, as one continuous whole. It underwent all kinds of changes and permutations—there were periods of relative peace, periods of warfare, periods in which certain understandings and styles of building were in demand, were practiced, and then receded, to be replaced by other styles—and these things all grew out of both social necessity and the ideas of ancient people about themselves.

The great Mayan civilization is an interesting case in point, and it relates, in a certain way, to the Atlantean thesis. There were stages of profound violence and warfare during various epochs of Mayan civilization as well as within the civilizations, including the Aztecs, that branched off from the Maya. There were periods of public execution in Aztec history, there were periods of human sacrifice, there were periods of ritual violence. This came in particular at the latter stages of those civilizations; it wasn't general and it wasn't necessarily common, but it did occur. People have sometimes wondered why these great monument builders, particularly in the later stages of their civilizations, went through periods of what seem like extreme ritual violence or brutality.

My friend, Ptolemy Tompkins, a great writer of esotericism, broached a theory about this, which I find brilliant, and I want to offer it here. Ptolemy has traveled extensively in Central America and his father, Peter Tompkins, was an independent archeologist, very much in the mode of a John Anthony West or Robert Schoch. Ptolemy noted that Mayan and Aztec civilizations in their later stages engaged in a lot of blood sport and blood sacrifice. As he wondered at this, he theorized that it is possible that, in earlier stages, these civilizations felt more possessed of a vital understanding of the interconnectedness of all things—they felt close to the gods or the cosmos, so to speak. Their knowledge and understanding of nature contained real profundity. But in later stages, it is possible that some of these insights were lost within both the culture and the individual. And sometimes when feelings of vitality and connectedness get lost, people engage in alternative ways of heightening a sense of thrill and purpose—and these ways can come in the form of violence.

Violence or the witnessing of violence can give the individual *a false feeling of life*. This was true of the murdering of martyrs, for example, in the Colosseum at Rome. Some apparently universal fissure in human nature makes us drawn to the violent, makes us drawn to bloodshed. It gives us a perverted sense of vitality. A brilliant modern mystic named Vernon Howard (1918–1992) used to speak of the "false feeling of life" we derive from hostility, anger, violent entertainment, and acts of both physical and emotional violence, including attacking people on social media. So, Ptolemy theorized that some of the great civilizations in their latter stages might have devolved into the practice of ritualized violence, which one could also say about our own civilization. They lost their connection as cultures and as individuals with the first principles of life. And, feeling bereft of those vital first principles and their life-giving properties, they resorted to violence for a false *thrill*—for the rush that one gets when feeling that all possibilities are open, all barriers have fallen, all paths are stretched out before you. It was a harbinger of the fall of some of these great civilizations.

Is violence as a replacement for life the general downfall of people and societies? It's a tantalizing theory, and it comports with the story of Atlantis as it was written about in Plato, and as Manly Hall wrote about it in *The Secret Teachings of All Ages*. Although the underlying factor that destroyed Atlantean civilization, so the mythos goes, was *hubris*. This is also seen in the story of Icarus, from the great Hellenic myth, who constructed wings of feather and wax. Feeling indestructible, he flew too close to the sun, the wax melted, and he plummeted to earth.

Arrogance is profoundly dangerous. Arrogance abets foolishness. It always has. "Pride goes before destruction, a haughty spirit before a fall," reads Proverbs 16:18. Arrogance is one of the most dangerous of human traits, and one could say that that simple truth—which is so easy to overlook in ourselves—is at the heart of the mythos of Atlantis. That great civilization tumbled to its ruin because of hubris and arrogance; because of unnecessary expansionism; because of the need to attack Athens simply as conquest.

Another factor that historically played into the fall of great civilizations was depletion of natural resources. At least that's the prevailing theory behind the disappearance of the Mayan civilization as a monument-building culture. Archaeologists have theorized, probably rightly, that resources were in such desperate need within the cities of the Maya, and that there had been such an exhaustion of immediately surrounding resources, that the cities themselves became unsustainable. Of course, it's impossible to avoid comparison with the environmental crisis of our current day. So presumably these cycles repeat, because human nature is constant. Human consistency provides us with another reason to look into the mirror that history provides us. And that mirror must be unclouded. Hence, understanding the rise and fall of the ancient civilizations is perhaps the best yardstick that we have of understanding and measuring our own circumstances. But when doing so, it is also important to remember that, although everything has speeded up in our lives, these ancient civilizations existed for vast stretches of time. For that reason, it is important not to be too general in extrapolating from their rise and fall, because there were many undulating waves in their history and these events played out across vast stretches of time.

It is also important to look toward the ancient civilizations, Egypt in particular, for their psychological teachings and psycho-spiritual teachings. The Ancient Egyptians possessed a profound understanding of how the individual mirrors the cycles of nature and the congruity between the cosmos or outer world and that which plays out within the individual psyche. Each one of the gods of Ancient Egypt is a kind of representation of the individual psyche; and the disputes, the alliances, the violence that sometimes played out among the gods provide deeply psychological and parabolic lessons in human nature.

One of the key parables of Ancient Egyptian religion is the war that broke out between the god Horus and his uncle, Set. A variant of the story tells us—and it is important to remember that the ancient myths rarely have one definitive telling but several versions—that Set destroyed his brother, Osiris, Horus's father; Horus's surviving mother was Isis. Set dismembered Osiris's body in pursuit of conquest. In so doing, he was challenged and defeated by Horus. Yet that traditional telling doesn't fully open a window on the drama of these ancient gods. I personally saw a magnificent bas-relief in Egypt of Set and Horus in embrace. The image joined both of their traits: the generative, life-giving qualities of Horus and the self-assertion and self-determination and usurpation of Set. It was necessary that these be joined, both for political and psychological reasons. This scene appears in a rare bas-relief in the Egyptian National Museum signifying an Old Kingdom effort towards unification.

Personally, I love the figure of Set. I see Set as the great usurper, the great revolutionary. I think, in a certain sense, he was similar to the rebellious serpent that we meet in Genesis 3. The ancients realized that life could not be complete without veneration of that rebellious, usurping force that urges humanity to move forward, that asserts the need to create, to generate, to produce, to fulfill, to tear down, and to remake. I have a beautiful, original papyrus of Set hanging at home in my apartment in New York City. Egyptologists and mythologists sometimes refer to Set as an animal of unknown origin. The "Set animal," as the deity is sometimes termed, has beautiful upright ears or horns emerging from his head. Scholars cannot quite place what animal this figure was based upon. His origin is a mystery. He is sometimes considered the god of the underworld but that is not quite right. In Egypt, scholars understand Set as the god of storms and the desert. He was fierce.

In many cases, we can recognize distinct animals within certain Egyptian gods: cats associated with Bastet and Sekhmet, which we will further explore; birds, and particularly the water bird called the ibis, associated with Thoth, the god of writing and intellect, whom we will also consider further; a falcon associated with Horus; a crocodile associated with Sobek, a militaristic and protective god sometimes seen as the son of Set, and many other recognizable animals. Because no *discernible* animal is reflected in Set, I venture that Set reflects a non-material energy; Set represents that urgent *calling* that we feel within to create, destroy, and remake. Set is the *human animal*, in a sense. Noble, powerful, rebellious, usurping, romantic, creative: he's one of the most tantalizing of all the ancient Egyptian gods.

And there were hundreds of such gods who weighed human behavior; who made determinations about whether people functioned with *nobility, rightness, loyalty, payment of debt*—those were among the ethics most venerated in Ancient Egypt. I believe that we focus too little on such expressions of life today. A passage appears in The Talmud, the collection of rabbinic wisdom which we will also encounter later, in which a master asks several of his students, "What is the mark of an evil man?" All the students provide compelling answers; but one of the students in particular says: "He who borrows and does not repay." And the master says, "I favor that explanation above all the others, because all the others are contained within it." That was a vital expression of wisdom, of truth, in Ancient Egypt: payment of debts, keeping of one's word, loyalty to others—not corruption, not blind fealty—but *loyalty* in a form of what we might today call solidarity, solidness, fellowship. Part of repaying debts is honoring where one has come from and who one's benefactors have been. These were some of the traits of life enshrined and honored in Ancient Egypt, and the individual was always under the reminder that there was a constant repayment of debt called for.

You see this repayment of debt in the recompense of nature. The night provides a comforting, enshrouding darkness—that same darkness illuminates the cosmos and gives succor and insight to humanity. In the West we sometimes use "darkness" as a negative. But how else would we be able to see the stars and the cosmos? Darkness is life-giving. It is a womb. The warming rays of the sun make possible the functioning of human life, the planting of crops, the harvesting of food. The darkness is its reliving counterpart in which things gestate. Everything is owed its due: We benefit from gods of the hunt, to whom we owe game, livestock, and sustenance. We benefit from gods of sexuality and procreation—including the great bull, a symbol of procreation.

When I was in Egypt in 2019, I was taken into a very deep cavern that's usually closed off to the public within the Valley of Kings. I was granted permission by a caretaker to lay hands on the ancient bas-relief of a bull. I can share with you, speaking just on a personal scale, that I felt this electricity shoot through me upon laying hands; it was a wonderful personal experience. I was also granted the opportunity to enter a pitch-black temple to Sekhmet, the beautiful goddess in the simultaneous form of a cat and a female being. At the complex of Karnak in Luxor I was led into this temple by a guide. There was an armed soldier posted outside, and the director Ronni Thomas and I were given the ability to enter this temple; and we got to perform a small ceremony to Sekhmet, which was just a magnificent experience. One could feel a living presence of the goddess filling this pitch-black cavernous space; and we had the privilege to lay hands on this ancient monument. It was an extraordinary experience, to which I will return later in the book.

All of what I am describing is just a *sliver* of what the ancients were in touch with. Their initiatory religions awakened in them traits and possibilities of human nature that are as real as the veins in your own neck, but from which we are often divorced and distant in the world today. And when we are divorced and distant from these things, we often replace them with the *false feeling of life* that comes from violence, hostility, cynicism, rampant sarcasm, or any of the things that run riot today in digital culture.

In Ancient Rome, of course, there was a general uptick of violence, military campaigns, and the continued, urgent necessity to protect the homeland. Mercenaries were often paid to do this. The public was bought off with docility through circuses, so to speak, and through violence in the Colosseum. For all that, I don't think we've taken proper measure of the civilization of Ancient Rome: how it venerated and enshrined beauty in its statues and monuments. The ideal of beauty spoke to the ancient Romans in such a compelling, crystalline way. The same is true of the Greek and other Hellenic civilizations. Even amid setback that beauty persisted. Beauty was a kind of centerpiece of their culture.

Indeed, no consideration of ancient civilizations is complete without taking measure of beauty. And, seen from that perspective, I don't think we should ever feel that our personal conception of beauty is something that's necessarily superficial or vain. Beauty appears in the great Tantric writings; in the Vedas, including in statuary and base reliefs and tapestries made by the Vedic civilizations; it is extolled within the Hebraic book, the Song of Solomon; beauty is celebrated within the statuary of the Maya; in the statuary of the ancient Chinese and Japanese civilizations; as well as Greek and Roman design and statues. The legendary Egyptian queen Nefertiti (c. 1370–c. 1330 B.C.) was said to be the creator of makeup, she was the first who adorned her face with natural substances to accentuate jawline and cheekbone and to decorate lips and eyes. She wore the magnificent oblong crown that you'll see depicted in many statues and bas-reliefs.

So beauty, too, was a centerpiece of the ancient civilizations, and I don't think that we today should just dismiss it as something temporal or superficial. Make no mistake—and you can walk through any museum and validate this for yourself—beauty was a fundamental part of the culture and religion of these ancient civilizations. But, as these civilizations grew devoid of purpose or depleted of resources, and as hubris or violence more routinely set in, such events also opened the door to decline and destruction.

Although I must add this following note, on which I will close. I see decline and destruction *less* as a lesson for civilizations and *more* as one for individuals. It's easy—too easy—to talk about the rise and fall of civilizations as some kind of macro concern, which somebody, somewhere ought to do something about; but I think these lessons are about the individual, as well.

The great twentieth century Egyptologist R.A. Schwaller de Lubicz (1887–1961) made the observation that the Temple of Luxor, which I recently visited, is actually in the shape of a human form; it takes the shape of the anatomy of man. For that reason he called it the Temple of Man. That is, among other things, a reminder that we should understand the ancient monuments and the ancient civilizations as *intimate parables of self.*

Hence, I close this chapter by cautioning against getting excessively distracted with the rise and fall of *empires*, which can almost serve to distance you from these lessons on a personal level. And, as noted in the previous chapter, philosophy must be personal; it must be practical, if it is anything at all. So, the question is: How do *I* deplete resources in my own life? How do *I* fail tests of loyalty and debt, broadly defined? How do *I* take from others what is not mine? How do *I* attempt to expand or perhaps to grab beyond what is necessary in my own life? How do *I* substitute violence and hostility for true vitality? It is when we see *ourselves* in the mirror that ancient civilizations hold up to us that we begin to decipher their most valuable lessons and secrets.

LESSON IV

_____ ୭ ୧ _____

Science of the Stars

The topic of this chapter is the science of the stars, or astrology. Astrology is one of my personally favorite topics. I've learned a great deal about classical astrology from Manly P. Hall; his astrological writings in *The Secret Teachings of All Ages* and elsewhere have been enormously helpful in marrying my understanding of astrology to astronomy. In the ancient world, the two arts were one and the same; they were not practiced along different but parallel lines (as they are today among the best astrologers). The capacity of ancient people to chart the movement of objects through the skies was one of the earliest and first signs of civilization, of shared destiny, of common practices, and of the cultivation of a polity of knowledge.

Astrology is a unique subject, in a sense, in our contemporary world, because it is one of the few practices from deepest antiquity that remains in circulation, that remains current, that remains part of day-to-day life. If you were to ask almost anyone from any walk of life, "What's your sun sign?" chances are, not only would that person be able to tell you, but he or she would also be able to tell you something about the sign's traits. That's something that I find quite remarkable and that I never take for granted. Of course, for many years modern newspaper horoscopes (today supplanted by online horoscopes) have been very popular. That trend came into play in the years immediately following the Second World War, and it helped bring a certain kind of astrological language into everyday life.

But the remarkable thing about astrology is that it has survived the ages, albeit not always intact but certainly recognizable from its origins in Babylon, Ancient Egypt, and Persia, and then as it traveled into the Hellenic cultures, into the religious practices of ancient Rome, where it took the form, roughly speaking, that we know today in the West. Although we are also the recipients of permutations, interruptions, and modern novelties and innovations that weren't necessarily part of the outlook of ancient people. We possess certain terms and points of reference that were not used to in the ancient world. The earliest references, for example, to the phenomenon of Mercury

Retrograde—a very popular concept today—in which the planet Mercury appears to move backwards from our vantage point on Earth, and everything is supposed to run backwards that involves Mercury, such as communication, commerce, and travel, only began to appear in Western astrology in the mid-1700s.

So, it's important to understand that while the astrology we practice today certainly does have ancient roots, it has also undergone many different variations; it's not precisely what was practiced by the ancients. And this raises an extremely important point, one that Manly P. Hall elucidated especially well in *The Secret Teachings of All Ages*, among other writings, and that is: our astrological system in the Western world does not actually match the cosmic objects in the sky as we experience them when we go outside and look at the night sky, or when we gaze at the night sky through a telescope. It's very important to understand this, because in late antiquity there was a split in astrological systems. Western astrology, the astrology that we practice today (sometimes known as tropical astrology) was formulated in the Roman Empire, thanks in large measure to the astronomer-astrologer, Claudius Ptolemy (c. 100–c. 170 B.C.). In about 150 B.C., Ptolemy wrote a book called *Tetrabiblos,* which codified the principles that we practice today in the Western world and upon which we rely heavily in the twenty-first century. The Eastern system of astrology, sometimes known as Vedic astrology or sidereal astrology, about which more will be said, branched off and went in a different direction. And this division in systems persists to this day.

The reason for the split is as follows: Vedic or sidereal astrology is based on the actual position of earth apropos of the other planets and cosmic objects. It is astronomically accurate. The system that prevails in the West, sometimes known as tropical astrology, is not always astronomically accurate; it does not reflect the actual position or placement of the planets and other celestial objects apropos of Earth. Its charts are different from what you will see when you go out and look up at the evening sky. The reason for the difference is that *the earth wobbles on its axis*. Because of this slight wobble of the earth's axis, what we see when we gaze at the evening sky is different from what our ancient ancestors saw. The cosmic objects themselves have not moved or changed course; rather, this slight wobble in the earth's axis creates a different *vantage point* from our terrestrial sphere when we observe the movement of the celestial objects.

This phenomenon produces what is sometimes called "the precession of the equinoxes," which means that the spring equinox today occurs in a different zodiac sign than it did in antiquity. When our ancestors in Ancient Babylon gazed up at the night sky, they witnessed the spring equinox, the dawn of spring that occurs around March twentieth, in the sign of Aries, the ram, which represents rebirth, renewal, and the initiation of projects. It was very natural that the ancient Babylonians associated the dawn of spring with the figure of the ram rushing in to herald the new.

Physically, the spring equinox occurs when the sun rises at the crisscross of two lines: the celestial equator and the ecliptic, the imaginary path that the sun makes through the sky, which is also the zodiac wheel. If you were to imagine our equator projected as a line out into space that would represent the first line. The other, the ecliptic, is the zodiac wheel, or the wheel in which the sun appears to traverse. Hence, if you were to imagine the celestial equator being projected out into space and if you were to imagine the ecliptic (the zodiac wheel) projected out into space, these two points crisscross at a certain point. When the sun rises at the crisscross, that's considered the start of spring or the spring equinox.

When the principles of astrology were originally codified in Babylon around the seventh to the sixth century B.C., the crisscross occurred in the sign of Aries. And, as noted, this all made perfect sense; there was a harmony and symmetry to it, because the ram is a natural herald of spring. However, because of this wobble in the earth's axis, the occurrence of this crisscross appears to *recede* through the zodiac signs by about one degree every 72 years. This doesn't occur in actuality, of course, but results from our vantage point on Earth due to our axial wobble. This produces *the precession of the equinoxes.*

Once every 72 years, the spring equinox effectively *moves backwards* by one degree. Each of the twelve zodiac signs is 30 degrees. So, the equinox will appear to cycle backwards through an entire sign over the course of about 2,160 years. It then enters a different sign. The equinox actually revolves around the entire zodiac wheel once every 26,000 years; that's sometimes called a Platonic year.

For centuries, our ancient ancestors experienced the spring equinox in Aries; but because of this precession of the equinoxes, later in antiquity the equinox occurred in the sign of *Pisces*. This was sometimes thought of as the dawn of the Christian era; Pisces is a fish and Christ was referred to as the "fisher of men." So, the equinox moved backwards, in effect, into Pisces, heralding the Christian age.

The next sign preceding Pisces is *Aquarius*, the water bearer, and some felt that early in the twentieth century the equinox precessed into Aquarius. Mind you, precisely where one constellation ends and another begins is not something that is always commonly agreed upon. And since we're talking about vast stretches of time, astrologers disagree about whether or not the equinox really entered Aquarius in the early twentieth century or whether it's happening now in the early twenty-first century. In any case, we're rather in the ballpark, celestially speaking. And

I am also referring, of course, to what is popularly called the *Age of Aquarius*. You may know the song lyric from the Broadway play and movie, *Hair*—"this is the dawning of the Age of Aquarius"—and that's exactly what the song was talking about.

A wide range of spiritual writers in the early twentieth century spoke of this dawning Aquarian age. A wonderful channeled reinterpretation of Christ's philosophy called *The Aquarian Gospel of Jesus the Christ* appeared in 1904 and helped popularize the notion of an Aquarian age. There was, and remains, a feeling of a possibility and excitement that, as the equinoxes enter the sign of Aquarius, we are embarking on a new age of education, spiritual search, individual liberty, mystical insight, and personal innovation— everything associated with the water bearer, the sign of Aquarius. That can sound fanciful, of course, but that is the ideal.

So, to recap: Aries the ram marked the opening of humanity's astrological understanding: Pisces marked the dawn of the Christian era; and Aquarius is said to mark this Aquarian age, this dawn of a new age of mysticism, education, and personal expansion.

What I am describing also marks a crucial difference between Western and Eastern astrology. As I said earlier, Eastern, or Vedic, astrology is astronomically accurate; it actually reflects the position of the celestial objects. The Western model relies on how the celestial objects appeared in an earlier era. This is not to say that Western astrology is "wrong." In the West, astrology remains keyed and attached to the original dates that were assigned to the zodiac. In the Western model, if you were a sun sign of Aries or Sagittarius or Libra during the Roman Empire, you'd still be one today. In the Eastern model, you would be a different sign based on the precession of the zodiac. In the West, the personal signs are fixed and seasonal; Western astrology, generally speaking, does not account for the fact that these celestial entities have moved apropos of our vantage point on Earth. (It should be noted that Western astrology, at least on a macro scale, incorporates sidereal insights insofar as it takes note of the changing eras—Aries, Pisces, Aquarius—associated with the precession of the equinoxes, which is an exception to its general approach.)

This "fixed sign" approach in the West was made as a concrete and informed *decision*. The decision was reached by the great astronomer-astrologer, Claudius Ptolemy, who I mentioned earlier. Writing in the Roman Empire, Ptolemy published his book, *Tetrabiblos* ("four books on astrology") around 150 A.D., and he basically said that the zodiac signs should remain fixed seasonally. He was aware that our views of the celestial objects were changing. He understood the precession of the equinoxes, he understood that Earth's wobble would produce a different night sky, but he made the decision, which became widely accepted in the West, that the signs of the zodiac were celestial or seasonal windows; they weren't to be strictly keyed to the vagaries of the constellations themselves. Yes, the constellations would appear to move, but the wheel of the zodiac, Ptolemy reasoned, should remain constant, because each sign and house occupying the zodiac wheel was understood as a kind of window onto the season that it was associated with. This is why Western astrology is sometimes called tropical astrology or seasonal astrology; the window of Aries is a window onto spring and should remain fixed, regardless of what stars we see in that window. Ptolemy believed that the wheel should be fixed according to season, regardless of whether the constellations that compose it shift position apropos of our vantage point on Earth.

The Vedic or Eastern astrologers disagreed. The Vedic astrologers associated with Hinduism and the traditions of India contended that astrology should be astronomically accurate and that the wheel should turn, in effect, to follow the constellations. So, the two systems, roughly speaking in the second century of the Common Era, diverged.

Which system is right? Which system should you, the individual, follow? It's up to you. It's wonderful to know about both of them. I've always said that I believe that the astrologer should know something about astronomy, just as the student of Kabbalah should know something about the Hebrew alphabet, and so on. I do believe it's important to have grounding in the traditions that we're studying even when we enter them from an esoteric perspective.

Now, there are many people in the East—and a not small number of people in the West—who defend the Vedic or sidereal system, simply because it's more accurate; it's where the constellations are from our sightline. Whereas others might say, "Well, regardless of where the constellations are, we follow the Ptolemaic system, in which we treat the houses as windows onto the different seasons. We leave them fixed." And frankly, most people who are interested in astrology never trouble themselves with it once, including many astrologers themselves—and, again, my contention is that the astrologer should have some idea as to what's actually going on in terms of astronomical phenomena.

And then you have a variety of other systems, such as the system used to forecast daily horoscopes, which is known as the "solar houses" system. In "solar houses," your birth sign is placed on the horizon line and then the daily horoscope forecaster or astrologer is simply looking at what is occurring celestially for your sun sign that day. That, too, can be defended. The sun sign and the horizon line, although they're different entities, are reflective of what's happening in the life of the individual. But I must note, it's a modern innovation. It's not something that our ancient ancestors were doing. That doesn't mean it's wrong; traditions must start somewhere. And because something is old doesn't mean it's right, and because something is new doesn't mean it's wrong or somehow lacking. But, again, I think we should be aware of what's going on in our thought systems. What system would you use, if you were to study both the Vedic and the Western systems? There are very good arguments on both sides.

Now, the system that I personally use is Western astrology. I suppose I stand with Ptolemy. I have studied both systems; I have experimented with both systems. In all fairness, I am no scholar when it comes to Eastern astrology. But my conclusions have led me to personally select the Western system. I honor the system of the East very deeply, and it is a system of astrological forecasting that is absolutely vital to the practice of the Hindu faith. When traditional Hindu couples get married, they often visit a Vedic astrologer, who will forecast for them a propitious day on which to set their wedding date. The Vedic astrologer might cast an overall marriage horoscope for them. He might offer suggestions as to favorable dates for different possibilities—such as buying a home or starting a family or whatever it may be. Astrological forecasting is a vitally important part of traditional Vedic culture.

Now, some of you may be aware that in some states, including New York State, where I live, there are anti-fortunetelling laws on the books. These laws go back to the 1920s, and I keep a close watch on the application of these laws because I do not want them to impinge on people's religious freedoms. These statutes are actually intended to protect people from con artistry where you might have a grifter posing as a psychic who is bilking people out of ruinous sums of money, persuading them to pay up in order to avert some disaster. That's the intended target of those laws. *But if those laws are too broadly or aggressively applied they conflict with people's First Amendment rights.* As just noted, in the Hindu faith astrology is part of traditional practice. So, law enforcement cannot summarily decide to start applying these anti-fortunetelling laws to astrologers; because most astrologers are engaged in an entirely defensible act of religious and self-expression; they owe explanation to no one other than their clients. It's just a note that I want to make, because I'm always keeping a watchful eye on those laws to make sure that they're not being overzealously applied, which would conflict with our Constitutional rights.

It is important to understand that the protection of your religious liberty is not dependent upon what label or term you may use, or that someone else may use to describe you; or what traits, whether false or accurate, are associated with that term. *All pursuit of faith is protected.* In 1999, George W. Bush, then governor of Texas, criticized the decision of military leaders at Fort Hood, TX, to accommodate the requests of Wiccans for a worship circle on the base grounds. "I don't think witchcraft is a religion," Bush told *Good Morning America*. That makes no difference Constitutionally. And the military has, for that reason, accommodated Wicca and any number of other nature-based faiths.

My personal experience in casting many different astrological charts for myself, for others, and my own studies suggest to me that the Western system really does provide a kind of thumbprint of character. There are many different, complex methods by which you can interpret a chart. I certainly cannot claim expertise in all of them. I have colleagues who really understand Western astrology to a razor's edge, and they are simply brilliant. But my approach, my astrology, personally speaking, is more the astrology of Manly P. Hall, of Carl Jung, of Henry Miller, of D. H. Lawrence. It's an astrology in which you look at *the basics of the celestial objects at the time of an individual's birth*. And, by the way, your birth time is pegged to when you take your first breath. You will find that you have a birth time on your birth certificate—which is necessary to cast a fully accurate chart—you need birth date, location, and time. Birth time is when a medical professional will record your first breath.

I believe, as did the figures I just mentioned, that the positioning of the celestial objects at the time of your birth does provide a kind of *thumbprint of character*. I've seen it again and again in my own life, and in the lives of others. I think the basic astrology of birth, or the natal chart, provides a kind of blueprint, a kind of rough sketch, of the individual's character. And I think the same is true of the various transits and progressions; the transits do suggest things that people are going through. I can vividly peg aspects of my life in which I made definite, discernible progress to a particular transit of Jupiter in my chart. That's considered my ruling planet because I am a Sagittarius and Jupiter plays a very important role in my astrological makeup.

Why should any of this work at all? If you talk to a critic, he or she will tell you it's completely imaginary; there's no scientific evidence for any of this. Their assessment may be correct, but they have no way of knowing whether it's correct, because they haven't studied astrology; in many cases, they barely know the first thing about it. Some critics throw around the word "science" all too easily. Science is a method, and the method gets applied well or poorly all the time. Most of the social science papers that were published a generation ago or even less are considered invalid in light of today's scientific methods. Within the social sciences, this occurs all the time; one methodology supersedes another and work that seemed valid twenty years ago is deemed invalid. And the same work that deemed its predecessor invalid will itself be supplanted. This is why some people question whether the social sciences themselves possess "laws" and should be considered as a science at all. Hence, the irony that many of the vocal critics of spiritual or esoteric belief systems emerge from the social sciences.

A blogger once surmised, in what I consider a false equivalent, that you shouldn't have to participate in an abhorrent system, like racism, in order to condemn it. He was attempting to defend his judgment of astrology, et al, by arguing that such methods are intrinsically irrational and thus require no personal familiarity or use. What the skeptic missed, however, is that racism and other oppressive outlooks result in *negative conduct*. They are systemic. Can the same be said of esoteric systems? In matters of faith, therapeutic philosophy, or esoterica, the sole measure is impact on personal behavior and consequence. How else would you evaluate a personal philosophy? If you cannot demonstrate negative behavior and consequence in any constant way, then what is actually being challenged? In such cases, the critic is stating a subjective preference not much different than arguing on behalf of a favored food or choice of music.

The question of what "works" or doesn't in therapeutic and spiritual systems is a more elusive target than we sometimes acknowledge. To cite another example, clinicians have difficulty studying recovery rates from Alcoholics Anonymous and other Twelve Step or addiction-recovery programs. This is because people flow in and out of such programs and it is difficult to say whether quitting a program constitutes a "failure," or whether the recovery of those who stick with it (which is obviously higher) proves an unqualified success apropos of overall enrollment numbers at the outset. In terms of study structure, which group do you count: *all* potential participants or only the long-haulers? And by what benchmarks? There are often periods of recidivism followed by a return to sobriety, and this can play out over many years.

Imagine how much greater is the difficulty of really making a determined study as to whether astrology can be keyed to intimate life events—which are sometimes *emotionally felt* events, and thus more difficult to identify and measure. Some researchers have done so; there are studies that have demonstrated a correlation between career and astrological makeup, and some of that material is quite intriguing. But, for all this, I haven't directly addressed the question: *Why should any of this work at all?*

Well, in lesson two, where we talked about the first principles of philosophy, I made reference to the Hermetic dictum, "as above, so below." That is the central idea of esoteric and occult philosophies, in both ancient and contemporary life. I'll be talking in greater detail about Hermeticism as a philosophy in our next chapter. But let me note that ancient cultures of every type—from Native American to Mayan to Babylonian to Egyptian to Hellenic to Persian—first began to organize themselves into societies and began to observe seasons and rituals based on their understanding of the movements of the celestial objects. This practice was both calendric and a sacred marking of time. Timekeeping was not only a vital activity to ancient cultures, but it was probably *what formed them into cultures* to begin with; everybody could agree on the necessity of planting seasons; everybody could agree (at least then) on the veneration of celestial objects or certain energies with which they were associated, not only regarding natural cycles but also the cycles of the psyche, cycles of self as related to nature.

As of this writing, I have no wonderful theory for you as to why astrology works, if it does. I have previously attempted a theory of delivery for mind causation, which I explore in my book *The Miracle Club*—but I do not yet have that for astrology, about which I must be frank. Of course, I could talk about correlations between the cycles of the moon and tides, the moon and reproductive cycles, and the manner in which cycles of the moon affect gravitational pulls on Earth, and that's all valid. It's not the most *romantic* explanation, but it's valid. Rather, I am interested in the fact that the calendrics, the timekeeping, and the celestial tracking practiced by the ancients was, in a sense, the very thing that *heralded their entry* into communities, into groups, into polities, into civilizations. And ancient people—separated by vast stretches of time, culture, geography, and language—all shared in this common activity, which was some attempt to attach earthly events to celestial events. And they believed—with a deeper understanding of nature than I think we can appreciate—that there was a correlation: "as above, so below." I am *not* ready to discard that wisdom.

From time to time, I hear from reporters who ask: "Why is astrology still popular? Has astrology grown *more* popular in the digital age? What keeps people attached to this stuff?" And, inevitably, the answer that they're fishing for, and the perspective that they already hold and expect me to repeat, is usually something about how in periods of economic crisis or personal insecurity people gravitate toward occult methods for security and answers. In other words: it's all emotional.

Or some commentators see the endurance of astrology as testament to the eternity of people being suckers, and so on. As you can surmise, I part with that, and the one thing that I always say to reporters is that *if* you're really probing the question of retentions of belief, you cannot, as a first principle, remove from the table all *possibility* that people remain attached to astrology simply because it works in some measure. If you remove that possibility, if you reject that even as a point of consideration, then are you really asking a question? Or are you instead just relying on someone else to reframe what you already believe?

There are lots of practices from the ancient world that we've discontinued; we don't use leeches anymore or ingest poisons once thought to be therapeutic, like mercury. Any number of religious and medical practices have been let go. Cruelties of punishment have been let go. But astrology, among other esoteric and spiritual practices, has endured. The extent to which it has grown in popularity is partly media and technology driven, of course. But astrology has always been with us; it was used in farmers' ephemerides going back to the Middle Ages. You can still find it in the popular *Farmers' Almanac* published today (which, by the way, is handy guide for the cycles of Mercury Retrograde). Farmers from antiquity up through the present use astrological methods to determine cycles for planting. So the practice of astrology endures in contemporary culture—from agricultural to psychological to divinatory—and I will not automatically remove from the table the question of its facility when asked why astrology has endured.

In addition to seeking single answers, we are often taught today to look almost exclusively for *sociological responses to beliefs*—or to smirk about "suckers born every minute," or some such. But such an approach does less to foster questions than to narrow them when it invalidates the experience of the end user.

We celebrate our ancient ancestors for the genius of their calendar and agricultural systems; for the psychological richness that they brought to their religious parables and myths; for their monuments and engineering marvels. Don't be too quick, along with all that, to neglect their insights into correlations between the human psyche and events in the cosmos. That is what the retention of astrology means to us today.

LESSON V

─── ❧ ❧ ───

The Hermetic World

I n this section we explore Hermetic philosophy. This is a philosophy from late Greek-Egyptian antiquity that underscores almost everything that we refer to as occult or esoteric in the Western world today.

I believe that Manly P. Hall is at his finest when writing about the philosophy of Hermeticism. *The Secret Teachings of All Ages* is actually a magnificent overview of Hermetic philosophy, a term that I will define shortly. Indeed, the ideas of Hermeticism run throughout the entire book. The mythical figure of Hermes Trismegistus, depicted in the book in a beautiful illustration by artist J. Augustus Knapp, is the presiding deity of every page of *The Secret Teachings of All Ages*. The figure of Hermes, the philosophy of Hermeticism, is the animating spirit of the book, as well as of this guide. And, again, I must tell you, you can find almost no better introduction to Hermetic philosophy than the chapter that Manly dedicates to the subject in the *Secret Teachings* and his references to Hermeticism throughout the book.

As noted, Hermeticism is really the urtext or the foundational philosophy of nearly everything that we regard as occult or esoteric in our world today. Ancient Egyptian civilization can seem fantastically distant from us today; and it *should* seem fantastically distant in a certain sense. As I was describing earlier, we don't even have a fully settled timeline of the antiquity of Egypt; but even if one goes by the traditional timeline, its antiquity is difficult to fathom. As I mentioned, when the ancient Greek historian Herodotus encountered the pyramids, they were as ancient to him as he is to us. This is a civilization that existed for literally thousands of years before the birth of Christ. It is a civilization whose practices, rites, mysteries, rituals, and secrets not only remain shrouded in the mists of antiquity for us, but our understanding of Egyptian hieroglyphs did not even dawn until the modern era.

Hieroglyphs are, of course, a symbolic, pictographic language. They have a phonetic correlate, but Western people were incapable of understanding hieroglyphs until the discovery of the so-called Rosetta Stone in 1799 by one of the historians who

Napoleon brought with him on his ill-fated invasion of Egypt. Napoleon brought with him to Egypt whole teams of historians, archaeologists, stenographers, and artists who could record some of the magnificent antiquities that his armies came upon. One of the most fateful discoveries that Napoleon's team of court scholars found was a stone tablet composed of the writing of three different languages: Egyptian hieroglyphs, Ancient Greek, and Demotic. This text was produced in 196 B.C. in the so-called Ptolemaic era, in other words the late stages of ancient Egyptian civilization that later produced what I am referring to as Hermetic philosophy. And because this document was composed of these three different languages (hieroglyphs, Greek, and Demotic), the Western world was, for the first time, able to fully decipher hieroglyphs.

I mention all of this to underscore how recent it was—the Napoleonic and post-Napoleonic age—that Westerners were even able to grasp the symbolical language of the Ancient Egyptians. Hence, think of how little we really know of the reaches of Ancient Egyptian civilization. This is why I say that Egyptian culture can—and should—seem fantastically distant to us. At the same time, modern seekers *do* possess a slender thread of authentic connection to the ideals, insights, and spiritual psychology of Ancient Egypt. This is not imaginary. This thread is thin; it is not easy to find; it has been broken; it has been interrupted; it has been tangled up or remade by modern innovations, insights, and novelties; but it *is* there, it *is* real, and it does connect esoteric seekers today to certain ideals and concepts possessed by our ancestors in Egyptian antiquity. And this connection, this thread, is formed by Hermetic philosophy.

The term Hermetic is often used today as a synonym for all things that are mysterious and arcane. It references late-ancient Egyptian philosophy. And, as such, it is a controversial term, because some will claim that the Hermetic expressions of the late Egyptian world were really Greek expressions, or Neoplatonic expressions, and they weren't authentically Egyptian at all, or they were Egyptian only in small measure. I think that's a historical mistake, which has plagued Western intellectual life and is slowly being corrected in our own era. Scholars are coming to understand the authentically *Egyptian* nature of Hermetic philosophy.

Simply put, in the late stages of the Egyptian empire—in the generations immediately preceding and following the birth of Christ—Ancient Egypt was occupied by Hellenic forces, both Greek and Roman. Egypt was ultimately dominated by the Roman Empire. This began with the conquest of Egypt by the Greek general and military ruler, Alexander in 332 B.C. Alexander the Great (356–323 B.C) was an extraordinary figure; not only did he dominate much of the known world during his lifetime, but he actually did not destroy or attempt to sublimate the traditions, philosophies, languages, and monuments that he encountered. Rather, in some cases, he actually attempted to embrace them. And he often preserved them, although he did place the territories that he conquered under his own financial and military domination. His generals were known as Ptolemies—that's where the term comes from—and Alexander proceeded to install these Ptolemies or generals as kind of viceroys, or figures in charge of the territories that he had conquered. This is why there exist a line of Egyptian rulers in late antiquity known as Ptolemies.

Now, part of the Ptolemaic reign in Ancient Egypt involved the figure of Cleopatra (51–30 B.C.)—who ruled Ancient Egypt roughly about fifty years prior to the death of Christ. And Cleopatra, though Greek, was, like Alexander, a widely venerated figure in Ancient Egypt, because she helped to restore the temple orders, mystery traditions, and initiatory rites and practices that had been fading first under Persian and later under Greco-Roman domination. The Ptolemies, however, were Greek in background, as was Cleopatra herself. They did represent foreign domination of Ancient Egyptian culture, and they did form into a kind of insular community of their own, often intermarrying to maintain their bloodline. Hence, for several centuries at the end of Ancient Egypt's lifespan, the ruling class was largely Greek, although the military power was Roman.

For all that, Cleopatra herself was widely venerated because she was seen as somebody who brought restoration to Egypt's splendor; she was seen as a ruler who could deftly and *carefully* negotiate with Roman military authorities to maintain some semblance of religious and governmental autonomy. She was considered a daughter of the great mother goddess, Isis, if not the reincarnate of Isis herself. And under Cleopatra's rulership, the arts, the great monuments, the practice of esoteric rites, rituals, and mystery traditions, and the temple orders themselves were restored. So she is traditionally regarded as an Egyptian ruler, even though she herself was of Greek descent.

The Ptolemaic ruling class tended to use the Greek language for official business and religious texts. And from this a remarkable development occurred in these late stages of Egyptian culture. A cohort of Greek religious scholars and esoteric seekers within the city of Alexandria, named of course for Alexander, began to *write down some of the philosophies of Ancient Egypt in the Greek language.* They encountered hieroglyphs, they encountered esoteric philosophy, rite, ritual, and spiritual and symbolic insights of the great Empire—and they began to write these things down in conventional Western form. The Greek language is, in essence, an expository language; it is a language of letters and sounds that are foundational to Western life and thought. Post-antiquity, Westerners could not read hieroglyphs so this became a singular record.

In addition to its hieroglyphic language, Egyptian philosophy, as with many ancient philosophies and religious systems, was conveyed through *oral tradition*. Things were passed on from mouth to ear: from priest to neophyte, from seeker to seeker, from initiate to initiate, from student to student. In fact, spoken word always precedes written word, *both in human history and in the life of the individual.* Infants learn to speak before they learn to write. It is a human truth that writing always follows speech, never precedes it. Western Scripture tells us: "In the beginning, there was the Word."

The work of many foundational figures in the Western world, such as Homer, the Greek poet and storyteller, began as oral tradition. The reason Homer's writing is considered so revolutionary is because he took things that were widely recognized as having traveled the lines of oral tradition and he became one of the first known figures to write them down. Stories and myths were originally recited by memory. Homer took these traditions and, in some cases, their mnemonic structure—memory-inducing devices that they contain so they could be memorized—and he rendered them into the form by which they became known for posterity.

The Hermetic philosophers of Alexandria in the late stages of Egyptian civilization, particularly in the generations immediately following the death of Christ, did the same thing. They, too, were dealing with material of deepest antiquity. They were dealing with ideas that *began* in symbol and oral tradition. This is why it's very important to remember that, regardless of the late-ancient construction of the Hermetic literature, a topic to which I will return, the material found within Hermetic literature itself is today becoming justly understood to be an authentic retention of some very ancient Egyptian ideas.

Now, there's a specific reason why this literature was called *Hermetic*. This term makes reference to the god of writing and intellect within Greek tradition, Hermes. But that doesn't quite get at it. When the Greeks encountered Egyptian civilization, they were enormously moved and touched by Egypt's god of writing and intellect, Thoth. Thoth is widely depicted throughout ancient Egyptian life, depending on the era. He appears as a figure possessing the body of a human and the head of an ibis, or a water bird. Thoth is frequently shown holding a clay tablet and a stylus, which he is using to make inscriptions. You will see all of this in J. Augustus Knapp's somewhat fanciful but beautiful depiction of the figure of Hermes or Thoth accompanied by an ibis. Egyptians venerated the ibis, a water bird, because they thought of it as a messenger of the gods. This creature was capable of existing within all the habitable elements: land, water, and air. It was said to traverse the elements to receive higher messages from the great over-mind, which the Greeks called *Nous*. So the ibis was seen as a divine messenger and a being of great intellect, which is why Thoth had the ibis as a head. And it's of course self-explanatory that this figure held a stylus in one hand and a clay tablet in another, because he is writing.

The Greeks were overcome with veneration of the figure of Thoth, and they often referred to Thoth as *Thrice-Greatest Hermes.* In other words, they believed that the figure of Thoth was *three times* as great as their own god of writing and intellect, Hermes. In Greek, this term translated into *Hermes Trismegistus.* That became a Greek term for Thoth, or Thrice-Greatest Hermes, a figure held in unique veneration by Greek-Egyptians who dwelt in the city of Alexandria. When Greek scribes and scholars began to write down symbolical Egyptian ideas and insights into the Greek language, they very often signed this literature with the name of Hermes or Hermes Trismegistus. Affixing the name of a venerated figure to a piece of writing was thought to give it greater gravity, authority, and weight. This practice was not uncommon in the ancient world; scribes and writers would sometimes append the name of Moses or Abraham to a piece of writing—even if it was far past the biblical era—because they felt that it lent authority. The Alexandrian scribes who wrote these things down are unknown to us; they didn't use their own names. They used the name of Hermes or Hermes Trismegistus. This is where the term *Hermetic* comes from.

The Hermetic literature arose from this fateful encounter between Greek and Egyptian civilization in the late stages of the Egyptian empire. Greek scribes and scholars wrote down unknowably ancient Egyptian traditions and ideas—undoubtedly intermingled with ideas of their own—which is why this work represents an extraordinary retention, or time capsule, of certain Egyptian ideas. This is why I say that Hermetic philosophy, which I will further describe, is a thread, however slender, that connects twenty-first century seekers to Egyptian antiquity. But the Hermetic literature itself, like the traditions upon which it was based, very nearly vanished.

By the 5th century A.D., Rome lost its grip throughout much of the Western world, and eventually the Eastern world. Rome entered a period of decline; its colonies and protectorates were basically freed from Roman domination—whether they wanted to be or not—as the Roman Empire frayed and declined. And these Hermetic manuscripts, to a degree, were themselves lost to time. When Europe entered the period known as the Dark Ages, there was a great deal of chaos, plague, warfare, and disorder almost everywhere; that wasn't all that was going on, but a degree of disorder prevailed. And some of the great writings that might have appeared in the Library of Alexandria (which eroded over time and collapsed in the late 3rd century A.D.) or that belonged to pre-Christian religious orders were, in some cases, spirited away into monasteries and were preserved and protected from the relative chaos of the Dark Ages. And this brings us to an extraordinary chapter in history that involves the re-emergence of the Hermetic literature and its great influence on the development of the Renaissance, and, ultimately, of modern life in the West.

The Renaissance, as we typically refer to it, reflected a gradual return to artistic expression, architecture, and cultural endeavors in Europe, which, roughly speaking, began in Florence, Italy, under the reign of Cosimo de' Medici (1389–1464). And a remarkable event happened in Cosimo's court around the year 1462. At that time, a Byzantine monk entered the royal court in Florence carrying with him a variety of scrolls written in Greek, attributed to the figure of Hermes Trismegistus. He presented these to the Florentine ruler, and Cosimo and his court scholars were absolutely overwhelmed with the possibility. The figure of Hermes Trismegistus had come to be viewed as an actual figure of deepest antiquity, a legendary teacher or prophet who may have been a contemporary, it was believed, to Moses himself; who may have been a contemporary, or a teacher, of Abraham. One of the passions of the Renaissance mind was the belief that somewhere in the distant past there existed a primeval theology, a pristine theology—this theology was thought to predate Judaism, Christianity, and all known religions of the world; and this primeval theology was believed to reflect humanity's earliest ideas about the nature of the cosmos and how we relate to

unseen principles of life. Cosimo and his contemporaries believed that this is what was presented to them,
authored by the great Hermes Trismegistus himself.
The scrolls were believed to contain the primeval theology that the Renaissance mind had theorized about,
and that, it seemed, had finally come into their hands.

Cosimo immediately directed his court transla-
tor, Marsilio Ficino (1433–1489), to discontinue his
translating of Plato from Greek into Latin, which
was the scholarly language of the day, and to turn his
attention exclusively to these Greek Hermetic manuscripts, which Cosimo hungered to read before his
death, which occurred just two year later. When the
translation was complete, religious figures, artists,
and scholars throughout the burgeoning Renaissance world were absolutely enthralled; because they
believed that they were reading humanity's deepest
antique principles.

Now, the Hermetic manuscripts, both in terms of
their ideas and their symbolism, wielded huge influence over Renaissance life. The symbols of Hermeticism appeared everywhere: the caduceus, the great
wand with two snakes wrapped around it; symbols
of Egyptian antiquity: pyramids, obelisks, all-seeing
eyes. Concepts of alchemy—including what we might
call psychological alchemy—became widely written
about, experimented with, and sought after within
the Renaissance world. A feeling of electricity per-
vaded the air; there was a sense that the earliest prin-

ciples of searching men and women had finally been discovered.

I'm making big leaps across history, because there is so much to cover, but in time a fissure developed around the Hermetic literature, which eventually limited and stymied its influence. The manuscripts that Ficino translated were called the *Corpus Hermeticum,* which came to number seventeen tracts that were later grouped with another Latin dialogue, *Asclepius,* for which the original Greek was not found. The *Corpus Hermeticum* was considered a direct line to the thought of deepest antiquity. But in the early 1600s, a classical scholar named Isaac Casaubon (1559–1614) made the critical discovery that there appeared references and styles of language within the Hermetic literature that earmarked this literature as having emerged from *late antiquity.* It was not, Casaubon determined, literature from the deepest reaches of primeval life; it was, rather, literature that had been written in the generations immediately following Christ.

In time, Casaubon's critical analysis led to a perception—and an overreach, I think—that the Hermetic literature, because its hoped-for antiquity had been dispelled, was somehow fraudulent or inauthentic. And, in time, this literature really fell out of vogue; it fell out of circulation. This is one of several reasons there aren't more quality English translations of the Hermetic literature today. There are some turgidly written Victorian translations; there are some English translations that emerged from the late Renaissance or post-Renaissance, but they weren't considered very readable or penetrable; and even by the early twentieth century, there were very few reliable English translations of the Hermetic literature. Even in our time, there are really only a couple in wide circulation: one is published by a scholar named Brian Copenhaver for Cambridge University Press; and another is published by Inner Traditions, produced by the scholar Clement Salaman and a team of collaborators. Those are two of the finest; the Copenhaver translation and the Salaman translation are both just excellent.

And they're both fairly recent. Until our own time, there really were few serviceable English translations of the Hermetic literature; and this resulted, in part, from the circumstances I just described. When the timeline was readjusted, people eventually made the *mistake* of thinking that this material itself was compromised—that it was unimportant or inauthentic. That judgment was an error; and this error, I think, deprived modern Western civilization of an important retention of Ancient Egyptian thought—thought whose roots ran deeper than the late-ancient iteration in Greek form.

As scholars are coming to understand today, the Hermetic literature, regardless of its timeline, *drew upon material that does authentically connect us to primeval Egyptian thought*. So, the hopes that the court scholars and the translators of the Renaissance attached to this Hermetic literature, their hopes that it represented a lifeline to oldest antiquity, weren't *entirely* off base. The form in which it reached them had been written down later. And this situation is not uncommon in the ancient world, as I was mentioning with regard to Homer, for example. And the ideas may have been augmented by Neoplatonism or other Greek philosophies. But the core content provides some of our deepest insight into Egyptian philosophy.

For the reasons I've just explored, I believe that the Hermetic literature is of unique value to us today, and that it should be read and it should be encountered by *all* of us who consider ourselves spiritual seekers.

Indeed, the Hermetic literature that was so influential during the Renaissance came to form a kind of catalogue of what later became known as occult spirituality; particularly in the work of a philosopher named Cornelius Agrippa (1486–1535), who published what he called *Three Books Concerning Occult Philosophy* in the early 1530s. The term "occult"—another word so often confused—is derived from the Latin *occulta* for *secret* or *hidden*, a term Agrippa and his contemporaries used to describe the spiritual and magickal* systems of the ancient world. Agrippa's work, heavily influenced by Greek-Egyptian Hermet-

---

* The spelling of "magick" with a "k," is derived from early modern English and I often use it in this book to distinguish occult practice from stage magic, as discussed in chapter XII.

icism (as well as Latin-Arabic magickal texts), forms an urtext of a great deal of what we consider occult practice today, including principles of astrology, ceremonial magick, sigils, spell-casting, divination, spirit conjuring, and much else. So the Hermetic literature, in a way, inspired and formed the backbone of a great deal of modern occultism, and there are remarkable correspondences between Hermetic literature and some of the practices that are carried on within our alternative spiritual culture today.

The academic publisher Brill has issued an anthology called *Gnostic America* in which I wrote a chapter that analyzes the correspondences—sometimes indirect correspondences—between contemporary New Age practice and ideas expressed in Hermetic literature. The parallels can be really quite remarkable. The chief correspondence, which you will find in Books I and XI of the *Corpus Hermeticum*, is the principle that the human mind possesses causative powers. Again, this returns us to the great Hermetic principle, "as above, so below." The Hermetic writers saw all of creation as emergent from a great over-mind, a great creative intellect, which, as I mentioned, they called *Nous*. And we, the individuals, were created in the image of *Nous*, an idea that later echoed in Western Scripture. As such, *we, too, are able to create with our own intellects, although we must abide by the laws and limitations of the sphere of creation that we occupy.* That is the contention of Hermetic philosophy.

For all of our connection to the cosmic, we are going to decay and die. This notion is echoed in the Book of Psalms: "Ye are gods, but ye shall die as princes." Hermetic literature can help us to understand that reference, because I think that reference, in a way, derives from its insights.

Hermetic philosophy further views creation as a series of concentric circles emanating from this one great mind. And each concentric circle, each cosmic framework, as it grows more distant from the center must also function under its own increasing set of laws, to which the beings or intelligences occupying that concentric circle must submit. So we, as descendants of this great over-mind, are capable of creating with our own intellects, but we are also limited by the cosmic framework in which we live. Human realization, human advancement, human initiation, and the experience of death, transformation, and recurrence can aid the individual in rising up through these concentric spheres, until the individual returns to the great source of all that is, the great over-mind.

This may sound very familiar to some of you who are interested in New Thought or other mind-metaphysics philosophies, as I am. You will find an extraordinary, though indirect, antecedent of those philosophies within the Hermetic literature. And it is astounding to me to find similar sets of ideas among different groups of seekers separated by vast stretches of time and geography. But keep in mind, a confluence of ideas does not mean that they were all drinking from the same waters or that the ancients were directly influencing, or are part of a continuum with, modern spirituality. The American pioneers of New Thought largely lived in rural settings, where perhaps the only book to which they had ready access was Scripture. They often reached their conclusions through personal experiment.* Very few English translations of Hermeticism could even have reached them within the confines of rural New England life in the mid-to-late 19th century, where many of these spiritual pioneers rose up. And yet, some of their insights do comport with insights found in the Hermetic literature. That is something to ponder because I believe it is a hallmark of universal truth when different groups of people, sometimes separated by vast reaches of time, geography, and language, arrive at similar sets of ideas. It's an evidence trail of truth.

When you begin your journey into Hermetic literature, I advise that you pay particular attention to Books I and XI, and also particularly to the Latin book called *Asclepius*. I think that those three books, each of which are quite short, best express the principles I was just describing, especially the Hermetic concept that your mind is a tool of creation; that you *can* create through the causation of thought in this realm, as we were created by *Nous* or the over-mind.

---

* I explore the development of the positive-mind movement in my book *One Simple Idea: How Positive Thinking Reshaped Modern Life*.

The Hermetic World   151

Book I is sometimes called "The Divine Pyman-der," or "The Divine Pymander of Hermes Trismeg-istus." *Pymander* is a term derived from Egyptian spoken phonetics that means something like "great shepherd." Book XI is a particularly useful dialogue between Hermes and his disciples in which Hermes describes the epic potentials of the individual, specif-ically in matters of mind causation. Book XI explores how, through the proper preparation—meditation, prayer, diet, or temporary fasting—the individual can begin to become possessed by the forces of the higher mind. The great spiritual seeker and scientist Eman-uel Swedenborg (1688–1772) described the influence of the higher mind as a "divine influx;" you'll find that quality, too, in Hermeticism. In fact, a great deal of contemporary spiritual thought can be found in extraordinary form in the Hermetic literature. This whole notion of being born again, or of undergoing a conversion experience, or of undergoing an awaken-ing experience, or of divine inflow—all of that exists within the Hermetic literature.

The third book I recommend is *Asclepius*, which is a dialogue between Hermes and his offspring and student named in the title. The book also features an agonizing and prescient prophecy of Ancient Egypt's decline. We haven't been able to find its earliest Greek antecedent, but there are references to it in other books that demonstrate its antiquity. Sometimes these ancient manuscripts simply got lost, and we don't have the original versions; we have translations, or transla-tions of translations. So today the *Corpus Hermeticum*, as it's traditionally understood, consists of seventeen books and the Latin work, *Asclepius*. Again, Books I and XI and *Asclepius* are wonderful places to begin your journey, and they encapsulate the very things I've been referencing.

Not all Hermetic literature is contained in what is traditionally referred to as the *Corpus Hermeticum*. Again, the *Corpus Hermeticum* is a collection of books that grew out of the Renaissance search for Hermetic literature; these were Greek works translated into Latin. But there were lots of other works, sometimes magickal in nature—sometimes ceremonial magick, sometimes astrological, sometimes alchemical—that bore the name of Hermes, or that were contemporary to the Hermetic literature. These works are some-times called "technical Hermetica." And this class of writings includes another work that does not appear in the *Corpus Hermeticum* and that, until quite recently, some scholars didn't even regard as an authentic work of Hermetic antiquity. But I've been quoting from it throughout this book. It is the text known as *The Emerald Tablet*. That's where the phrase, "as above, so below," appears: "True, without falsehood, certain and most true, is that that which is above is as that which is below." *The Emerald Tablet* is fancifully depicted by J. Augustus Knapp in his illustration of Hermes where it appears hovering above the sage's outstretched hand.

The Emerald Tablet—which in some respects is the centerpiece of psychological alchemy and the centerpiece of Hermetic thought—has not been found in its original Greek form. It exists in Arabic. It dates back to about the 8th or 9th century A.D. in its Arabic form, and, for that reason, it has never been canonized within the Hermetic literature. We don't have the original Greek manuscript; we only have, really, what might be considered a very late ancient or early Middle Ages Arabic version. However, *The Emerald Tablet* has sufficient correspondences with other, older Hermetic works, so that today it is largely considered a valid part of Hermetic literature. Although I should note that if you purchase one of the translations that I was referencing earlier, you will not find *The Emerald Tablet* translated into English. But you can find translations of *The Emerald Tablet* elsewhere online. One of the very first English translations of *The Emerald Tablet* was made by the great physicist, Sir Isaac Newton (1641–1727), who venerated *The Emerald Tablet*. In fact, if you go online, you'll find that Newton produced a very serviceable English translation of *The Emerald Tablet*, which makes it accessible to contemporary seekers. He was translating it from a later Latin edition. So there exists a whole network of Hermetic writings that you won't find grouped with the *Corpus Hermeticum*. For that reason, people sometimes refer to the overall Hermetic writings as the *Hermetica*, a term that's more encompassing of some of the more explicitly magickal and so-called technical works.

There exists a roughly contemporary occult book that I think serves as a reasonable retention of certain Hermetic ideas. It is a popular occult book that some of you reading these words may have read or heard of: *The Kybalion*, which was published in 1908 under the byline of Three Initiates. The book presents itself as the commentary on a hidden work of Hermetic wisdom dating to deep antiquity. I have walked through the details and history of the book in a wide variety of writings, including my *Kybalion Study Guide*, and I'll note in brief here that Three Initiates was a pseudonym used by the brilliant New Thought writer and publisher William Walker Atkinson (1862–1932) in the early twentieth century. Atkinson frequently used pseudonyms; he wrote under the name of Yogi Ramacharaka, Theron Q. Dumont, and Magus Incognito; perhaps his most famous and enduring was the byline under which he wrote *The Kybalion*, Three Initiates. Rumors and stories abound online as to the identity of the Three Initiates; some people invoke the name of Paul Foster Case (1884–1954), a great American occultist. But that timeline doesn't really match up. The fact is, in addition to other historical evidence, Atkinson identified himself as the sole author several years after the publication of the book in an entry in *Who's Who in America*.

Other documentary evidence also confirms him as the identity behind Three Initiates.

I don't want to get lost in the drama of any of this; what's more important is: *The Kybalion* is far more than a novelty of early twentieth century occult literature. At one time in my career, I made the mistake of underestimating *The Kybalion*; I thought it was contemporary New Thought, Atkinson's specialty, dressed up like an ancient Hermetic book, which was the kind of dramatic device that Atkinson used—but *The Kybalion* is also a great deal more than that.

As I pursued my own education into Hermetic literature, I eventually returned to *The Kybalion* with fresh eyes. One summer, several years before this writing, I reread the book five times consecutively. It's a short book but also a somewhat dense book; it's not easy to get through and it doesn't disclose its insights very readily. In fact, Atkinson makes the point that he purposely provides relatively little in the way of concrete methods in *The Kybalion*, because he believes that it will be more useful to the seeker to work out his or her own methods.

As I embarked on these serial readings of *The Kybalion*, I came to realize that the book *does* possess authentic modern correspondences with some of the ancient Hermetic literature. Atkinson was operating off of just a handful of translations that were available to him in his own era, including, I think, a translation that was produced by an English scholar named

G.R.S. Mead (1863–1933) in 1906, two years before *The Kybalion* came out. Mead—who had been a secretary to the great occultist and co-founder of the Theosophical Society, Madame H.P. Blavatsky—was a classical scholar in his own right, and he had a command over ancient and biblical languages. And Mead was extremely ambitious; he produced a three-volume work called *Thrice Greatest Hermes*, in which he made a vast translation of all the different iterations of Hermetic literature, of which the *Corpus Hermeticum* was just one part. Personally, I find Mead's translation pretty tough going. The three-part work is magisterial in terms of its scope, breadth, and comprehensiveness; but the prose can be very heavy and wooden; it is often marked by a kind of late-Victorian formality or affect, which is difficult for most twenty-first century readers to get through.

But I do believe that Atkinson heroically marshaled his way through Mead and a range of other Victorian or immediately post-Victorian translations. Using what source material was available to him at the time, Atkinson made a pretty sturdy distillation of certain Hermetic ideas within *The Kybalion*. One of the ideas—and I think one of the most book's closest resonances with Hermetic philosophy—is that everything that exists, including your own psyche, is in a state of *polarity*. "Every stick has two ends," as the great spiritual philosopher G. I. Gurdjieff put it. This is a boundless spiritual and physical law—all truths are two, like yin and yang—and Atkinson depicted this law with psychological poignance.

Our emotional states themselves exist in polarity. So, for example, if you are feeling stuck in a state of *fearfulness* or *anxiety*, the sliding scale of that emotional state is fundamentally connected to *courage*. You can actually slide the scale toward that positive polarity. If you fix your mind on the principle of an emotion that is at the opposing end of the one you're experiencing, you can actually *reverse polarities* within yourself. You cannot change a point of polarity into something to which it is unrelated; you must try to locate within your own psyche whatever the polar opposite is of the emotional state that you're going through. So, what is the opposing polarity, for example, of *depression*? You might say, it's *enthusiasm*. What is the opposing polarity of fear? As noted, you might say, it's *courage* or even *enterprise*. What is the opposing polarity of *anxiety*? Well, you might say, it's *confidence* or even *maturity*. Atkinson's point is that, as much as our emotions can seem to run away from us, if you can locate the opposing polarity of the emotion that you're experiencing, you can take advantage of that understanding and proceed along the sliding scale to its opposite. This inner task is made easier if you can, in effect, understand or picture your emotional life as a sliding scale of polarities, in which you identify the opposite pole and, through an act of mental concentration, move towards the opposing polarity. This is because, so teaches *The Kybalion*, opposites are of the same nature. Again: "as above, so below."

The idea of polarity has its philosophical roots in Hermeticism. This is one of the many reasons why I personally feel that you are poised for great discovery as you enter into the Hermetic literature, if you so choose, because Hermeticism forms the foundational system that underscores so many of our mystical, esoteric, and occult philosophies today. Manly Hall, in *The Secret Teachings of All Ages*, explains this history in splendid fashion; he helps clarify this history; and he also provides serviceable translations of some of the Hermetic literature, which obviously predate the contemporary translations that I was referencing earlier.

Manly's chapter on Hermes Trismegistus is one of the finest parts of an epic book; I think it's one of his best accomplishments. And I encourage you not only to read it but to *use it* as an entry point to your own reading of the Hermetic literature. And then you can, if you wish, use this foundation to approach or, as in my case, re-approach *The Kybalion*—a book that I came to understand as vastly more important, more significant, and more powerful than I had initially realized. So much so, that recent to this writing, as I have described and will return to, I visited Ancient Egypt to work on a feature documentary, *The Kybalion*, with director Ronni Thomas, and to identify the manner in which the book intersects with certain aspects of Egyptian thought.

That visit helped me gain greater understanding of some of the concepts of polarity, mental causation, and humanity's capacity to rise up through these concentric spheres. It was a true journey of discovery. And all of it—all of it—rests upon my exposure to the Hermetic literature. The Hermetic literature and the philosophy of Hermes is the ancestor to what we seek, and I'm filled with joy for you that this is an open door. I encourage you to enter.

LESSON VI

—— ๑ ๐ ——

Hellenic Mysteries

W e now turn to Hellenic mysteries, the mysteries of the Greek world. As I was describing in the previous sections on primeval civilizations and Hermeticism, Greece was, to a very great extent, the inheritor of a great body of ideas that existed in an earlier form in Ancient Egypt. That thesis is extremely important. I recommend as background reading not only *The Secret Teachings of All Ages* but also the wonderful book *Black Athena* by the historian Martin Bernal, who does a masterful job of tracing and exploring the wisdom of the North African milieu of Ancient Egypt and the manner in which it got absorbed into much of Hellenic life, particularly in Ancient Greece.

It often strikes me today that we should include an element of history in *everything* that kids learn in school. I think this is true of the study of mathematics, for example, because our knowledge of mathematics in its earliest form springs from both the Egyptian and the Greek worlds; the Greek philosophers, in particular, saw mathematics as a kind of key to the nature and meaning of the cosmos. Today, of course, we use mathematics in all kinds of pursuits: arithmetic and calculation, engineering, finance, and so on. It's a necessary tool for getting things done, getting things constructed, understanding how things work in architecture, and, of course, mathematics relates to everything that we do to develop transport, civil engineering, and the maintenance of our world. But mathematics began as a kind of sacred science; just as astronomy and astrology were joined together in the ancient world so, too, was mathematics seen as a sacred art, which could unlock the building blocks of creation, and allow men and women to construct and to create things in their own sphere. And these things would be created according to principles of measurement, tone, and geometry that ran throughout nature, that ran throughout the makeup of the cosmos. Again, we encounter the indispensable insight, "as above, so below."

Manly P. Hall keenly understood and helped to revive the principle in *The Secret Teachings of All Ages* that all of our worldly arts and sciences—

including mathematics, architecture, engineering, and geometry—began with humanity's intent to know itself. For the Ancient Greeks, mathematics was a sacred science, which would assist the individual in this all-important task of self-understanding. One of the great progenitors of this idea was the Greek philosopher, Pythagoras. Pythagoras lived and worked in the 5th century B.C., and he was the founder of an academy, or mystery school, in which he invited initiates who wished to study the principles of music, geometry, architecture, and mathematics, and to understand how these principles could essentially unlock higher realities to us.

Many of the core basics of mathematical formula as it exists today date back to Pythagoras. For example, he arrived at the idea that the number 10 is kind of a base number, an essential building block that can be used (and is today used) as the basis of a comprehensive numerical system. He also presented what is known as the Pythagorean theorem—sometimes expressed as $a^2 + b^2 = c^2$—which codifies the dimensions of the right-angle triangle and a vast array of shapes that follow from that; the Pythagorean theorem is a key part of our modern geometry, engineering, and architecture.

Pythagoras identified the golden mean or golden ratio as a natural symmetry that appears in nature. In using the golden ratio as a design principle, the smaller part of an object bears the same ratio to the larger part of an object as the larger part bears to the whole. In a calculation, the golden ratio is approximately 1.618. Within that formula appears the recipe for great harmony and beauty; for and the construction of buildings, bridges, and monuments that have survived as testaments to beauty and functionality as such things coexisted in the ancient world. The golden mean runs throughout the architecture of Egypt, Greece, and Rome.

As mentioned, the golden mean, or the golden ratio, is repeatedly encrypted in nature. This formula occurs over and over in the natural world—in the shell of a snail, in the shape of a flower, in the latticework of a leaf. You find these different instances recurring throughout the natural world reflecting a kind of holy proportion of harmony in which the ratio of the smaller part to the larger part equals the ratio of the larger part to the whole. Based on his preternatural observation of nature, Pythagoras helped to identify and establish the golden mean as a core principle of architecture, engineering, and design.

Pythagoras also identified a theory of musical orderliness and a series of octaves that can be detected in the spaces between the planets themselves. This is called the "music of the spheres." The philosopher believed that musical notes or octaves—as with numbers, as with principles of geometry—could be discovered in their primary form through observation of the natural world. And these things repeat across not only the objects of natural life—including the dimensions of the cosmos themselves—but they can be detected and used here on earth, not only in musical instrumentation, but for construction of every kind, and for measuring experience within ourselves. In short, Pythagoras discovered a kind of "creation code" within the cosmos and brought it to earth. He was a Promethean figure.

Pythagoras also pioneered the very recognizable symbol of the pentagram, the five-pointed star, which is the symbol of the individual, with a head, two arms, and two legs. It's a magnetic symbol; it's an entrancing symbol. The pentagram, oddly enough, has come to take on sinister associations in popular culture today. But it's a beautiful, magnetic symbol that represents humanity itself. Again, this is an example of Pythagoras finding symmetry within the expression of organic life.

As noted, a great deal of the arts and sciences that Pythagoras brought to us were, in a sense, *sacred sciences* through which the individual could detect the mechanics of creation, and serve as a creator, including an architect or engineer, within the sphere that we occupy. This fulfilled the Hermetic principle that we are *born to be creators*; we are extensions of the overmind; and we, too, create within our physical framework as great Mind creates within the concentric circles of the universe, in which all things are organized into one whole.

Now, Pythagoras never wrote anything himself, at least nothing that's come down to us; no writings that emerged from Pythagoras have reached us in modern times. The writings that we possess about Pythagoras and about his ideas all come from his students, in the same way that Plato's dialogues are derived largely from the work of Socrates. We have a master who existed, who was a historically verifiable figure, but who communicated, at least as we are aware today, through oral tradition. Others who followed him, primarily his students and sometimes students of students, wrote down the ideas that came from master.

This is among the reasons why I have been saying that Greek-Egyptian Hermetic writings are so important, and why they almost certainly reflect thought from deepest antiquity, *because antique men and women tended to communicate first and foremost in an oral manner*, from the lips of the teacher to the ear of the student. And then, as in the case of Pythagoras, it was often the students who wrote things down.

Pythagoras taught his students at an academy reputed to be in Croton. Manly P. Hall idealistically designed his campus, the Philosophical Research Society, on the speculative model of the ancient academy of Pythagoras. Manly was explicit that he wanted the Philosophical Research Society to be a reflection of the mystery school of Pythagoras—a place where the seeker could come, unencumbered by dogma or doctrine, and just ask, *What is? What is this world in which we live?* So, Manly was inspired by Pythagoras—an image of whom, as depicted by the artist J. Augustus Knapp, appears in a dedicated chapter of *The Secret Teachings of All Ages*. In Knapp's portrait a lyre or harp appears the master's feet. This represents his model of the music of the spheres. Also in the image there appears a right-angle triangle, whose dimensions the philosopher mapped out through the Pythagorean theorem. Knapp supplies a variety of other objects as well, including pyramids and triangles, which Pythagoras saw as the essential building blocks of life. Pythagoras also believed in the sacred dimensions of the numeral 3, which identifies the three points of the one-dimensional triangle, which itself can be extrapolated into other shapes, including, of course, the pyramid. Pythagoras saw the numeral 3 as the foundation of all design.

I noted earlier that I wish that a little history got mixed in when school kids learn about mathematics, because I would like them to understand that these things are not calculations and formula alone, though they certainly are that and they're very important on those terms; but, in addition, these things are part of humanity's *indestructible wish to know itself.* Our conception of the arts and sciences began, and had some of its earliest expressions, in Egypt, Persia, and Greece, as a *sacred language*, which would help the individual understand his or her correlation to the cosmos. Ancient Greece, like Ancient Egypt, had its own series of initiatory mystery traditions in which teaching occurred through actual experience, sometimes in the form of passion plays, rituals, and dramas.

Earlier I referenced the development of occult philosophy during the Renaissance, and I want to return to that for a moment, because the term, "occult," like the pentagram, has developed a sinister reputation, at least colloquially among some people in the modern world. But the fact is, the term occult, as noted, is simply derived from the Latin term, *occultus* or *occulta,* which means *hidden, secret* or *unrevealed*. It was how many Renaissance philosophers referred to the ancient philosophies that they were discovering or rediscovering, philosophies that belonged to the vanished temple orders, academies, and religions of the antique world, and hence had been largely lost from view during what we call the Dark Ages.

And one of the key facets of occult thought—and you can find this in the insights of Pythagoras—is that esoterica is not *secret* so much because it's withheld or kept away from people; but rather it is secret in the sense that it requires *experience*; it requires initiation, of a sort; it requires getting your hands dirty. You really must be *involved* in the drama of a search. You must have a certain degree of preparation, and perhaps a certain degree of mentorship.

Pythagoras formed his mystery schools and study circles because he wanted to personally facilitate the advancement and experience of the individual. It was only through experience, he believed, that the individual could really come to know him or herself. And this echoed throughout the mystery traditions, including those of Ancient Egypt to which Greece is indelibly linked. These mystery traditions later echoed in a reconstituted form in the rites of Freemasonry and other societies dedicated to internal and ethical refinement, which was the *ideal* of Greek philosophy.

In *The Secret Teachings of All Ages*, Manly P. Hall explored certain aspects of Greek life that had been lost to modernity, but for which he displayed an extraordinary instinct. In some cases, he accurately captured ancient events in ways that other scholars of his day, in the 1920s and 1930s, were apt to miss. One such episode involved the Oracle at Delphi. The Oracle at Delphi was a female figure who would sit in a cavern at Delphi that was filled with fumes and mist. Various statesmen, orators, diplomats, educators, philosophers, and generals would come to visit the Oracle and ask her to prophesy the future. The Oracle was known as the Pythoness or Pythia. As I mentioned in the opening lesson, a woman named Pythia was the one who first exposed me to *The Secret Teachings of All Ages*. As Manly depicted in the *Secret Teachings*, and as you can also see from the book's illustration by J. Augustus Knapp, the Oracle of Delphi sat entranced on a kind of massive, golden tripod. As she sat there draped in robes in this mist-shrouded cavern, she would, as Manly described, imbibe fumes, grow intoxicated, enter a trance, and provide prophesies and foresight.

Now, in Manly's day and for many decades after, this portrait of the Oracle of Delphi was considered fanciful; it was considered myth. It had first appeared in the writings of Herodotus, but modern authorities considered it more legend than fact; most believed that there really wasn't a woman actually seated on a tripod, in a cave, with the mists—it was considered all too theatric. But ten years after Manly's death in 1990, archaeological findings at Delphi located exactly such a cavern with the very physical characteristics that Herodotus had described,** and that Manly later echoed in *The Secret Teachings of All Ages*. And this image—once thought to be mythical, once thought to be legend—was restored to academic recognition.

So, this is one area of several—earlier I noted his predating of the traditional timeline of Ancient Egypt—in which phenomena that Manly wrote about in this great underground book later came to be validated or at least debated by modern science. This is one of the reasons why, in our own time, Manly is just beginning to attain greater recognition within mainstream scholarship. To be sure, this recognition is

---

* You can learn about this in the 2006 book, *The Oracle: The Lost Secrets and Hidden Message of Ancient Delphi* by William J. Broad.

very slow in coming, and it is somewhat limited, but it is occurring.

University of Chicago scholar of myth Mircea Eliade (1907–1986) did a great deal in the twentieth century to bring respect to the study of ancient myth and esoteric traditions. Eliade confided to a colleague of mine, philosopher Jacob Needleman, that it was Manly P. Hall and *The Secret Teachings of All Ages* that initially awakened his passion to study esoterica and myth as a young man. Eliade was a widely respected scholar of mythology who dramatically advanced the field—and he named Manly as inspiring his earliest ideals. For my own part, I make the same claim.

Now, Manly felt that the initiatory process was a prerequisite to all religion itself, was a prerequisite to all philosophy itself—that it was impossible to really come into an understanding of psychological truths about yourself and your connection to the natural world without some kind of mentorship or initiatory process. This can be difficult to find in our world today. In particular, many seekers face the question of who to trust. I wrote the following passage in an article called "How to Spot a Sketchy Spiritual Guru" at Medium:

> The one key to not getting burned on the spiritual path is using *aggressive commonsense*. Always be prepared to speak up for yourself and to say no if you feel an activity or commitment crosses a line. A

philosopher I know once put it this way: "A real esoteric group is very difficult to find and very easy to
fall out off. A fake group is just the opposite." Make
that your yardstick. If anyone starts applying undue
pressure or attempts to isolate you, or if a leader
asks that you suspend your discretion in favor of
his, take a step back. There is no better guarantee of
personal safety than using your own applied judgment. When you discover and wield that judgment,
you may also find a large part of what you came
looking for in the first place.

Manly also believed that the Ancient Greeks possessed a core insight regarding deities. The ancients
personified unseen energies that we live under—and
they would personify these energies with names like
Athena, Hermes, Jupiter, or Dionysus. *The ancient lexicon of gods were deified versions of energies that course
through men and women, and that exist independently of
us.* That is one of the reasons why I often counsel people that you possibly, *possibly*, may discover something
extraordinary in your life if you identify a deific figure
from the pantheon of mythology, and perhaps seek to
form a kind of devotional or petitionary relationship
with this figure. Is that really so strange or odd? As
we've been reviewing, the ancients had a deep and profound understanding of nature—much deeper than
we do today, and on a profounder scale. They not only
personified energies but they would seek *actual abid-*

ing relationships with these figures. Now, if a person, at least as a matter of philosophical experimentation, is willing to consider the prospect that all emanates from one great intellect—one over-mind, or *Nous*—it could be theorized that there exist different aspects of this one great over-mind. And these different aspects and characteristics could announce themselves as the personified energies that the ancients named and venerated.

A living intellect, I think by its very nature, must possess emotions of a sort. Ethics arise from emotions, sympathy arises from emotions, empathy arises from emotions. And it could be theorized that if these expressions of the over-mind were at one time the subject of human veneration, and that veneration has largely dissipated in the modern world, *perhaps* these energies are lonely, in a certain sense. It might be open to you, the individual, to pursue a relationship with a personified divine energy with which you resonate. And that relationship could possibly prove enormously promising and helpful to you. It's a personal experiment that one can undertake. I embrace practical religious experiment, as long as the consequences are entirely personal.

It is interesting to consider that figures within the Hellenic world who were exemplars of rationality, engineering, calendrics, and mathematics had dedication to these deific energies. The lettered Roman emperor, Marcus Aurelius (121–180 A.D.), for example—who wrote his wonderful book of ethics that is today called *Meditations*—venerated Jupiter or Zeus; that happened to be his personal form of worship. So these deific figures and the ideals that they represented were profoundly present in the lives of Hellenic men and women. That does not mean they were right; but nor does the transformation of religious mores mean that they were wrong.

The Hellenic world also possessed, of course, a wonderful lexicon of psychological myths and parables. In a certain sense, myth is truer than history, insofar as myth announces who we are; myth brings insight into human nature. Whether or not the events of a myth are actual is beside the point; and in some cases, as with the Oracle of Delphi, Manly demonstrated that events that were thought to be merely mythological were, in fact, true. But whatever the events, a myth is a universal language that speaks to every facet of life and exposes both the foibles and the promises of human nature.

One element of Greek mythology, which later resonated within Judeo-Christian tradition, is that gods and deities often come to you disguised as wandering strangers, people who may be in need of help or hospitality. And those who provide hospitality or help to these disguised gods often meet with untold riches, which is probably a principle that should remind you to practice kindness toward strangers. (And many people who we think we already know are, in fact, strangers.) There is a divine or esoteric element to the practice of hospitality.

Most people in our world know the myth of Icarus, a young man who constructed wings of feather and wax and who flew too close to the sun—in his hubris, Icarus's wings melted and he fell back down to earth. Everyone immediately understands the psychological dimensions of that story. I think this is a more useful parable than Atlantis because it is personal. I encourage us to see these lessons within ourselves rather than in a more general sense.

The Roman god Janus bears two faces and has two identities; and I think we probably all feel that there are two identities fighting for prominence within our psyches. This may be called a plus-self and a minus-self, each challenging the other for dominance. This, too, repeats throughout our religions: the stories Cain and Abel, Jacob and Esau, and, in some versions, Set and Horus. This notion of there being two beings locked inside of us repeats in literature, including in modern works like *Dr. Jekyll and Mr. Hyde* by Robert Louis Stevenson, *William Wilson* by Edgar Allan Poe, and Stephen King's *The Dark Half*. And I think that many of us harbor the instinct that we are so divided, that within us there are always two forces. What would happen—and I challenge you in a practical way—if you were to experiment with that myth on a very personal level? If you were to actually and literally invite in that which represents the plus-entity in yourself? Do so persistently—do it by words, do it by prayer, do it by reflection; open up all doorways and possibilities to yourself; because, again, while the events of a myth may or may not have actually occurred, the applications are universal. Myths were humanity's earliest psychology and hold personal possibilities that run deeper than may first appear.

Mythical or symbolic animals possessed distinct and powerful traits in the Hellenic world. The familiar consort of Minerva, the goddess of wisdom, was an owl, which is one of the ways in which an owl has come to be seen as a symbol of wisdom as well as a messenger. The snake was seen as a symbol of rebellion, usurpation, slyness; again, this, too, echoed in Hebraic scripture as the snake in the Garden. Obadiah Harris, the past president of Manly P. Hall's Philosophical Research Society, shared a wonderful story with me a few years before his death in 2019. Obadiah said that when Manly Hall used to ready himself in his office each Sunday morning prior to delivering his weekly talk, he would pause before his altar and rub a wonderful little Egyptian statuette of a cat. It was a black onyx model of Bastet, one of the Egyptian cat gods. He would rub this little cat for wisdom because a cat has the ability to see in the dark. Many people felt Manly displayed a preternatural ability of speaking extremely fluidly and at great length without notes. I'm not suggesting a connection but I did like the story. And this little cat really existed—I held it in my hands—but it has unfortunately disappeared from Manly's office. The current PRS president, Greg Salyer, and I are searching for it. We'd like to re-select this little cat into existence.

Everything, *everything*—from a vessel, to an animal, to a building or monument—was seen to pulse with life and possibility in the Hellenic world. The Hellenic world, and Egypt before it, have formed the blueprint, the layout, for our own cities and large-scale civilizations in the West and in other parts of the world. Look at the layout of Washington, D.C.—populated as it is by obelisks, domes, and archways; by Romanesque and Hellenic temple designs, some of it inherited from ancient Egypt and much of it employing the golden mean of Pythagoras; sports stadiums echoing the Colosseum; highways echoing roads of the same name that were devised in ancient Rome; waterways, irrigation canals—all of these things came from the Egypto-Hellenic world. The blueprint of our physical civilization derives from their world.

In many cases, when ancient Greco-Roman temples were demolished or buried, their foundations were turned into building sites for Notre Dame and other expressions of Christianity throughout the Middle Ages. So many things that we know today as great Christian monuments literally sit upon original foundations of Greek, Roman, and sometimes Egyptian temples. Look at the familiar image of the Madonna and Child, an image that repeats throughout the world today, and has for centuries. The inception of that image was a statue of Isis, the Egyptian earth mother, with Horus, her holy offspring. And, in fact, many early Coptic Christians remade statues of Isis and Horus into early statues of Mary and Jesus.

We stand on the shoulders of the Egypto-Hellenic world in almost everything that we do, in almost everything that we build, and in almost every way that we see ourselves in current life. Again: "as above, so below." All is interconnected. If you wish to understand the basis of our chemistry, mathematics, psychology, religion, and so on, you can locate antecedents within the Hellenic mysteries, which themselves owe a profound debt to Ancient Egypt.

Know yourself—and part of knowing yourself is understanding the base upon which you stand, which is to a great extent Egypto-Hellenic in nature.

The Role of Secret Societies

The question of "secret societies" is one of the most controversial and dramatic in all of esoteric spirituality. In a sense, it is particularly controversial at this moment in the twenty-first century because we are living through a period in America, and in other parts of the world, where people are suffused with a kind of *us-versus-them* mentality. A certain degree of conspiracist thought has always been popular within American history, going back to the anti-Masonic scares of the early 19th century, and we seem to be experiencing an upsurge of this kind of conspiracist thinking today, in which a "hidden hand" is thought to be manipulating our destiny.

It's worth commenting on that before getting into the question and the history of secret societies. I think that within American culture today, there is a deep and justified hunger for *transparency*. People feel like there are holes in the straight story, people feel like there are forces at work—financial and governmental—that do not necessarily have their best interests at heart, and they feel manipulated and locked out of decision-making processes. I think this instinct is correct. But I think this instinct also gets perverted and misdirected into conspiracist thought, in which some sort of perhaps historically real but fictitiously reimagined secret society (the Illuminati, most frequently) is cited as wielding nefarious control over human affairs. People speak in terms of different groups, like the Council on Foreign Relations; Bohemian Grove; the Bilderberg Group; Skull and Bones; the Deep State; Freemasonry, of course; and other organizations, some historically real but reimagined along the lines of being some secret force in human affairs.

The problem I have with this outlook is that it frequently results in this us-versus-them mentality. It is, in certain ways, almost antithetical to the spiritual search, because the conspiracy model locates problems in the world as existing *out there*, among *them*; and those of us who are trying to expose the problem—so goes the kind of mood that you find within conspiracist culture—are somehow always the *good guys*. It's never the mirror that we look in for the problem. It's never or rarely our own relationships that we scrutinize. Or our own ethics. But,

rather, the notion is that manipulations and mech-
anizations that oppose the best interests of human
flourishment are perpetuated by *some other* force,
that's out there somewhere. This, in the ultimate
sense, perpetuates an angry, tribal mentality. This
way of thought almost never leads to policy ideas or
reforms; or to understanding the economic forces
that strip the individual of decision-making ability, economic forces that often conceal their profit-
making apparatus, so that the individual doesn't
realize when he or she is being taken advantage of,
such as by health insurers. Rather, the conspiracist
model tends to cement a view of life in which the epicenter of good is usually located in *me*, the observer,
and the epicenter of bad is always *out there* in a secretive, shadowy apparatus.

Not that one shouldn't be concerned with unseen
policies, economic manipulation, and a paucity of
social equality—those things are urgent. But I con-
tend that anything that directs us, first and foremost,
away from self is ultimately antithetical to the search.
I believe that the wish for greater transparency—
and the suspicion that we're being moved around by
larger forces, and that we deserve greater insight and
decision-making capacity—is healthy and important. It is justified. But I very often find that *instead* of
looking at, say, the pricing policies of pharmaceutical
companies, or at predatory credit-card or mortgage
lenders, or at the grossly inflated profits reaped by

health-insurance companies who continually narrow the range of benefits payable to the consumer, or at the problems of banking deregulation, which contributed to the mortgage crisis and, hence, the Great Recession of 2008, the reverberations of which are still being felt today—instead of looking at such things, considering such things, asking about such things, and determining *policies* that are going to correct such things, which are entirely within reach, we get waylaid into delving into chimeras, into notions of secret societies or occult power centers, where no solutions or causes lie. And often where nothing lies. If I was an unaccountable Big Pharma exec, I would consider conspiracy theories my best friend. Keep looking *over there*—and not at me. Or at yourself.

The notion that secret fraternities or societies are controlling things is not only simplistic, and not only (usually) in our present day part of a kind of repeat-circuit loop of references, premises, and suppositions—in that vein, I cannot tell you how many times I hear people use the term *Illuminati* without any definition or historical grounding—but conspiracist culture often *misdirects the human gaze from the real problems and the complexities* of abuse of power in our economic and governmental system. Again, the emotional hunger behind conspiracy theorizing is *right*; it's a hunger for transparency. *But* that hunger gets misdirected by a kind of ideologically entrenched conspiracist thought—this obsessive search for a hidden hand—

and devolves into an us-versus-them schema, usually ending in paranoia of a kind, and usually devolving into theories that demean or dehumanize other individuals and groups. Eventually, almost all conspiracy theories, as they're practiced in the twenty-first century, lead to an exaltation of self and a suspicion of other. That is the primary problem I have with the conspiracist outlook when it is practiced as a kind of dogma.

None of this is to say that there have not been secret societies of a sort in human history, and that these secret societies have not wielded influence. Humanity has always had a penchant for forming into fraternities, mutual-aid societies, and communities of interest. And humanity, of course, always has a penchant for intrigue and self-interest; so, to some extent, those factors will always be present in whatever community or grouping we find ourselves in. But what we're really concerned with in this chapter is the *actuality and role* of secret societies as a veritable force for ideas, insight, and the preservation of esoteric ritual, rite, and practice throughout the last several hundred years of history. That is an entirely legitimate area of inquiry when done with a sense of critical thought and historicism.

Now, Manly P. Hall, in *The Secret Teachings of All Ages* and at other times, actually took very positive measure of what we would call secret societies, including Freemasonry. Manly was a Freemason himself. He wrote several books extolling the virtues of Freemasonry as an initiatory organization dedicated to the refinement of the individual through ancient symbols and passion plays, which encrypted ideas about ethical development and about the inner proportions and possibilities of the individual. Historically speaking, Freemasonic practices include dramas and rites that depict the passage of the individual from ignorance into understanding; mastery of esoteric symbols as codes to development; internal democracy; abstention from tale-bearing or rumor mongering; and the principle that legitimate rank and privilege do not come without personal advancement. These are some of the ideals actually practiced within Freemasonry historically; this sufficiently attracted Manly, so that he became a Freemason in the 1950s, and shortly before his death, he was awarded the honorary 33rd degree in the Scottish Rite, its highest designation. One of the last talks he delivered was to a gathering of Freemasons in Los Angeles.

Manly also took positive measure of the historical movement called Rosicrucianism or the Rosicrucians. This name is adopted by a variety of modern groups. And, as we'll see, historically Rosicrucianism may have been more of a thought movement than an actual organization.

Manly also made reference to that most controversial of groups, the Illuminati—frequently heard about today on late-night radio and online posts, but rarely understood as an authentic historical entity. Since the Illuminati is the source of so much misunderstanding today, that is where I will begin. Indeed, every time I step onto a basketball court, some well-intentioned kid will see my tattoos and ask me, "Are you a member of the Illuminati?" And it's not even clear what anybody actually means when they put that question to you. I have been accused of being the public face or a PR agent for something called the Illuminati; I'm supposed to be their cover, so the story goes on certain websites.

The Illuminati, in our own day, has become a catchall phrase for some sort of nefarious hidden force. Supposedly all kinds of influential figures belong to this group—from Barack Obama to Jay-Z to Lady Gaga to Pope Francis—and some of these people are thought to disclose their affiliation through the use of symbols in their songs or media or during Super Bowl halftime shows. Why exactly the Super Bowl or a Disney movie would be a venue to suggest one's secret allegiances, I'm not sure; but the idea behind these stories is that we're being manipulated, and, again, it's *those guys*, the *Illuminati*—always someone else, someone other than the being who gazes back at me from the mirror—who is the source of the problem. And people sometimes associate the beautiful symbol of the eye and pyramid on the back of our dollar bill, about which I'll say more in the following chapter, as some sort of code or symbol for the Illuminati.

In a sense, the real story is very different, but no less remarkable. I always tell people that actual history is, in many regards, more fantastic than anything fantasy holds. We could learn so much if only we really wanted to probe the *actualities of history*, rather than engage in fantasizing, which admittedly—and this is another attraction of conspiracy theory—is dramatic; it's entertaining, it's alluring, it's fun. It's much more fun than understanding why your health insurance company is capable of declining perfectly valid claims and whether insurers have done market research that finds that, if you deny a certain number of valid claims and make people wait a certain number of minutes on hold, ten percent or some odd number of people will just go away in exhaustion. If you want to find evil, look there. So much in our financial life requires greater transparency; and yet, the policy requirements are difficult and sometimes confounding. Instead, we get lost talking about figures like the Illuminati.

There was, indeed, a real organization called the Illuminati. It was founded in Bavaria in 1776 by a philosopher and lawyer named Adam Weishaupt (1748–1830). Weishaupt was a remarkable and interesting man. He was a radical democrat, who believed ardently in separation of church and state; who believed that rank, and privilege, and the role of the aristocracy should not translate into holding governmental, legal, or parliamentary positions; that government should be representative; and that every individual should have the freedom to pursue his or her own religious ideals. He believed in radical ecumenism. Weishaupt felt that the ideals of the ancient religions of Egypt, Greece, and Rome could be revived and could be used as initiatory rites to refine the individual in the modern age. He practiced a kind of mystical or primeval Christianity, although he rejected *organized* Christendom and the economic benefits granted to the Church.

At the time, the government of Bavaria, as with many governments across Europe, was completely intertwined with an official state church; the two formed a DNA strand of power. Hence, state-sponsored religion was given enormous legal and economic benefits, all of which Weishaupt wanted to bust up. And if some of this sounds familiar, bear in mind that it's not accidental that Weishaupt founded the Illuminati in Bavaria in 1776—a date that was very important to him, because he identified with some of the most radical ideals of the American founders, especially Thomas Paine and, to a degree, Thomas Jefferson (although Weishaupt was much more interested in initiatory religion and spirituality than Jefferson was). And Jefferson knew about Weishaupt, which I'll say another word about.

Weishaupt was also friendly with the philosopher, Goethe; the composer, Mozart; and a wide range of artists, philosophers, and political reformers who agreed with his ideas about the establishment of a civic democracy, the protection of the individual search for meaning, and the separation of church and state authority. Those were Weishaupt's *primary* ideals. And he wanted to form revolutionary cells within Bavarian society and in other sectors of European society to oppose the church-state complex, and to help disseminate, agitate, and advocate for these reformist-radical ideas within monarchical societies.

Weishaupt also had, as I mentioned, a deep personal interest in the rites and rituals of the mystery traditions of Persia, Egypt, Rome, and Greece. He was interested in the ideas that grew out of the occult Renaissance across Europe. He was interested in the Hermetic literature, which we discussed earlier. He believed, quite rightly, that threads of ideas and symbolism had reached modern people from deepest antiquity, and these threads could sometimes be found within the Hermetic writings; they could be found within some of the occult practices that developed and were refined during the Renaissance; and they could be found within the rites and rituals of Freemasonry, a group that he venerated.

In short, Weishaupt devised a plan to form a renegade Freemasonic movement, which was called the *Illuminati*—the illumined ones. He intended to assemble a cluster of like-minded political radicals to secretly infiltrate Freemasonic lodges, which is why I call him a renegade Freemason. In so doing, Weishaupt intended to remake these lodges into vehicles for political reform or revolution. Now, seen from one perspective, Weishaupt had good reason to be secretive because the Bavarian government brutally punished its political enemies; and, in Bavaria and other parts of Europe at that time, if you were considered a provocateur who advocated overthrowing the prevailing church-state order, you could meet with harassment, arrest, jailing—or worse. Hence, there were reasons for secrecy that went beyond the drama of "secret societies;" and, due to this factor, Weishaupt was attracted to another secretive body, or clandestine might be a better way of putting it: Freemasonry, which not only operated in many respects below the radar of government authority, but also had the same taste and penchant for occult and esoteric symbolism, and the rituals and rites of personal initiation and refinement, as Weishaupt did. So, the agitator considered it a perfect marriage.

That's one part of the picture. Then there is the ethical question of conducting your political program under the screen of secrecy. Mahatma Gandhi, who had early involvements with the Theosophical Society and was a lifelong admirer of the occult movement, stated that he never actually joined any esoteric organization because he believed that secrecy is ultimately at odds with true democracy. Thomas Jefferson, a contemporary of Weishaupt, saw it differently:

although Jefferson had no taste for esoteric spirituality, he nonetheless wrote admiringly of Weishaupt. In a letter from 1800, Jefferson defended Weishaupt, noting that the renegade essentially believed in the refinement of the individual and in the practice of some of the civil reforms that had preceded in the U.S. Jefferson concluded that if Weishaupt lived in the new republic—where, he wrote, no secrecy is required in pursuit of these ends—then clandestine behavior wouldn't be necessary. But Jefferson felt that because Weishaupt lived and functioned in a more politically and religiously oppressive society, a degree of secrecy was forced upon him.

Weishaupt marched into this program to infiltrate Masonic lodges and turn them into political vehicles. I've given you two points of view on the matter. Is it defensible to enter any organization with an ulterior purpose? Personally, I believe in transparency. But I'm speaking from a twenty-first century perspective. Someone living in an oppressive, church-state apparatus in 1776 could easily and justifiably see things differently. In any case, Weishaupt's efforts didn't get very far. He interjected himself into a few lodges, he wrote a few tracts, he attracted a few confederates, but he also quickly aroused the suspicion of the state. Within nine years, the Bavarian government passed two sets of laws that effectively outlawed all secret societies. And the scent trail of the Illuminati goes cold after that.

Of course, some like to say that the Illuminati merely went deeper underground. That's speculation, at best. Consider that the next time historical writers addressed the question of the Illuminati was to theorize that the secret sect laid behind the French Revolution. A variety of conspiracist pamphleteers began to argue that this overwhelming revolution couldn't possibly have swept away the old order overnight; there had to be some hidden mechanism behind it. Thus reenters the Illuminati, recast as a kind of conspiratorial villain, and described in almost completely fictitious terms. Consider: the Bavarian government outlawed the Illuminati within about eight or nine years; the group effectively is disbanded and dispersed; but pamphleteers following the French Revolution insist that the old order just couldn't have dissolved so quickly.

Revolutions and dramatic political reforms have a discordant, deeply disorienting effect on anyone attached to the old order. People are sometimes shocked that the old world they once knew could be upended and vanish so apparently quickly. Rarely do they take the time to look at or understand the cumulative social causes that provided an antecedent, which can be traced out and predicted if an observer really applies scrutiny to the matter. Nonetheless, it can feel shocking when change finally occurs, regardless of the buildup; it can feel sudden, jarring, and disorienting. It's easier, simpler, and more tempting to under-

stand that change as having been the product of some
kind of hidden plan or schism, rather than social conditions that proved inevitably unsustainable.

Even when events are cumulative, change itself
seems sudden. If you backtrack a year from the mortgage crisis of 2008, which triggered the Great Recession, it is possible to detect (at least in hindsight) that
trouble was on the horizon, that so much of the secu-
rities industry and its mortgage-lending apparatus
was unsustainable. But few voices, including financial "experts" at leading brokerage houses, made any
such observation. And when the crash occurred over
the course of a weekend, there was panic. The events
themselves felt *sudden*; it felt like prosperity had gone
boom-and-bust, almost literally in the space of 72
hours. I watched a relative who was a partner at a
major bank rush into work on a Sunday shell-shocked
at what was occurring. Suddenly, a vast banking concern like Bear Stearns closed down. Bear Stearns
was a household name in the banking world, almost
like Chase is, and it crashed and vanished in about 72
hours. And that's just one financial institution.

Financial change, unexpected election results, and
mass protests can be part of a great contextual chain,
yet the event itself still feels sudden. Hence for figures
who had been attached to the aristocracy or the church
structure, or their sympathizers, the French Revolution felt unreal. And it was easy to redirect attention to
a neighboring "secret society" that had been outlawed

by another church, by another aristocratically based government, that might have been the hidden hand behind this supposedly inexplicable reversal. And this cycle of conspiracism continued. The Illuminati theory got revived after the Russian Revolution, after Vatican II, and other social events in Europe into the early twentieth century.

A variant of the hidden-hand concept got inadvertently revived by President George H.W. Bush (1924–2018). In two addresses to joint sessions of Congress, on September 11, 1990 at the start of the first Iraq War and on March 6, 1991 at the war's end, the elder Bush described the emergence of a "new world order." His use of this phrase at the dawning of the digital era caught the ear of conspiracy theorists, who interpreted it as code for world domination by groups such as the Illuminati or a hidden global elite.

If you read the speeches themselves, Bush, validly or not, was making reference to the possibility that, with the conclusion of the first Iraq War, there could be a new era of commerce, peace treaties, cultural exchange, and so on; it was a bit of fanciful idealism. He drew upon a phrase, New World Order—or New Order of the Ages—that appears in Latin in the Great Seal of United States, a topic we will explore in the next chapter. Bush's phrasing, which has now been surpassed by "Deep State," was interpreted as a catchword for unseen forces, and it drummed up a new chapter of conspiracy theorizing around the Illuminati, a group that has not actually existed for close to 250 years.

Those are the facts of the Illuminati's existence and the perpetuation of its mythos. As noted, I think we should seek to understand the group's radical democratic ideals, and its attachment to the occult and esoteric traditions of antiquity, as an *alternative* to a church order that had grown grotesquely calcified. I think Weishaupt should be understood as a radical political reformer, in the same way we understand that about somebody like Thomas Paine, even if one has misgivings, as I do, about Weishaupt's secrecy. This was Manly's understanding of the Illuminati, and my wish is that students could be educated about this history, so that they might find such a group inspiring, if flawed, rather than frightful and fantastical.

Likewise, there are a lot of fanciful ideas around Free-masonry, which rivals the Illuminati in its reputation for skullduggery, most of it unfounded. Freemasonry, on which I commented earlier, is a historically fascinating and, in some ways, justly mysterious group, because even within the Freemasonic order itself, where you can find some truly first-class historians, there's no consensus as to the order's origins. The group's founding remains the subject of debate. Masonry may be the only modern organization for which that is true.

On an idealistic level, some will say that Freemasonry goes back to the builders of Solomon's Temple;

some will say it goes back to the builders of the pyramids; some will say, more traditionally speaking, that it goes back to the stone-making guilds, the cathedral building guilds, of the Middle Ages. I believe there is historical validity to that latter outlook. I'm not sure that it covers *all* the bases, because there are aspects of Freemasonry that are deeply esoteric in nature, and we may never have the full story. But it is possible that the order began among the great cathedral builders, at least in part.

Regarding the timeline of Masonry's development, we possess a few important and tantalizing signposts. One of the most significant is the diaries of British esotericist and antiquarian Elias Ashmole (1617–1692). Ashmole wrote in his diaries of 1646 about being inducted into an order of Masons, and that this induction ceremony had a spiritual and esoteric quality. This account is very useful, because it's one of the first and earliest explicit references to Freemasonic practice found on the European continent. It wasn't until more than a generation later, in 1717, that the Grand Lodge of England actually emerged aboveground with the public declaration of its existence. That's the crucial year in the history of Freemasonry. These dates are significant bookends because—while they are certainly not the only pertinent dates and other, earlier references than Ashmole can be justifiably linked to Freemasonry—the Ashmole diaries are inarguably clear; they make it plain that he was inducted into a Masonic order of esoteric spiritual outlook.

Freemasonry, like the Illuminati, has always had a tense and uncomfortable relationship with church authority, in Europe in particular, because Masonry as it emerged on the public scene in 1700s promulgated a belief in God and a radical ecumenism but *existed outside of the authority* of any church structure. And, as it happened, there were major figures who emerged from the folds of Freemasonry, including the Italian democratic revolutionary Giuseppe Garibaldi (1807–1882), who actually fought militarily against church authority in Italy and other parts of Europe. It's important to remember that even into the 1870s there were still monarchies in control in Europe. And this was true into the 1900s in Russia. It wasn't until the 1870s, under pressure from unifying Italian democrats, that the church officially disbanded its private army and militia, allowing for the emergence of a democratic republic of Italy. Garibaldi, a Freemason and revolutionary, militarily opposed the church; there was a civil war going on in what is today the modern state of Italy, which hinged on the effort to disband the Vatican as a separate and independent military fiefdom. So, religious or monarchical military power was a fact of life in Europe up through very late into the 19th century and in Germany and Russia into the twentieth century. Masonry generally opposed this.

That an organization—of students, scholars, merchants, bankers, farmers, political figures, and artists—would group together in a manner outside of church authority was no small thing. Again, this further gives you some idea of why clandestine behavior was sometimes necessary—Masons for much of their history were functioning outside of sanctioned authority. Yes, there was a certain drama to Masonry's attachment to secrecy; yes, there was a certain esoteric quality to it—although I would defend anybody's right to assemble in private—but there was also a political necessity. For generations, Masonry in Europe promulgated principles that you couldn't easily pursue aboveground; indeed you could suffer severe consequences, as did the Illuminati which was rendered illegal.

Like the Illuminati, Freemasonry also promulgated the belief that the ancient mystery religions—of Persia, Egypt, Greece, and Rome—had left behind certain scent trails, certain threads, which Masons believed they could piece together and reassemble into rites and rituals. Masons also sought to revive a variant of the rites of the Hebrew priests, who presided over the Temple of Solomon and the Tabernacle in the Wilderness in the early religious structures of the Hebraic world. Freemasons attempted to forge these surviving threads into ceremonies, dramas, and passion plays that would foster the ethical development of the individual. They drew upon occult symbolism—

the pyramid, the all-seeing eye, the obelisk, the skull and crossbones, the pentagram, the Star of David—which Manly P. Hall writes about in *The Secret Teachings of All Ages*. These symbols were seen as keys that could ignite self-understanding.

I'll say more in the next chapter about the very unique way that Freemasonry played out within the U.S. colonies. I think, in a certain sense, that Freemasonic ideals reached their fullest fruition in the life and the experience of some of America's most idealistic founders. It was in the United States, rather than in Europe, that Freemasonry was able to express its fullest political and spiritual vision. With glaring contradictions, of course. And because Freemasonic lodges tended to reflect local customs and mores, in Europe, where there was greater class and social stratification, Masonry tended to evince a greater degree of clubiness and mutual aid, and this probably remains so today. I do not perceive that kind of cliquishness as a large part of Freemasonic culture in the United States today; but I think some of that attitude has more or less persisted in parts of Europe.

In the past couple of generations, there have been certain scandals in Europe—including in Italy and England—where people who were fellow Freemasons within law enforcement or finance were involved in certain acts of collusion, or so the accusations went. I take those charges seriously, not because they suggest something innate to Freemasonry so much as they do to human nature in general: all of our endeavors, all of our groupings, carry the risk of devolving into the practice of self-service or the perpetuation of local prejudices. That's a fact of human life and it occurs everywhere; that it would occur within Freemasonry is no surprise.

But the essential ideals of Freemasonic practice in Europe were to create a spiritual and intellectual order that existed outside the dogma or doctrine of church and state. Masonry's great innovation was *radical ecumenism*; any individual could join, provided he voiced belief in one creator, and, so went the ideal, people from any walk of life could be a member and attain rank and privilege only as they passed through the degrees, passion plays, rites, and rituals that had been structured to reward responsibility rather than bloodline. So, in other words, Freemasonry, in its ideal, was supposed to be a radical meritocracy. And it generally practiced internal democracy, electing its leaders based on members' preferences rather than inheritance. These were radical ideas back in the early 1700s; they sound to us like Civics 101 today, but at that time they were threatening to the established order. I'll be saying more about Masonry and politics in our next chapter on the secret history of America.

In addition to the Illuminati and Freemasons, the best known so-called secret society in modern history is Rosicrucianism. Manly Hall writes a great deal about

Rosicrucian doctrines and philosophy in *The Secret Teachings of All Ages*. There are, in fact, many self-styled Rosicrucian organizations that cropped up on the alternative spiritual scene in the U.S. and other parts of the world beginning in the early twentieth century and that continue today. But Rosicrucianism as a historical fact can be traced to the years 1614 to 1617, during which time there appeared in Germany three anonymously written manuscripts, which caused a great sensation. The first one, appearing in 1614, was called the *Fama*, or "our fraternity," and it declared the existence of an "invisible college" of eso-teric seekers who had as their aim the promotion of a healthful, just civic society—where there would be free hospitals; free education; and the free practice of religion; and Christian, Muslim, and Jew could all live together. And, again, if these ideas sounded radical in the early practices of Freemasonry, you can imagine how much more radical they must have sounded in 1614 in post-Renaissance aristocratic Europe.

About a year later, there appeared another secret manuscript circulating in Germany, this one referred to as *Confessions of the Rosicrucian Brotherhood*, which gave further voice to and explanation of this hidden brotherhood, which was said to have emerged from the initiatory travels of a certain pilgrim who entered a mysterious tomb bathed with white light, and found ciphers, codes, and messages that conveyed to him the existence of an ageless wisdom—a perennial philosophy that taught the principles of self-refinement and, again, that called for the establishment of a just civic order and social polity, and the establishment of hospitals and colleges—and that this "invisible college" of Rosicrucians was an unseen force that would propel society forward. This is probably what inspired Adam Weishaupt over a century later to found the Illuminati.

And finally, in 1617, there appeared the third and final Rosicrucian manuscript of the era, the *Chymical Wedding of Christian Rosenkreutz*. The *Chymical Wedding* was a spiritual allegory, somewhat in the vein of the book *Pilgrim's Progress*, in which a young man, Christian Rosenkreutz, is called to a palace to help oversee a magical wedding between a king and a queen. Embedded within this allegory is a late-Renaissance understanding of the Hermetic literature and the nature of psychological alchemy. One of the key ideals of alchemy—and something that you'll see repeated again and again in alchemical woodcuts and drawings from the Renaissance—is the notion of *unifying the male and female forces* within the individual; unifying the capacity, classically speaking, for intellect and emotion; intuition and industry; suggestion and birth. The notion being that the masculine and feminine sides of human nature must become rejoined into the *divine hermaphrodite*—making reference to Hermes (the god of writing, commerce, intellect) and Aphrodite (the keeper of wisdom, beauty, and art). The marriage of the divine hermaphrodite is voiced within the principles of psychological alchemy, symbolized within the joining of polarities in Hermetic philosophy, and retold as an allegory in the Rosicrucian tract of the *Chymical Wedding of Christian Rosenkreutz*. The young Christian—a seeker, pilgrim, and philosopher—*is to help the king and the queen, the metaphorical man and woman, rejoin and become the one great being that fell into two pieces after the fall from Paradise.*

It is worth asking: Was there any Rosicrucian order? Was there an actual Rosicrucian brotherhood? It is not entirely clear. Rosicrucianism, I think, can be more accurately understood as a *thought* movement. Certainly there were key figures behind it—these unsigned manuscripts came from the hand of *someone;* and it may have been a cluster of people who were interested in promoting revolutionary and spiritual ideas without necessarily being part of an actual order or brotherhood. That doesn't make what they did any less valid, any more than an idea is valid because it's old or new, popular or obscure. Some historians have theorized that Rosicrucianism may have been composed of some disgruntled followers of the magician, John Dee (1527–c.1608/9), who was forced into exile after the death of Queen Elizabeth in 1607; and that's entirely possible.

Others have theorized Rosicrucian ties to Freemasonry, including the groundbreaking British historian Frances Yates (1899–1981). In her 1972 book *The Rosi-*

crucian Enlightenment, Yates argued compellingly that Rosicrucianism formed the earliest vestiges of esoteric ideas that later emerged as Freemasonry. And the timeline really matches up, because the Rosicrucian manuscripts appeared in the early 1600s; the diaries of Elias Ashmole appeared not much later, in 1646; some other, roughly contemporaneous references appeared in literature, poetry, and religious expression; and what is called Freemasonry, in the form of the Grand Lodge of England, emerged aboveground in 1717, about a hundred years after the last Rosicrucian manuscript appeared. That leaves sufficient gestation for Rosicrucianism to have transformed from a thought movement to an actual initiatory brotherhood—which continues today, and which I will be talking about in terms of its influence in the United States in our next chapter. This is real occult history—not fantasy but the true currents of the unseen quest to know.

What I've outlined is part of the actual history of so-called secret societies, more of which can be read about and understood in *The Secret Teachings of All Ages*; in the work of Francis Yates (who's a wonderful historian, whose work should be engaged by any student and lover of Manly Hall); and in anthologies like *The Secret History of America*. And, of course, you also can find quality translations of the Rosicrucian manifestos, and I encourage you to read those as well.

It's critical to understand that these groups really did exist and do exist, but not to get lost in the lurid misrepresentations that populate paranoid postings online; but rather to look at these groups and ask, "What were they really doing? What were their ideals? And, how can their successes, shortcomings, and outlook help inform and propel forward our own highest ideals today?"

The Secret History of America

W
e will now explore how some of the ideals and principles inherent within the secret society tradition, as described in the previous chapter, played out in key aspects of the structure, culture, and spiritual and civic life of America.

It's important for me to take a step back for a moment and describe to you something about my own orientation. I must be very careful as a historian of the esoteric not to overcompensate or overindulge in a kind of idealistic portraiture of some of what I am describing. Because concurrent with the emergence of some of these fraternities and thought movements and the ideals that they represented there coexisted deeply conflicting and contradictory actions and forms of governance in the American colonies and in other parts of the world. Just as the so called "Rosicrucian Enlightenment," a phrase belonging to historian Frances Yates, and the ideals of Freemasonry were playing out, there coexisted grotesque countervailing forces. Sometimes these forces intermingled.

In the American colonies in particular, where Masonry played a fairly decisive role in the formation of the republic, two deeply contradictory waves of history played out in early American life and well beyond. One was the destruction of the Native American civilization. I don't think that we as a society have ever fully come to terms or come to acknowledge the horrific destruction practiced over the course of centuries against the Native American cultures. President Andrew Jackson, himself a Mason, appears on our $20 bill; but we possess little realization or understanding of the brutal policies that Jackson and others carried out against Native American civilization.

An idea can never be destroyed, and some of the ideas, both civic and religious, that were practiced within Native American culture have in fact endured. Benjamin Franklin, for example, was well aware of some of the governmental structures of the Seneca Nation, the Onondaga Nation, and other tribes that had formed into polities or unified bodies—where disputes were sometimes settled by treaty, by agreement, by diplomacy—and these things did have some influence on him and a few of the other founders. And, of course, some of the great religious parables, designs, dances—beautiful, expressive and deeply esoteric aspects of Native American spirituality—do persist and are practiced. But the terrible displacement that that civilization experienced, the terrible disease and *violence* that was visited upon that civilization by the colonial government, is something that we as a nation have never really come to grips with.

The same is true with the centuries-long crime of slavery. When I was writing my first book, *Occult America*, I read all three of Frederick Douglass's memoirs—Frederick Douglass, of course, being the abolitionist hero and voice of human dignity in the 19th century. As I was reading Douglass's memoirs (all of which are enormously readable, and vital and important reading), I just fell to my knees, I fell to my knees, in some cases literally, at this history of brutality and what it meant to children to be born into bondage—to be ripped away from their mothers and parents at very, very young ages and raised in just horrific conditions—and how this was perpetuated over hundreds of years. It's a history that we *think* we know. And yet we don't know it; we've never really come to a serious moral *reckoning* of that aspect of our national history, however easily the names of figures like Harriet Tubman or Frederick Douglass or Booker T. Washington (who was born a slave) come to our lips. I don't think we've ever fully come to understand what was done, how it was done, and the generations-long legacy of this brutality—which, of course, persists in various forms in the twenty-first century. That's a national crime that I don't think we've ever really come to terms with. That may change in our generation.

For the purpose of exploring some of the unseen esoteric dimensions of civic and political life in America, I want to do something that is somewhat ahistorical. I want to jump outside of the linear timeline for just a moment in talking about the unseen history of America; because I could start from the Freemasonic experience and easily jump forward from the emergence of the Grand Lodge in 1717 to the dedication of some of the most crucial American founders to Freemasonry—and that's important, that matters, and I will get to it—but I want to say something about the manner in which *esoteric spiritual movements and reformist or radical political movements grew intertwined*, because that's real history, too. That's a history that Manly P. Hall recognized in *The Secret Teachings of All Ages*, and, again, it's a much truer and more valid form of historicism than anything that swirls around conspiracy theories.

On that note, I want to say an important historical word about the life of the abolitionist, Frederick Douglass (1818–1895). Douglass was a great rationalist, a purveyor of education, an advocate of human dignity—and historians don't often detect an esoteric undercurrent in Douglass's career or in what he described as the most important episode of his life, which played out when he was about 15 years old. Douglass was born into slavery; he was torn away from his mother at a very young age and forced to live on a plantation in the state of Maryland, many miles away from the plantation on which his mother was enslaved. His mother was a woman who would walk for *hours* to see him when he was young, to give him a bar of soap, or to give him a ginger cookie that she had made; he was otherwise completely separated from her.

At a young age, Frederick, in early adolescence, was removed from plantation life in the town of Saint Michaels and taken by his slaveholders to the city of Baltimore. He spent several years in Baltimore, where he was actually able to teach himself to read. The female head of his household began to teach Frederick to read when he was in young adolescence, but when her husband found out about it, he strictly forbade these literacy lessons, because, he said, if you teach him to read there will be no controlling him. So these lessons were abruptly halted. But Frederick had learned enough so that he was effectively able to continue his lessons on his own. Living at the time in a city, he was able to find scraps of newspapers, discarded books or publications, even labels on products; and he was able to take the rudimentary knowledge that he had gained and build on it, so that sooner or later he was fully literate—which many adults, both free and enslaved, at the time were not.

Just as abruptly as Frederick had been taken from the town of Saint Michaels and moved to Baltimore, his owners (so to speak) again uprooted him and returned to Saint Michaels, to plantation life. And the master of his household said, in effect, it's going to prove difficult to control a city kid in a rural environment, so rather than just putting Frederick back to work on the plantation, he decided to loan him out for a year to a brutal local slave master, named Edward Covey. Covey had a reputation as being a "breaker" of slaves; he was very sadistic and brutal, and he was proud of his reputation. Frederick's owners made the determination that a year of back-breaking work under Covey would reacclimate Frederick to the servitude demanded of him in Saint Michaels.

So at the start of 1834, Covey took control of Frederick's life. Frederick worked on his farm and Covey, true to his reputation, dispensed horrible beatings and acts of cruelty. He beat Frederick so badly once that the teen fled Covey's farm and returned on foot to his old slave masters in Saint Michaels, and he begged them to take him back in. They refused. They turned him around to Covey's farm.

After returning, Frederick was hiding in the woods outside of Covey's farm—cold, starving, still caked with blood, and not knowing what to do. While Frederick was in the woods, he was happened upon by an older man, also a slave, named Sandy Jenkins. Sandy was considered a wise and sympathetic figure, and he took Frederick to his cabin in the woods, cleaned him up, and gave him something to eat. Frederick said that Sandy had a reputation locally as "an old adviser." Sandy, he wrote in 1855, "was not only a religious man, but he professed to believe in a system for which I have no name. He was a genuine African, and had inherited some of the so-called magical powers, said to be possessed by African and eastern nations."

Now, this is very important, and I write about this further in *Occult America*. What Frederick was referencing when he called Sandy someone who practiced the old ways was an African-American system of magick, which retained some of the West and Central African spiritual practices and combined them with certain beliefs and practices in America. It went by the name *hoodoo*, with an *h*. It was not Vodou; Vodou was entirely different, and the two are often confused and conflated by observers. Vodou is a proper Afro-Caribbean religion, with its own pantheon of deities, religious authorities, rites, ritual, and practice. Hoodoo was different.

Hoodoo was a series of practices that grew in part from the Yoruba nation in West Africa. Hoodoo practitioners, who remain active around the United States today, combine spell work and magick with some spiritual ideas from Catholicism, Judaism and other faiths and groupings in America, including Pennsylvania Dutch folklore and hexing.

No one is precisely sure about the etymology of the term, *hoodoo*, which is rendered lowercase. It's not a permutation of Vodou. Hoodoo may have derived from the word *huduba*, a term used among the Hausa people of West and Central Africa, which meant to sort of cast a spell on someone or do some sort of trick on a person; but it's not entirely clear if that was the point of origin of the word. In any case, hoodoo arose as an African-American, initially slave-based, tradition of magick, spell work, root work, and botanical remedies. Hoodoo's ritualistic supplies and means of magic-making often came from native herbs and everyday household objects—objects that an enslaved person might be able to get his or her hands on, like wild or garden roots, herbs and flowers, and nails, pins, jars, perfumes, and soaps. In practice, hoodoo was a system of ceremonial magick and spell-work that was meant to help everyday people get through the struggles of daily life.

And this tradition continues today; hoodoo is very often focused on the practical necessities of day-to-day living: dealing with money problems, legal trouble, an unfair boss, a troublesome neighbor, issues of romance or broken hearts, and so on. Hoodoo is for the workaday needs of men and women taking on life in tough circumstances. And for that reason, among many others, I love hoodoo. Hoodoo formed a part of my own spiritual practice for many years and continues to today. I believe in the practical application of esoteric and occult ideas. I believe these methods should meet men and women where they live and should form a response to the necessities and urgencies of ordinary life.

And so Frederick described Sandy as a practitioner of this system; but what he was referencing was *unrecognized* by many mainstream historians. Hence, for generations Douglass's three memoirs have been available on the public scene, but the thread of esoteric influence that he described was *unrecognized*. Most scholastic historians didn't look any closer when Frederick said, in effect, that Sandy was a kind of root worker or a root doctor—terms still used in hoodoo today—and that Sandy could employ roots, botanicals, and natural objects to work spells.

So, to continue our narrative, Sandy took Frederick back to his cabin, he bathed him, he gave him some food, and he said that the teen would have to return to Covey's farm; there was no real choice—if he escaped and got caught he would be killed. However, Sandy also provided Frederick with what the writer called a "magic root"—a hard, spherical root—to keep in his pocket on his righthand side. Sandy told him that as long as you carry this root, you will be protected, you will be *okay*.

Now, from the description, I have almost no doubt that the root that Douglass described is one native to the American South, called *jalap root*. It dries into a hard, spherical nub, and it is a *venerated* magickal item within hoodoo. Within the parlance of hoodoo, it's generally called John the Conqueror or High John. John the Conqueror is used to bestow virility, strength, and power. A principle of "like-attracts-like" appears in most occult practice. And jalap root, John the Conqueror, dries into a hard, tough, spherical nub, which actually resembles a male testicle; that's what it actually looks like. And, again, in the practice of like-attracts-like, natural objects are thought to bestow, or *enhance*, those faculties that they resemble or represent or to which they are symbolically related. So Sandy told Frederick, you must carry this with you and Covey will not be able to hurt you. Frederick was skeptical but he gratefully accepted what he called the "magic root"— John the Conqueror—and he went walking back to Covey's farm.

The following day, when Covey encountered Frederick on the farm, surreptitiously carrying his "magic root," Frederick was absolutely shocked to discover that Covey was downright polite to him; the teen couldn't believe it. And he thought, maybe there *is* something in what Sandy had given him. But he soon realized it was *Sunday*, and Covey was a Sunday Christian; he would pull back during the Lord's day of rest, but, when nightfall came, the old Covey returned. The next day, Monday morning, Covey grabbed Frederick by the neck, dragged him into the barn, and he took out a whip with which he was going to give him a horrible beating. But this time, as Frederick wrote, something happened. Something rose up within him, and instead of submitting to Covey's beating, he fought back. The two men—the 15 year-old Frederick and Covey, the so-called "breaker of slaves"—struggled together for about two hours; and Covey, he wrote, could not get the better of him. Eventually, after two hours, just exhausted, Covey gave up. Covey relented.

Frederick wondered at this, because, even though the man couldn't get the better of him, he was surprised that Covey pulled back. He thought maybe Covey felt some sort of personal embarrassment; because, again, he was supposed to be this fearsome breaker of slaves, and maybe Covey didn't want it to get known locally that he was incapable of getting the better of this 15-year-old. So they never spoke of it again. And Frederick thought about his *magic root*; and he wrote that while he wasn't given to folklore, maybe there *was* something to this magic that had been bestowed upon him by a trusted "adviser," Sandy Jenkins.

And something more occurred, too. Frederick described this moment of fighting back against Covey as *the inner revolution of his life*. He wrote about this episode in all three of his memoirs; it's the core episode of each book. Douglass said that he realized for the first time that he could never, ever be subjugated again; that there was a force within him that *would be free*. He might not *yet* be free as a physical fact, but he had become free internally. And he vowed that he would seize the first possible moment to become free physically—he would watch for it every hour of his life and however long he remained in bondage he would never again be made to feel like a slave *in fact*. Within him, he wrote, there arose this indelible sense of selfhood, of independence; he was capable of standing fully erect.

In the years following—it took more than four years—he eventually fulfilled and acted on his vow to be physically free at the first possible moment. He made two escape attempts, and the second succeeded and Frederick fled to New York. But precedent to his physical freedom, was his internal freedom—it was *the revolution of his life*. And he said, in all three memoirs, that he had to wonder if maybe some of Sandy's belief system had rubbed off on him, as well. He always spoke of Sandy with deep veneration.

Now, I must be clear: Frederick Douglass did not identify himself as a follower of hoodoo or any magickal system. Douglass believed in self-education in the deepest sense. Douglass was concerned—and he wrote about this too—that upon any misfortune some of his fellow slaves would immediately jump to the conclusion that they had been hoodooed or cursed, or that somebody had cast some magick against them. Douglass inveighed against this form of what he considered superstition; he felt it kept people in a kind of mindset of dependency. So it isn't as though Frederick was some closeted believer in magick. He was not. But, again, he did write about the episode three times over the course of his memoirs, and he always cracked open the door just enough— just enough—to say, well, perhaps Sandy knew a thing or two.

I share this story with you, not only because it sheds light on the life of a critically important moral voice in American history, but also because it demonstrates an important principle: which is that esoteric search—occult practice, radically ecumenical spirituality, the individual search for meaning—almost always infuses the individual with a sense of his or her own selfhood, with a sense that the ethical and internal search is a *birthright* that belongs to every individual; that the search cannot be controlled, conditioned, or taken. The search, like a question, is indestructible. And, usually, when people come into some sense of a personal, individualized spiritual search or an awakening episode, it results in changes in their outer life, as well; it results sometimes in a greater degree of self-assertion or even in the kind of personal revolution that Frederick described. There has always been, particularly in American life, an intimate connection between religious radicalism and social or political radicalism. In a certain sense, you cannot open one door without opening the other, because the search invests the individual with a sense of his or her innate right to self-development. The episode that transpired between Sandy and Frederick helped instigate that revolution within Frederick; I think he would be the first to make that point.

A similar social-spiritual revolution emerged roughly contemporaneously with the rise of the movement called Spiritualism, which involved séances or the talking to the dead, and the suffragist movement. Both emerged around the same time in the mid-19th century and in the same locale of central New York State. I write about this extensively in my book, *Occult America*. In the first half of the nineteenth-century, a section of central New York State served as the spring-board for a great deal of religious and political innovation in America and the world. It was often called the Burned-over District. This area was a snaking piece of land that ran east to west across the state, from Albany in the east to Buffalo in the west. It began as a carriage trail—today it is U.S. Route 20—used by New Englanders who flooded into central New York after the War of Independence.

Whenever there are migratory flows to a new area, very often people leave behind family ties, congregations, and church memberships that they belonged to back home, and they become ripe constituents for new ideas, both social and religious. And so the Burned-over District, because it was a kind of great artery through which New Englanders ventured west across the nation, became, as one historian termed it, a "psychic highway," through which new religious ideas flowed. These relatively liberal New Englanders poured into central New York State, sometimes to set-tle, sometimes to use it as a channel to fan out into other portions of the country, and they left behind the traditions of New England, which they might have grown up with, and hence they were open to new ideas. The area was called "burned over" because it was said to be ignited by the fires of the spirit, and it was a place where everyone belonged to some sort of new religious movement, evangelical upcropping, or metaphysical church.

Spiritualism was among the new ideas that sprung up in this area—or, put differently, an old idea given new life. It began just outside of the city of Rochester, New York, in the winter of 1848. Two young girls, Kate and Margaret Fox, grew up in a Methodist household in the village of Hydesville. Bangs and raps were heard through the Fox cabin, and the adolescents told their shocked parents that they had worked out a system of communication with the spirits: those knocks and bangs and raps were a code with the unseen world. A variety of journalists, clergy, and scientists descended upon the Fox cabin, and many concluded that these two young adolescent girls, Kate and Margaret, seemed to have actually worked out this system of bangs and raps that could allow them to communicate with the beyond. The two girls became enormously popular, and thus was born the modern movement of Spiritualism. All across the country Americans, with surprising rapidity, began to assemble themselves into séance circles and clubs. Thousands of Americans grew enthralled with the idea of contacting the dead.

Why did Kate and Margaret become popular so quickly? Why were their claims so widely embraced?

I think it's because they were speaking to a very deep need, which is actually one of the best ideals in American life: a zeal to *do it yourself*, to cut out the middleman, even in matters of metaphysics. Many Americans believed that they required no clergyman or man in the robes to serve as a gatekeeper to the unknown; if these two kids living in upstate New York can do it, then it stands to reason that I can do it too, or so went the attitude of many believers. Spiritualism as a social movement appealed to people's instincts of self-assertion. And, of course, in an era before modern medicine, Americans staggered under childhood diseases, early deaths, farming accidents, and so on; death was a palpable presence everywhere and people had very little capacity to deal with it. There was no such thing as grief counseling. Calvinist Protestantism provided no kind of therapeutic compensation. Spiritualism gave that to people in a certain way; believers were soothed, were made to feel like they could go on in life if they could reach the spirit of a departed loved one.

And, again, seekers were roused by this idea that if these two adolescent kids from a cabin are capable of communicating with the spirit world, then maybe the ability to prophesize or to reach the ineffable doesn't just belong to some lost biblical age, but that signs and wonders are available to us today, here in the New Jerusalem of America, as some people referred to the nation. Many people wanted to feel that no one held the turnkey to their search, to their abilities, to their capacity to pierce the veil to the beyond—they felt that they required no bells and incense and approbation, but that the great mysteries were as close as the kitchen table.

A unique and important social opening arose from Spiritualism—and in a manner that few historians have recognized. *Spiritualism was vital to the development of the suffragist movement,* or the movement for women's voting rights, and for this reason: in the decades that immediately followed the experience of the Fox sisters, as Americans assembled into séance clubs and circles, it happened that *most spirit mediums were women*; and as mediums they were looked to as authorities, as guides. Spiritualism opened the door for the first time in American life for women to become recognized as religious leaders, at least of a certain sort. Women who wanted a voice in the civic culture and religion entered Spiritualism because that's where they could function as authorities. In 1848, the same year of the Rochester rappings, there occurred the historic Seneca Falls conference for women's rights, roughly in the same neighborhood. The Seneca Falls conference occurred 40 or 45 miles east down Route 20, the "psychic highway." For about one generation in American life, you could not find a women's rights activist who had not spent some time at the séance table and vice versa; the two movements were dramatically intertwined.

Spiritualism had opened a door that could never again be closed. And it provided a forum for more than table rappings. Many of the Spiritualist clubs had their own newspapers and meeting spaces. They were often ardently progressive. Spiritualist newspapers opposed capital punishment and supported universal suffrage and abolitionism. In a sense, the "spirits" themselves were progressive. Mediums often depicted heaven as a place that contained all the world's people—Blacks, Jews, Catholics, vanquished Indian tribes, people from all different nations and races. This cut against the orthodoxy that only congregants of a recognized church could be saved. Spiritualism was innately *progressive*.

I could do a twelve-chapter series on this point alone, because there are many extraordinary figures who found prominence through America's alternative metaphysical culture. One is Mother Ann Lee (1736–1784), the founder of the Shakers, and an early American religious leader who established the first Shaker village in the Burned-over District outside of Albany in the village of Niskayuna. Today it's called Watervliet, but the earlier Native American term Niskayuna was used when the Shakers ventured there in 1776. You can visit Mother Ann's grave there today. She played a major role not only as an early female religious leader but as someone whose villages marked the most visible manifestation of communal spiritual life in the new nation.

Or Jemima Wilkinson (1752–1819), a spirit medium from Rhode Island, who called herself the Publick Universal Friend. Wilkinson spoke throughout New England and then migrated into central New York. During the War of Independence, she was one of a very few figures who could cross battle lines and speak to both colonial and British troops. Followers of the Public Universal Friend, who migrated into central New York in the years immediately following the War of Independence, actually did a great deal to settle central New York. They founded a town called Jerusalem, which is still there today. And the mansion they built for their avatar is still there, as well. These people helped crack open the door not only to an independent spiritual search in America—something occurring before the framing of the Constitution—but they brought about actual social progress: they provided voices for people who had been excluded from the religious and civic sphere.

The indestructible wish to peer into the beyond, and to do so on one's own terms, had myriad social consequences. Hence, it is important for me to describe these and other episodes as a key aspect of America's unseen religious history. All of these people at once highlight some of the great social failings of the nation even as the presence of religious freedom, I would say a dramatic amount of religious freedom compared to the old world, allowed them, amid national fractures and hypocrisies, to demonstrate *how the advent of inde-*

pendent or esoteric spirituality brings with it ultimate consequences of personal freedom and social opening. Some people think the occult is characterized by sinister secrets and nefarious hidden hands—the stereotypical circle of people in dark robes passing among them a skull and drinking from it God knows what. Whereas, the *actuality* of occult spirituality in American life is that is often went hand-in-hand with radical assertion of selfhood.

We as a culture have not fully understood the extent to which spiritual and social experiment go hand-in-hand—*that* is the truer story of the occult in America than any kind of fantasies about shadowy orders and secret societies. That's real history, and it's more fantastic than anything fantasy ventures. I want kids—and adults—to learn this history, because it is a mirror; it tells us who we really are. I began this book by talking about the imperative to *know thyself.* How can I know myself if I don't know the foundations beneath my feet? That's why I love occult history, because it gets at what's beneath the floorboards.

In the previous chapter, I alluded to the social changes fomented by Freemasonry. Masonry played a vital role in the best developments that played out in American life. Again, Freemasonry, as I noted earlier, is sometimes depicted as a concealed hand—a secret society that does not wish us well—yet in the American experience nothing could be further from the

truth. The fact is, Freemasonry, as a thought movement, made a huge consequential journey across the
Atlantic from the European continent to the American colonies, where it commanded the allegiance of
some of America's most critical founders, including
George Washington, Benjamin Franklin, Paul Revere,
and John Hancock. An outsized number of Washington's generals were Freemasons. An outsized number
of the signers of the Declaration of Independence and
the framers of the Constitution were Freemasons.

Freemasonry extolled the principle of *radical ecumenism*; it believed in the protection of the individual
spiritual search. Masonry believed that the spiritual search could not be bound by any one doctrine,
dogma, or congregation, and certainly not by government interference or stricture. Freemasonry was one
of the first organizations in modern life to consistently
profess that perspective. And Freemasonry as a fraternal order existed in America for decades prior to
the Declaration of Independence and for decades
prior to the Constitution; hence, it helped *inform* some
of the attitudes of religious liberty that resulted in
the creation of those governing documents. Masonry
certainly wasn't the only influence; there were lots of
influences, including the work of Enlightenment-age
scholars like John Locke. Thomas Jefferson, whose
writings prefigured the First Amendment, was not a
Freemason and he had no interest in esoteric spirituality; but he had an interest in radical individual-

ity, albeit incompletely. The same was true of Thomas Paine. So, Masonry was one among many influences; but it was an important channel, and it certainly touched the lives of Washington and Franklin.

It is difficult for us today to understand just how rural a place America was in its colonial and immediately post-colonial years. Philadelphia had little more than 500 houses by 1700. It was an agriculturally based society; there really wasn't much civic culture beyond farm and church. There were a few public houses and places for practicing commerce; but church, farm, and family life were pretty much what most people functioned within. Hence, if you were to enter into sworn allegiance with a fraternal order like Freemasonry that in itself represented a huge commitment. That kind of allegiance opened up a whole other artery of existence, a whole other venue for exchanging ideas. That kind of commitment, in an ardently agrarian and culturally limited society, placed a profound impact and influence on one's life and thought.

Recent to this writing, I published a new introduction to *The Temple and the Lodge* by Michael Baigent and Richard Leigh. The authors creditably explore Freemasonic influences on America's framers and revolutionists, noting: "Most colonists did not actually read Locke, Hume, Voltaire, Diderot, Rousseau, any more than most British soldiers did." But a significant number of thought leaders took vows to Freemasonry. Freemasonic ideals, which included religious inclusivism, separation of church and state, and belief in the sanctity of the individual, forged a bond and shared outlook. Baigent and Leigh—in what I consider a stretch—even suggest that Masonic sympathies blunted British commanders' fighting resolve against the colonists.

Masonry had a liberatory impact on America in other ways. There exists today an African-American Masonic tradition called Prince Hall Masonry, and its history is important to understand. Now, it was once believed that Prince Hall Masonry emerged in the American colonies in 1775. That date often appears because it was cited in the archives of the Massachusetts Historical Society a few years later, so it was always considered a valid reference; but the date is wrong. Two outstanding historians, John L. Hairston and E. Oscar Alleyne, have recently and definitively established its founding year as 1778. Details and primary documents appear in their monograph, *Landmarks of Our Fathers: A Critical Analysis of the Start and Origin of African Lodge No. 1*. And this is important in the unfoldment of a certain aspect of American history.

Prince Hall Masonry was and remains an African-American-based Masonic order founded by Prince Hall, a free Black man and leather worker who lived in Boston. Along with about 30 African-American colleagues, Prince Hall aimed to form a Masonic Lodge;

without getting into the granular details here, the men received a grant to form a kind of Masonic Lodge, which they named African Lodge No. 1. The first Grand Master of African Lodge No. 1 was Prince Hall, so the movement later came to take on his name.

Prince Hall's signature appears on two of the earliest petitions against slavery circulated in the American colonies. The first was in 1777. The second was in 1778, the year of the founding of African Lodge No.1. I want to note this very carefully, so that it's not misunderstood: Prince Hall Masonry actually reflected the first Black-led abolitionist movement in American life. And it was Freemasonic in nature. I am not saying that abolitionism grew out of Freemasonry; abolitionism had many different contributing factors, and Freemasonry did *not* always play a noble role in these struggles. Freemasonry, as with any human organization, is characterized by the local mores, practices, and prejudices of its members and communities. So, naturally speaking, there were Freemasonic lodges that stood on the wrong side of liberatory history. But the *ideals* of Freemasonry *were on the right side;* and African Lodge No. 1 ought to be properly recognized as the first Black-led abolitionist movement in American history. That's the history that you won't hear about from the conspiracists, who have all kinds of closed-circuit notions and references about Masonry. Or they defer to this imaginary idea that there's somehow a secret order *within* Masonry, concealed by the overt charitable work, civics, and Shriners Children's Hospitals, which are a magnificent philanthropy, by the way. There exists evidence of no such thing as an inner, dark Masonry.

In short, I view Masonry as an organization that we should be very proud of in American life; it has helped us to bear out some of our most important ideals and it has affirmed some of our deepest ideals. Masonic philosophy also contributed to the beautiful eye-and-pyramid on the back of our dollar bill; that symbol is not a leaf directly from Freemasonry, but I believe it was inspired by Freemasonic values.

On July 4th, 1776, the Continental Congress formed a subcommittee to design a seal for the new American republic. This subcommittee was chaired by Benjamin Franklin, himself a Freemason. In 1781, the committee introduced and Congress ratified its proposed Great Seal. On the front of the seal appears the familiar image of the American eagle, with olive branches and arrows clutched in its claws. And on the reverse appears this mysterious eye-and-pyramid—a pyramid capped by a floating eye of providence, indicating that our earthly works and material progress (the pyramid) are incomplete without higher understanding (the providential eye). The pyramid is surrounded by the Latin slogan, *Annuit cœptis novus ordo seclorum*: "God Smiles on Our New Order of the Ages." I have it tattooed on my left arm. That's one of the sources for the term "new order," which we considered in the previous chapter. The founders saw this term as heralding the nation's connection to a chain of great civilizations, extending back to Egypt, Persia, Greece, Rome, whose architecture marked the new republic. All of these nations and their temple orders honored the esoteric search, the inner search. The most idealistic founders saw the new nation as a place that would protect the individual search for meaning. The "new order of the ages" was meant to associate America with the *rebirth* of civilizations that enshrined the search, that preceded us in ancient history, and that recognized the polity between the individual and the cosmos: "as above, so below."

Masonic principles played an important part in the establishment and creation of this symbol and slogan—which, by the way, did not actually appear on the back of our dollar bill until 1935. It was put there by two Freemasons: President Franklin Roosevelt and his Secretary of Agriculture, who later became his second Vice President, Henry Wallace. Wallace, a Freemason and Theosophist, was a true explorer into esoterica and the occult. He first raised the idea of placing the eye-and-pyramid on some kind of coin or commemorative currency. Wallace felt that reestablishing a connection to the Great Seal—which at that time was used largely for official business and was unfamiliar to most Americans—would help revive the spirits of the nation. Roosevelt was so taken with his idea that he decided they wouldn't just conscript the Great Seal to a ceremonial coin but rather would place it on the back of the dollar bill itself.

Roosevelt personally—and in his own handwriting on an early design—supervised the placement of the eye-and-pyramid on the back of the dollar bill: and he placed the pyramid in a position of primacy. In the Western world, we read from left to right; left comes "first" as your eye travels across the page. Roosevelt moved the more conventional American eagle from a position of dominance and, in his own handwriting, the records of which exist in the US Treasury Department, reversed the order of the symbols so that the eye-and-pyramid occupied the place of primacy on the left.

*Annuit cœpti*s *novus ordo seclorum*: God smiles on our new order of the ages. It's a beautiful principle that shines as a beacon for what Freemasonry introduced and sought to affirm in our national life. Manly P. Hall writes about the idealistic dimensions of the American founding, the best of our ideals. There's so much more to explore on the topic. I suggest that you also read Manly's anthology, *The Secret History of America*, where he writes about these topics in greater detail, and I further explore this dimension of his historicism in my introduction. In that book I also explore Manly's influence on different American figures, most notably President Ronald Reagan, who actually met with Manly P. Hall and quoted him in his speeches, albeit without direct credit. I write about some of these episodes in my *Occult America* and *One Simple Idea*, which is a history and analysis of the positive-mind movement.

The Secret Teachings of All Ages posits the presence of "secret society" members at crucial moments of American history, a topic I consider in chapter one of the *Seeker's Guide*. I encourage you to delve into that material in Manly's work, because it's important that we, in the opening decades of the twenty-first century, *recapture* this beautiful esoteric aspect of our history—and not allow it to be sensationalized, nor cede it to people who think about these things from the perspective of paranoia. Manly suggests that there is a bridge—a real and discernable bridge—from the ideals of esotericism to the activities and the structures of our day-to-day lives. Let's find that bridge and walk over it together.

LESSON IX

_____ ୨ ୧ _____

Mysterious Beasts and Natural Wonders

Manly P. Hall actually dedicates a great deal of time and illustrations in *The Secret Teachings of All Ages* to allegories, myths, and legends of strange and mysterious beasts and natural wonders. It's a topic of perennial fascination in our own time; everybody is fascinated with Bigfoot, among other mythical creatures. Are they real? What do they represent about the recesses of our psyches? What role does mystery play in our world? And what allegorical role have mysterious beasts played within the annals of esoteric and mystical philosophy?

Well, let's get right down to it. Is Bigfoot real? Very possibly. I have a friend who is an executive within digital commerce—a very rationalist, even materialist person—and he has crunched the numbers for me and demonstrated that many millions upon millions of square miles around the earth—just on the surface itself—are unexplored. He adjoins that fact to various testimonies of a Bigfoot or yeti-like creature over the past century or so, and determines with what he considers statistical accuracy the overwhelming likelihood that Bigfoot or yeti, or some kind of undiscovered simian creature is real. I will leave that to the investigators; I take it seriously, of course, but it's not my particular field of study. I do feel, however, that the human wish to discover mystery in a world that can seem overly mapped out by satellite imagery is a perennial and insuppressible wish. I think at each epoch of progress in the world, whether it's the Industrial Revolution, the digital revolution, or revolutions in travel or communication, there has always appeared a reassertion of reports, testimonies, and claims of strange beasts and phenomena.

The legendary paranormal researcher Charles Fort (1874–1932) began his career, like Manly P. Hall, within the reading room of the New York Public Library. In 1919, Fort wrote his first book, *The Book of the Damned*, in which he endeavored to catalogue diffuse reports of strange anomalies from newspapers around the world: floating airships with no visible means of projection, frogs falling from the sky, spontaneous combustion, strange lights—all kinds of weird reports that Fort believed poked holes in the straight story of science and materialism, which was in the ascendancy at that time. It wasn't that Fort was anti-science or anti-materialism—he was anti-*orthodoxy*. Fort believed that as soon as we get into settled notions about the world and its events, we begin to create a dogma that closes us off to questions and channels us into a kind of intellectual tunnel vision, whereby we cannot allow for the possibility of anything that goes outside of the straight story. Fort, in a kind of proto-type for the critically minded paranormal investi-gator, was attempting, above all, to poke holes in the straight story, to demonstrate how materialism didn't seem to cover *all* the bases of life, at least if one took account of the persistent reports and testimonies of anomalous phenomena from around the world.

Some people considered Fort a genius. Novelist Theodore Dreiser was a great admirer of Fort. He said, "To me no one in the world has suggested the underly-ing depths and mysteries and possibilities as has Fort. To me he is simply stupendous." Whereas H.G. Wells called Fort "one of the most damnable bores who ever cut scraps from out-of-the-way newspapers." Person-ally, I have a particular love for Fort, and for those peo-ple who thoughtfully explore anomalous phenomena, because what they are doing, at their best, is poking holes in orthodoxy; they're raising questions where questions really aren't supposed to be raised. And let's face it: anomalous discoveries demonstrably occur. Sometimes we discover the persistence of species that were supposed to be extinct. There are certainly lifeforms on this planet—and very probably on other planets, as well—that we haven't yet codified or characterized within our catalogue of scientifically verified categories or species, including in the ocean depths. Very recent to this writing, Chinese archaeologists revealed that they had found fossils pointing to the existence of a previously unknown form of dinosaur that had webbed wings; they provided an animation video of what this dinosaur might have looked like, which was run on the website of the *New York Times*. And I thought, well, there's proof of dragons, of a sort. I'm joking, mostly, but we're making discoveries all the time that are strange and wholly off center.

These things are not confined to earth. In our own time, for example, we have found evidence for the existence of microbial life and liquid water on Mars. When I was growing up, if you spoke of "life on Mars" it was considered science fiction. But in our generation, we have found the distinct possibility of one-time microbial life on Mars in the form of fossils. So talk about poking holes in the straight story—I think that was the best instinct from which investigators like Charles Fort were operating.

Manly Hall was unwilling to write off possibilities of anomalous beasts or strange creatures. And, of course, many such accounts historically were symbolical, allegorical, and mythical. But, still, Manly would write with some ingenuousness, for example, about the existence of gnomes—or what he called "conventional gnomes"—or what also might be called fairies, leprechauns, or little people. And such stories span the globe. You find stories of little people from every continent and nation: in West Africa, Ireland, Appalachia, Polynesia, Central America, and so on. Every culture, separated by vast distances of geography and language, has its own tradition of stories—some of them quite ancient—about mysterious little beings.

In Central America, particularly in the nation of Belize, which is an English-speaking country on the Caribbean coast, many people talk of the existence of little men or *aluxes*, who are said to live up in the highlands. I've visited Belize twice and several years ago a taxi driver was taking my friend and I up to a jungle lodge, a kind of an eco-lodge, way up in the hills. And he told us, "As soon as I drop you off, I'm gonna just tear out of this place." He said he was frightened to be there. And I asked, "Why? What are you talking about?" And he said, "Well, there are these little men who live up in these hills. And when you see one of them, you'll get so scared that your voice will get caught in your throat. You won't even be able to talk; it's just so scary." And I really didn't like this, because I thought he was just trying to play scare-the-tourists. Like he said, when he dropped us off he sped away.

So, we checked into the lodge, and the next day we were canoeing down the river. The river was dead silent. I don't even recall hearing birds. I started saying how I didn't like that cab driver trying to scare us; I felt that the guy was just sort of teasing us and I didn't appreciate it. As I was talking and rowing, suddenly, out of nowhere, at a moment of complete silence, a boulder came rolling down a hill and splashed in the water in front of our canoe. And I thought, well, maybe I should hold my tongue. One of the legends is that if you talk about the little men they appear.

Legends and stories continue to abound in Ireland of the existence of leprechauns. And these things are taken very seriously. In 1999, Irish authorities rerouted a major highway under construction in County Clare to avoid running past what was known as a fairy bush, which is the domain, so it is said, of these little beings. The fear was that if you run a highway through a fairy bush you will incur their wrath, and they will cause accidents. A folklorist and historian named Eddie Lenihan, with whom I've worked, helped prompt the change. Eddie and others sometimes refer to leprechauns as "the other crowd." They don't like to actually say their name, because these are figures of mischief; and people fear that if you speak their name you're inviting them in.

So even modern highways are sometimes affected by our belief in "the other crowd." Some scoff at this, but I personally like the presence of mystery in our world. I don't *want* to live in a world without mystery. I don't want to live in a world where there aren't questions about what exists in the shadows or what snaps a twig in the night. *Sometimes* these questions and legends may point us in the direction of unacknowledged truths. Other times they point us to allegorical truths.

Esoteric history and occult history teem with stories of mysterious beasts who deliver prophecies or some propitiously timed message. The ancient Egyptians, as I noted earlier, venerated water birds. They gave Thoth, their great god of writing and intellect, the head of an ibis, a water bird. The ibis was said to be capable of existing within all elements—water, earth, sky—and it could traverse the earthly realm and go to the heavens, so to speak, and receive messages and bring them back down to us.

Vedic culture, too, bestows beastly traits upon some of its deities. The elephant-headed god Ganesha, whom I've honored as the patron of this book, is considered one who lowers barriers—an elephant being an enormously powerful, formidable animal. The monkey-headed god Hanuman is also a remover of obstacles, a dexterous being whose beauty is on the inside.

One of my personal favorite mythic beasts is the beautiful waving cat from Japanese and Buddhist folklore. You'll find this symbol of good luck in the windows of shops in New York City, Los Angeles, and elsewhere. The legend goes that once a Buddhist monk was standing on a hillside and he saw a cat, which began to wave at him. Seeing the cat wave at him, he walked towards the strange animal—and in so doing walked out of the way of a falling boulder, which would have crushed him. Thereafter, the waving cat became a symbol of good luck.

We also have the Great Sphinx, a being with the crouching body of a beast or lion, head of a man, and sometimes the breasts of a woman. One of the messages of the Sphinx, among many others, is that divine beings are capable of combining the traits of different lifeforms, human and otherwise, and that people, like gods, can embody strengths and powers from multiple animal forms.

The zodiac sign of Sagittarius, for example, is the centaur with the torso and the head of a man, with the presumed intellect that accompanies it, but also the physical and the emotional strength of a horse. It's a fiery beast animated by a powerful emotional and artistic spirit, which is why the centaur or Sagittarius is seen as the sign of philosophers. Its emotions are powerful but can also run wild, both a strength and weakness.

In many cultures, from Indio-South American to European, the serpent or snake is regarded as a symbol of great wisdom. The ancient Greeks venerated the snake as a dispenser of wisdom: the wand or caduceus held by the god of intellect, Mercury, is entwined by snakes; sometimes the wand is also depicted with ribbons flowing from it, but a more traditional depiction shows snakes as givers of wisdom and insight.

The snake narrative appears, as well, in Western Scripture, in Genesis 3, which I believe has been misread and misunderstood within our culture. I want to take a moment to look at this most consequential of narrative of a mythical beast, the serpent or snake, and the gifts and insights it dispenses.

To begin with, I do not believe that any one exclusive meaning can be derived from Scripture. The books of the Old and New Testaments were written across hundreds and hundreds of years by the varying hands of different men and women. Not every book considered contemporaneous with Scripture made it into Scripture. There are, of course, Gnostic Gospels and so-called Apocrypha, that are not represented or recognized within every Scriptural tradition. For example, the Catholic Church recognizes the four Books of Maccabees, whereas those passages are not canonized within Hebraic Scripture, even as the story of the Maccabees themselves underscores the holiday of Hanukkah. And there are lots of Gnostic and Apocryphal Gospels, including moving and important books, that did not make the cut of canonization, which, too, was the work of man.

Myths contain psychological truths and insights into human nature, and the most enduring, I believe, also hold great metaphysical truths. What is Scripture but a vast compilation of myths? I use that term, of course, in its highest iteration; I do not use myth as something that's synonymous with falsehood or mere legend. Rather, a myth is an urtext; it's a parabolic story of the human situation. In that sense, one could say that myth is truer than history because myth captures human nature, as well as metaphysical truth, in many cases. Now, Eve's encounter with the serpent in Genesis 3 is, next to the act of creation itself, perhaps the most important myth within Scripture. And I wonder if we've read it correctly.

Very often the serpent or snake in Genesis 3 is seen as some deceptive or trickster figure; across centuries the snake of Genesis came to be associated with Satan or the Luciferic. And the serpent, so we're told, deceives Eve into eating an apple from the Tree of Knowledge of Good and Evil, which she's also been told is the one tree in the Garden from which neither she nor Adam may eat. As a result of Eve's disobedience, the first couple is expunged from the Garden, sent away East of Eden. They clothe themselves and Adam is conscripted to earn his living by the sweat of his brow, while Eve is conscripted to suffer pain in childbirth. And their two first sons, Cain and Abel, get into an act of fratricidal violence, with Cain slaying Abel. And so goes the story of the supposed fall of the human race, instigated by the serpent, which Western culture conventionally associates with the Satanic.

But I think we've made a misreading of Genesis 3. I think there's a more esoteric reading of Genesis 3, and a more affirming one. Adam and Eve, we're told, were children in Paradise. All their needs were accounted for; they didn't have to work, they didn't have any decisions to make, they didn't have any rules to follow—except for one. The Maker who put them in this supposed garden of paradise raised within the Garden a forbidden tree, a Tree of the Knowledge of Good and Evil. Reference is also made in Genesis to a Tree of Life, and some biblical scholars have argued that the Tree of Life and the Tree of Knowledge of Good and Evil are the same tree in the midst of paradise—a forbidden tree from which they are told not to eat.

It's worth asking the question: What kind of paradise is it when you're placed into a garden where the one tree from which you are forbidden to eat is the very tree that would open discernment to you? The very tree that would give you the capacity to measure, to decide, to create, to reason, to select, and to distinguish between good and evil; in other words, grant you the capacity to become truly human? What kind of paradise is it when everything is done *for* you? When you function as a kind of pet who is kept rather than a being who is capable of distinguishing between good and evil? We're taught, *as above, so below*, but how can that principle be true for the individual if he or she is barred from eating from the Tree of Knowledge of Good and Evil?

And does the snake really *deceive* Eve? The snake informs Eve, disturbs Eve, and the snake challenges Eve with the question: Why *don't* you eat from the Tree of Knowledge of Good and Evil? She replies, we've been told that if we eat from that tree, we will die. And the snake responds, you will surely not die. As it happens, the snake *is* telling Eve the truth. Eve does pluck an apple from the Tree of Knowledge of Good and Evil— or perhaps the Tree of Life—and eats it and does not die. Not only does she not die, but she is *illumined*; she is given knowledge of good and evil, she is given the capacity to measure, to really exist as a human being. She brings the apple to Adam, and he requires very little coaxing to eat it himself. Colloquially and historically, Eve is often depicted as the seductress, the woman who is the agent of humanity's fall. But in the text itself, Adam requires little convincing and Eve actually serves as the catalyst who opens humanity's eyes. If Adam is mythically seen as the first man, it is Eve who can be seen as the first *person*.

Now, the result of this disobedience is also that the Creator pushes them out of the Garden and punishes them: they must work and labor for their food. And their two first offspring, Cain and Abel, are the victims of fratricidal violence, in which Cain slays his pious brother. But again, consider: isn't friction the inevitable cost of human creativity? If we were kept like pet poodles in a garden somewhere, of course there would be no friction. There would be no sweat involved, there would be no pain involved in bringing forth the fruits of the earth and in propagating the species. There would be no dispute. There would also be no growth. Would we be able to fulfill the principle, *as above, so below*? That principle couldn't hold true if we were living in paradise, where the only forbidden fruit was the one that brought intellectual and creative illumination. Friction is necessary for humanness.

It seems to me that the snake in the garden was a great usurper, a great rebel, a great instigator. He overturned the prevailing order of things. He was, in that sense, a dispenser of wisdom. He was a psychopomp, he was a guide; he directed humanity toward the knowledge of good and evil, toward *actual* life, rather than merely kept existence.

As I mentioned, the ancients considered snakes as dispensers of wisdom, as keepers of great secrets, and as guardians of the esoteric. It was only later that we came to see snakes as objects of fear and derision. It was only later that snakes were associated with maleficence. I think that in our era we can appreciate the snake anew as an instigator of understanding, revolution, nonconformity—and *constructive* disobedience. The great Cleopatra used to wear the bracelet of a snake. Initiates of various mystery religions and traditions in the Hellenic, Egyptian, and Persian worlds would wear rings or other emblems with the symbol of a snake. The ouroboros, the snake consuming its tail, is a symbol of infinity, renewal, and eternal recurrence. The snake was and remains a central figure in the esoteric bestiary. Perhaps it's time to take new measure of it.

The symbols and the mysteries of the natural world have always figured into the traits and the understandings that we wish to foster within ourselves. The sala-mander is another beautiful figure, which in esoteric tradition is said to be a beast capable of surviving fire. If you are interested in Tarot cards, the subject of our twelfth and final lesson, you're probably aware that the cards illustrated by artist Pamela Colman Smith (1878–1951) in the early twentieth century include a salamander in some of the images. Some querents look at Smith's cards and wonder: what is that intrigu-ing little beast doing there? Smith is employing the sal-amander in its mythical sense as a beast that changes color, proves uniquely adaptable, and can survive circumstances that would take the life of another. The salamander, though small, is extremely fast and adaptable. In Tarot, the salamander is a mark of resil-iency.

Many different beasts have figured into our imag-inations as bringers of good luck. I previously men-tioned the waving cat. For many years in America—and this still goes on in some areas—people would carry a "lucky rabbit's foot" as a talisman of luck. Franklin Roosevelt himself carried a lucky rabbit's foot during his first campaign for president. That rabbit's foot is now located in the Franklin Roosevelt Archives and Library in the Hudson River Valley in New York State. Rabbits were seen by the Greeks as a sign of good luck and fertility, because rabbits prodigiously procreate. But the lucky rabbit's foot entered modern life along a different path. Actors and actresses have always been known for being superstitious, probably with good reason. At one time in the U.S., before the advent of the modern accouterments found in makeup bags and toiletries, actors would carry a rabbit's foot rather than a powder puff in their makeup cases and use it to apply facial powder. And as time passed, commercial powder puffs replaced rabbit's feet, and they transformed from something carried for the purpose of utility to being carried instead for luck.

The cat has always played a special role in allegorical and religious history. Cats, of course, were venerated by the Ancient Egyptians. There were two major cat gods: Bastet and Sekhmet. Now, Sekhmet, whom I mentioned earlier, is an extraordinary Egyptian deity who is a little bit like the Sphinx in reverse; Sekhmet possesses the body of a woman and the head of a cat. Sekhmet is the goddess of boldness and instigation. Sekhmet helps you defy odds and get things done in the world. When I was in Egypt and was permitted to enter an off-limits temple of Sekhmet at Karnak, it was an otherworldly experience. We went inside of this pitch-black temple chamber and—not fully discernible because of the darkness—there was this magnificent, enormously heavy, carved statue of Sekhmet in the center of the chamber. We performed a ritual in honor of Sekhmet, asked for her assistance, and it was probably the highlight of the entire trip for me. I just felt this influx of energy within my whole body, within my being, and I was permitted to touch the statue and to kiss the statue; it was a very, very rare opportunity to actually be able to lay hands on a monument of such deep antiquity. And it was a hugely moving experience. We exited the temple in a state of deep silence. I later learned, when I returned back home, that there have been a number of visitors from the West who had that very experience at that same temple, some of whom have written books about it.

In his private office, Manly P. Hall, as I mentioned earlier, used to have a beautiful, small, hand-carved Egyptian statue of a cat, which he left on his personal altar. In 2005, I was told by Obadiah Harris (1930–2019), who was then the president of the Philosophical Research Society, that each time Manly prepared to exit his office to enter the campus auditorium to speak, he performed the symbolic act of rubbing of the head of the cat, because a cat, as a being that sees in the dark, can give you the powers of illumination. Now, I always enjoyed that story, and I wanted to repeat the act myself, but the cat statuette has gone missing. But I do remember its placement on Manly's altar, I do remember Obadiah personally showing it to me, and I was touched by the story.

Cats are also said to be the familiars of witches, the roots of which probably date to the witch crazes in Middle Ages Europe and beyond. At that time, local women—often older women, widows, single women, the very people targeted in the witch crazes for generations—would sometimes care for cats. At that time, cats, due to their overpopulation, were generally seen as a form of pestilence in Europe. The Egyptians actually saw them as a form of *anti-pestilence*; they loved cats because, among other things, cats would go after mice and rats that would get inside of grain supplies. But around the Middle Ages, many Europeans feared that the continent was being overrun by cats. Older women who sometimes took up cats to care for and feed fit the profile of accused witches, hence the association.

Similarly, certain beliefs held that Satan came in the form of a black dog. According to a British legend, Satan fell from heaven into a blackberry bush and got dyed black, and hence black canines became associated with the demonic. In another contrast, the Ancient Egyptians and Greeks viewed dogs as creatures of great loyalty. And the Hebrew word for dog is *kelev* rendered in English as the name *Caleb* (which is the name of my older son); the term for dog and loyalty are synonymous in Hebrew. Obviously, we modern people share the view of dogs as creatures of loyalty and companionship, but they were sometimes viewed in a fearsome way, especially when black.

Hence, you can detect this enticing, intriguing network of correspondences between traits and properties possessed by these beasts and beings from mythological history and the lives that we lead, or strive to lead, in the world as it actually is. And these beasts—as with the cat in Buddhist or Egyptian tradition, or the snake in esoteric tradition—can serve as messengers, as bestowers of power. Or, as in the case of Ganesha, the elephant-headed god, as those who lower barriers. Above all, I think that the persistence and the experience of mysterious beasts, both in allegory and in actual history, ever deepens our connections with and ability to derive wisdom from the natural and unseen world.

LESSON X

_____ ❧ ❧ _____

Mystic Christianity

This chapter on mystic Christianity began as a lecture at a propitious moment in the history of the Philosophical Research Society. It was delivered on the celestial anniversary of the very day—and almost to the very moment—that ground was broken for the construction of the auditorium on Manly P. Hall's campus. The campus itself dates to 1934, but the auditorium was built as an addition beginning on May 16, 1959, with ground broken at 12 noon. I delivered these words in their spoken form just a few minutes past that exact point of the 60th anniversary. And one of the people who contributes to life at PRS created an astrological chart for the original groundbreaking of the auditorium and found an extraordinary comportment of transits that matched that moment, 60 years later, almost to the minute that ground was broken on that day. So we came full circle, in a sense, at a key time in PRS's history.

In a certain sense, all of Christianity is mystical in nature. All of Judaism, all of every world faith, is mystical in nature. Because the term *mystical* really means a direct experience of the divine, the individual's direct experience of higher powers. Seen in its most primeval form, Christianity is, by its very nature, a mystical faith. In a certain sense, the ancient world *needed* Christianity as it was originally brought. One could talk about different kinds of *Christianities*, one of which is called Christendom: the institutional Christianity of church structure, hierarchy, dogma, doctrine, and strictures that arose centuries after the death of Christ, when the New Testament was canonized and a system of bishops, cardinals, and popes was put into place, among other tiers of rank and order. That organization made Christianity into a worldly institution, into an institution crafted by human hands, and filled with the same issues of authority that virtually any human institution faces. But the Christianity that we're talking about in this chapter is the Christianity of the Sermon on the Mount, the Beatitudes, and Gospels, including those Gospels that are canonized and those that might be considered Gnostic Gospels, which were not included in the final selection of books that composed the New Testament. It's the Christianity of

Christ himself, at least according to surviving record, which is the religion that Thomas Jefferson (1743–1826) professed to belong when the founder constructed his heterodox distillation of the four Gospels, sans miracles, which is colloquially known as *The Jefferson Bible*. Jefferson said that the Christianity in which he was interested arose solely from the words and ethics of Christ, at least as they've reached us today.

Manly P. Hall writes frequently, and with deep veneration, of mystical Christian traditions in *The Secret Teachings of All Ages*. To a very great extent, Christianity is part of one continuous whole with everything else that Manly writes about in the book. Christianity was a response, in many ways, to the needs felt by everyday people in the ancient world for a religious practice of ethics, a practice that honored the lives and the experiences of ordinary individuals who were not part of any temple order, and who had no special privileges in society. It was a religion for the working person, for the everyday person, who wanted to seek his or her own direct contact with the divine. In that sense, the message of Christ was mystical in the fullest meaning of that word.

Part of the reason Christianity was able to win vast allegiance and popularity among different groups of people in the centuries following Christ's death is that, for many people in different parts of the world—North Africa, the Mediterranean, Persia, various other lands and places that had once been occupied by the Roman

Empire—the temple orders of antiquity had become corrupted. In their degradation—and it's a part all human affairs, including Christianity—these orders bestowed privileges according to inherited or aristocratic position; according to money, offerings, tithes, and sacrifices tended to priests and keepers of the faith; according to a rigid system of rules and hierarchy, where some people were permitted entrance to the temple and others were not. There was, in a sense, a crying need—first felt in the Mediterranean Basin, but later felt in other parts of the world as well, including Egypt—for a religion that was at the service of the everyday working person, the kind of background that the figure of Christ himself was said to have emerged from. He was a carpenter's apprentice, born of a poor couple, who practiced the Judaic faith; they occupied no special position in society. And here was this 12-year-old boy in the temple who seemed able to debate, to challenge authority, and to emphasize the *spirit of faith* above the *letter of law*.

The elevation of authority and structure had created fissures within Judaism at the time that Christ himself emerged. Within Judaism there exist to this day two polarizing concepts, which could be referred to by the Hebrew terms, *halakha* and *aggadah*. Halakha means the *letter* of the law. Aggadah means the *spirit* of the law. And Christ enunciated his message as one of restoring the *spirit of the law*. He believed that too much formality had crept into Jewish experience, rite, and ritual, and that this formality needed to be displaced in favor of aggadah, the spirit of the law. So Christ, it is recorded, would offer dictums like: "Be not concerned with what goes into your mouth"—regarding dietary laws—"be concerned with what comes out of your mouth." He would pose the question, "Was man made for the Sabbath, or was the Sabbath made for man?" And the response that he would bring was that the Sabbath was made for man. He wanted to break up the calendrics, sacrificial offerings, formalism, and ritualism that had calcified around Judaism at that particular stage under the domination and taxation of the Roman Empire, which itself presented a significant burden on local religions.

So, in that sense, Christianity, in its most primeval form, is inherently a mystical tradition insofar as it was brought to break up structures. Of course, it also replaced these very structures. As early Christianity developed into a more formalized faith, it attempted to coopt existing festivals and markers, so that Christmas itself is timed to the solar new year. Some of the practices of Christmas, such as the adoption of a Christmas tree, reflect earlier pagan, agricultural, and seasonal practices. Easter is timed to the spring equinox, which was celebrated universally as a time of rebirth throughout the pre-Christian world. The later holiday of All-Souls Day, sometimes called All-Saints Day, or All-Hallows Eve, was keyed to autumnal agricultural festivals that existed throughout the

Celtic world, which honored ancestors and the spirit realm. In many regards, institutional Christianity comported itself to the rites, rituals, and calendar of the nature religions.

The symbols of Christianity were themselves in harmony with symbols of the ancient world, as you will discover in *The Secret Teachings of All Ages*, including the widespread depiction of the universal mother holding her child. This can be seen as Isis and Horus in one iteration, or the Madonna and Child in another. And, in fact, in the age of Coptic Christianity, during the late stages of Ancient Egypt, statues of Isis and Horus were sometimes refitted into the image of Mary and Jesus. For that same reason, Christian churches were often built on top of the sites of ancient Roman temples; such was the case with the great Cathedral of Notre Dame in Paris. Contrary to how we view history, there was not a sharp and decisive break between the traditions of the pre-Christian world and Christian world so much as one world morphed into the other. History is not composed of rigid lines.

Timelines and dates often give us the misimpression of a kind of neat linearity in history, such as when the Roman emperor Constantine the Great (272–337 A.D.) converted to Christianity around 312 A.D., which we are taught to see as a decisive break with the past, whereas beliefs, practices, and governing styles often comingle for long periods. Although Constantine effectively made Christianity into the state faith, he actually practiced a coexistent form of Christianity and worship of Jupiter, as did many people within the Roman Empire. It required generations and generations until Christianity took the shape that is somewhat familiar to us today. And, in fact, one of the dynastic emperors who followed Constantine, Julian (331–363 A.D.), sometimes called Julian the Apostate, actually attempted to rollback Christianity as the official state religion. Julian began to restore some of the pagan and Jewish temples. But his reign was short-lived, from 361–363 A.D., so his program wasn't universally felt. (This, by the way, is why Julian is a popular baby name among some Jewish parents, as is Alexander, the conqueror who was seen as more or less friendly to Jewish worship.)

Hence, it is important to understand that we cannot necessarily seize upon a simple date, event, or conversion experience in the life of a ruler and say that this is when official Christendom took over Rome or other parts of the world. Again, many people in the court of the Emperor Constantine, and many everyday citizens, practiced concurrent forms of so-called pagan worship married to Christian worship, and this went on for decades. So, in a sense, we can say that the Emperor Constantine was a Christian—but not in the form that we would necessarily recognize today.

Early Christianity was spread by oral tradition, primarily—as were virtually all teachings of the ancient world—and its teachings could strike people, and continue to strike people, with an overwhelming sense of possibility, portent, and hope. Because, Christianity, in its most basic form, summons the individual to a *personal relationship* with the divine. And its requirements in its early form were very few in a ritualistic or ceremonial sense, unlike later social requirements that got tacked on to it, which included various ceremonial structures, very few of which appear in the New Testament, and, when they do appear, they're primarily Jewish in nature, such as the Passover supper that we call the Last Supper. But, rather, the message of Christ called, first and foremost, for *forgiveness*— that was the chief demand that Christ placed upon the individual—and, finally and ultimately, *love*. In the Gospel of John, Christ tells his disciples, "I have one more commandment to give you, in addition to the Ten Commandments, and it supersedes all the others; and that is to love one another." The loving of one's neighbor is the core ideal of *original* Christianity.

The esoteric teacher, G. I. Gurdjieff said it would be a tremendous honor to be called a Christian; but an individual cannot authentically be called a Christian unless he or she possesses love of neighbor; that is the actual *practice* of Christianity. Isn't it so revolutionary in its simplicity? Isn't it so beautiful in its primal calling to the individual? You don't have to join a temple order. You don't have to put any name on yourself. You don't have to claim kind of privilege, lineage, or caste.

You simply have to possess the wish to forgive and to love. That is mystical Christianity. Go through the canonized Gospels and the Gnostic Gospels backwards and forwards, and that is the essential message. Artifice and accouterments got added later on by formalists and interpreters, as is always the case with any religion; but the original message is one of love and forgiveness above all else. This is what the divine is set to bestow upon the individual, and this is what the individual, in turn, is obligated to bestow upon his or her neighbor. What a message of extraordinary, beautiful simplicity.

Inherent within Christianity is, of course, the experience of being "born again," of dying to one's existing self and being reborn in a realization of one's direct relationship with God. Now, I've spoken of accouterments or add-ons to Christianity, and I don't mean to suggest that all of those are necessarily of a limiting or an authoritarian style. I personally have gone through periods of deep interest in saint veneration as it's practiced within the Catholic Church. In fact, I think saint veneration is, in its own way, one of the most wonderful mystical variants of Christianity, because, again, it allows an individual to forge a direct relationship with an intercessor, whoever that may be. And it is reasoned that the spirits of certain people who led lives of perfection on earth are capable of interceding directly with the divine. It doesn't close the door to issuing your own prayers directly to the divine; but rather it opens the door to requesting the aid of a powerful ally, who may possess the station or ability to convey your prayers to the highest power and bring you signs and wonders, miracles and possibilities, here on earth.

I went through a very trying time in my own life about seven years prior to this writing, and at that time I developed a profound interest in cultivating personal relationships with different Catholic saints, including the figure of Mary. And to this day, actually, I wear around my neck everyday a symbol that's referred to as the Miraculous Medal. It shows Mary standing on top of the globe with her feet pressed on a snake, and on the back of the Miraculous Medal is the letter M surmounted by a cross. That image is encircled by 12 stars, which could be seen as the 12 signs of the zodiac or the 12 apostles. One day I was strolling through a Catholic bookstore in New York City—never discount the life-changing potential of bookstores—and I happened upon a pamphlet about the Miraculous Medal. I felt magnetically pulled towards it, a pull that has endured within me today. I do not draw lines among traditions. I do not abide barriers or partitions in my search. Hence, if I express interest in one branch of the search, which might on the surface seem contradictory to another branch, I suppose I say to that: "Bravo, let there be more contradictions. Let me overflow with contradictions." Because I do not believe that anything humanity has come to understand as a doorway relating to some kind of invisible help or unseen force is ultimately in contradiction to another doorway. I want to drink from many different wells, and I have been nourished and sustained by different wells. I made a pact, I made an agreement at that time in my life, that I would wear the Miraculous Medal around my neck, and that I would always wear it. And I've kept that agreement; that's a personal commitment of mine.

I was very attracted to the esotericism of the symbol of Mary on the Miraculous Medal, which emerged from a Marian apparition or visitation encountered by a nineteenth-century French nun, Catherine Labouré (1806–1876). In 1830, Catherine experienced a series of visions of Mary in the chapel that adjoined her convent in Paris. She witnessed this wonderful image of Mary standing atop the world with rays of light emanating from her hands, these rays of light being love and forgiveness dispensed to humanity. And then the apparition revolved, and on the reverse side of the apparition appeared this magnificent esoteric symbol of the letter M, surmounted by a cross. And beneath the letter M were two hearts—one that was aflame and one that was pierced by a sword—and then 12 stars surrounding the entire image. Catherine was instructed to have a holy medal cast of this image, which was left to human interpretation to decipher. The experience of Catherine Labouré really ushered in the modern era of Marian visitations. Several epochal visitations followed from that period, including the visitations at Lourdes and Fatima. Catherine's visitation, in a sense, marked the Marian era. It inaugurated a phase in which the veneration of Mary grew specifically pronounced within the church, and remains so today.

Now, of course, during the period known as the Reformation in sixteenth-century Europe—from which the Protestant faiths emerged—there was a renewed call for simplicity within Christian practice. And various figures, including Martin Luther (1483–1546), decried the excessive bonds between church and state power, and the manner in which the wealthy and aristocratic were granted dispensations *for purchase* within the church and given other privileges. The challenge to Christianity—their protest, which formed the heart of Protestantism—was that the faithful needed to return to a simpler, more direct form of practice; one that did *not* recognize dictums and rulership from a pope or any one central figure; one that did not offer dispensations according to contributions or offerings; one that did not venerate the images, icons, or relics of saints; one that, in fact, even downplayed *all* imagery in favor of a direct relationship to the divine. So, even Protestantism in its earliest form—which is today sometimes associated with more conservative expressions of Christianity—was itself a mystical impulse, a wish for a restoration of that unencumbered, ineffable bridge between the everyday person and the divine.

This is what philosopher Jacob Needleman has called the "genius of Protestantism."

Many parables, myths, lore, and legends emerged from early and Middle Ages Christianity, probably the most popular of which are the tales of King Arthur and the quest for the Holy Grail. The term Holy Grail is frequently heard today, but if you turn back the pages of history you'll discover that it's not altogether clear what the Grail itself was thought to be. Some believed it was the goblet from which Christ drank at the Last Supper, the Passover supper; some believed that it was some sort of a banquet plate; some that it was an incense holder; some believed that it was a chalice encrusted with jewels; some accounts describe it as a jewel that came loose from Lucifer's crown after the fall from heaven. The idea was that, somewhere, this object—although people didn't always agree on its nature—had been spirited away by early evangelists or other faithful. And if one could find it—and, again, the mythology and the parables differ—he might be granted ultimate power; or, more commonly, the discovery of the Grail would signal a kind of worldwide revolution, a rebirth of Christianity, in which there would be direct, fuller, and richer contact between the individual and the divine.

So, Western enthusiasts have for centuries been thrilled and aroused with this idea of finding a Holy Grail. We wish for tactile connections between the ineffable world and our own. It seems to me that's why, in some branches of Christianity, particularly Catholicism and Eastern Orthodoxy, there exists a deep and enduring attachment to relics—some people are in search of, or believe they have found, splinters of the original cross; different churches and cathedrals will place, either up on the altar or in shrines, relics of saints' bodies: bits of flesh, spots of blood, fragments of fingernails, and strands of hair. There exists a feeling that these worldly objects provide a kind of empirical footbridge between our world and the next, and I honor that practice.

And, of course, in the eyes of many Christians, today remains an era of signs and wonders. This is typified by numerous figures fairly contemporaneous to our own time, such as the Catholic saint Padre Pio (1887–1968), who was said to display the stigmata on his hands and to bleed from his hands. There is a large church on the west side of Manhattan, not far from where I live, which has preserved a variety of relics and objects that belonged to Padre Pio, including gloves and bandages that he wore over his hands when he was experiencing his weeping stigmata. You can see these wrappings marked with blood. They are there for veneration and for the individual to witness as he or she sees fit.

So the age of signs and wonders, so to speak, is not necessarily, within the Christian paradigm, part of a unknown past that will never reintroduce itself; but rather the concept of miracles is honored within

Catholicism and Pentecostal and Charismatic congregations, among others. Miracles and healings are subject to extremely rigorous testing within the Catholic Church today. In fact, one of the things that I deeply appreciate about the Catholic Church is that it is among the few institutions that actually undertakes meticulous research of paranormal claims. There are, for example, a variety of steps to sainthood, including strict verification of at least two miracles said to have been performed by the individual while alive. Very frequently these are said to be medical miracles, such as spontaneous healing. It would surprise most people to know of the vigor with which the Church investigates these mystical claims; because if the Church beatified a certain figure and the historicism or the claims involved were later found to have gaps, and this figure's authenticity were called into question, then it would challenge the church's authority to be able to make such designations to begin with. Although hundreds of saints have been beatified within the past few generations, many by Pope John Paul II (1920–2004) who was sympathetic to the practice, you would be surprised at the intensity of research that surrounds this process and its investigations. The Catholic Church routinely investigates and refuses to validate many claims of miracles, Marian apparitions, or other forms of visitation. The Church holds such claims to a high standard of corroborated evidence, witnesses, exclusion of other factors, and documentation. In that sense, the Catholic Church is, in my eyes, one of the most responsible investigators of supernatural claims in our own time.

You will continue to find within all branches of Christianity today claims of miraculous healings. In both Protestantism and Catholicism, people report spontaneous recoveries or remissions, and there are many such stories. Until the late 1960s, healing crusades, usually as part of tent revival meetings, remained popular in the U.S. This should not surprise us because early Christianity and the record of Christ's ministry on earth, in many respects, took the shape of a *healing ministry*. Most of the miracles ascribed to Christ and the apostles are miracles of healing. Not exclusively so—there are the loaves and fishes, water into wine, and walking on water—but the miraculous acts that Christ was reported to have performed most consistently involved healings. That remains a basic part of Christian practice today, although most denominations—Catholicism in particular—have long insisted that the individual also get quality medical care, in addition to whatever spiritual work may accompany their convalescence.

We know very little about the life of Christ as it appears in the Gospels and the Gnostic Gospels. We are told that he was born to a relatively poor couple in Nazareth—a working Jewish family whose father was a carpenter and whose mother was miraculously impregnated. And we know little about the years that were said to have transpired between his birth and his first emergence as a teacher at the age of 12. His parents were part of a caravan that was going to Jerusalem to pay taxes and to make sacrifices, obeying the ritual and state laws of the day. Within the caravan on the way home they discovered that they were missing their son, and, shocked, they rushed back to the temple and there he was. At the age of 12 their son was holding forth within the temple—questioning, challenging, offering parables and insights—and at that moment it became apparent that this was no ordinary child. This was a being marked for greatness.

And later, when he grew older—again, the interim years are largely unknown—he emerged out into the world and began to deliver sermons and parables. The Beatitudes, a part of the Sermon on the Mount, was one of his first great public statements; its sayings and expressions ("blessed are the poor in spirit") form, in many regards, the ethical backbone of Western culture. Many of the expressions that we're familiar with today, many of the moralistic concepts that we're familiar with, such as turning the other check or abstaining from judgment of a neighbor, attained currency from the Sermon on the Mount. It is significant that Christ spoke on a mountain, which is a natural pyramid, long considered a kind of bridge between the human and the ineffable. And, of course, a mountain is in the wilderness—it's not a cathedral, it's not a temple, no one is paying dues or has assigned seats, there's no hierarchy, everyone can come and just gather around. So, Christ dispensed his wisdom to a great festival of the people signaling its egalitarianism. And he fed them; he produced the loaves and fishes. In esoteric spirituality, food means transmission. As he proceeded with his ministry, challenging formalism and dogma, he attracted the ire of religious and state authorities, culminating in his crucifixion, said to occur at age 33.

I happen to have the number 33 tattooed on my right bicep. This is also the number of the highest degree in Freemasonry. Becoming a 33rd-degree Freemason is basically an honorary degree but it's considered, in Scottish Rite, the crown of Masonry. The number 33 reoccurs in various mystical traditions and aspects of Scripture. It came to be seen as a number that connotes the miraculous, including harmony between the individual and the heavens.

After the reported death of Christ, his apostles spread throughout other parts of the world, and were said in the Book of Acts to be capable of performing miracles and healings in the Master's name. And as generation after generation passed, Christianity went from being a persecuted minority religion to being adopted, as I noted, by the Emperor Constantine—although, again, adopted in his own way; he combined it with worship of Jupiter. Constantine and the populace comported Christianity with the calendar of the pagan world. The word *pagan* itself is not one that I particularly like using, because of its earliest connotations: it is a Latin-derived term that came into use in the Roman Empire meaning *villager*, or somebody from the backwoods or boondocks, so to speak. Because news of Christianity traveled relatively slowly, many people in outlying districts continued the old modes of worship and dedications. And these people, to whom the news of Christianity had not yet reached, were considered by some to be kind of backwoods folks, hence called pagans or villagers, meaning people who persisted in the old ways. The term has a derogatory tone like hillbilly.

Early in Christendom in 325 A.D., the Council of Nicaea decided on the church's central rules and structures; decided which books were going to be canonized in Scripture; which books were going to be deemed Apocrypha, or works of dubious or questionable authenticity; what acts of worship were considered sanctioned and which would be considered heretical. And as Europe entered the period of the post Roman Empire—the Dark Ages, the Middle Ages, the medieval period—the church became indelibly established as a very top-down, hierarchical institution, which eventually led to the Protestant revolution in the 1500s, after which Christianity branched out in different directions and permutations.

There also existed a historically suppressed Gnostic Christianity; a Christianity that never enfolded into the structures of the Council of Nicaea; a Christianity that harbored independent interpretations of the message of Christ—including one interpretation that the God of the Old Testament is a kind of evil God or *demiurge* who controls and manipulates humanity through designees sometimes called *archons*. Whereas the God of the New Testament is a God who brings love, forgiveness, and illumination, as represented by Christ. Some Gnostic groups—and their beliefs varied widely—emphasized so-called Apocryphal books, such as the Book of Enoch, which depicted the presence of fallen angels (watchers) and their giant offspring (*Nephilim*) who corrupt the earth.

Some Mediterranean-based Gnostic sects combined elements of Christianity and Judaism with retentive practices from the ancient temple orders, and thus created a kind of syncretic faith that honored the Christian message but continued with the initiatory and esoteric practices of pre-Christian antiquity or included in their lexicon Persian gods, such as the sun deity Abraxas. These sects and groupings were sometimes violently eradicated by Christian troops and governments in a manner that brutally contradicted everything that Christ had taught. It is a perpetual and universal fissure in human nature that revolutions become their opposite; everything slides from one polarity to another. Hence, a religion that was brought to the world in the name of love and forgiveness engages in the violent destruction of some branches of Gnostic or so-called heretical Christianity; and later sponsors and sustains mass violent inquisitions, murdering and torturing untold masses of people—from Jews to accused witches to deposed Knights Templar to accused heretics of all sorts.

Institutions grow corrupt because institutions are the work of human hands. This is as close as we have to a law of human nature. An idea that's brought forth to liberate calcifies into a justification to persecute even greater numbers of people, at least in many cases. This drearily repeats across history.

However, we still have the search—and that's the way out. Nothing can ultimately destroy the independent spiritual or ethical search. You can read *The Secret Teachings of All Ages*. You can read the Gnostic Gospels. You can read the canonized Gospels. You can read the Jefferson Bible for Christianity's ethical teachings without reference to miracles. And you can devise your own search.

You can come into the message and the meaning of Christ's *original* teachings, inasmuch as we have them, without label, membership, or fealty to anything or anyone. That, too, was a fundamental part of the message that the teacher brought. That's the mystical heart of Christianity. The trait of human nature to slide from an ideal to its opposing polarity can be *exited*; and the exit lies in the direction of your own search.

LESSON XI

_⟋ ⟍_

Kabbalah and
the Hebrew Masters

Kabbalah is a term that very simply means *tra-dition*, and seen from a certain perspective—and this is the perspective that I will take—all Jewish practice can be understood as Kabbalah.

Historically, the term Kabbalah is most commonly associated with two works, the *Sefer Yetzirah* and the *Zohar*, which were produced in late antiquity and later refined during the early medieval period. They reflect a broad range of mystical and esoteric practices within Judaism. These were rabbinic works, which is to say they were devised by Jewish masters, rabbis or rebbes, after the fall and the final destruction of the Second Temple in Jerusalem in 70 A.D.

The post-Temple age in Judaism is referred to as the Rabbinic Age, sometimes formally dated to the completion of the Babylonian Talmud in the 6th century A.D., though certainly in development earlier. It is an era in which the priesthood and temple order no longer existed; the system of sacrifices that had characterized Judaism in the ancient world was gone; and the Jewish people themselves were dispersed around the world—to other parts of the Mediterranean; to parts of North Africa and various parts of Persia; to various reaches of Western and Eastern Europe; and to parts of Asia.

After the final destruction of the Temple in 70 A.D., and in the generations ahead, ongoing tensions with the residents of Jerusalem and surrounding territories led the Roman Empire to finally expel the Jewish people from the biblical lands—not entirely, but in large measure. And as the Jewish people became a kind of wandering and dispersed nation, the rabbinic system developed so that individual teachers or the presiders over synagogues and congregations (rabbis or rebbes) became the keepers of the faith, so to speak; became those who interpreted Jewish practice for the faithful in an era that was no longer presided over by descendants of the priestly class, the Cohens and the Levites, terms that later formed popular surnames.

This is the era from which emerged two great branches of Jewish practice: Kabbalah, in the form of works such as the *Zohar* and the *Sefer Yetzirah;* and the Talmud, which was a compendium of dialogues among different Jewish masters and among students and teachers. The interlocutors would probe a vast range of ritualistic, ethical, and mystical questions. Again, all of Judaism can be seen as part of the Kabbalist tradition, because Kabbalah simply means a tradition or transmission or received revelation. And, as with Christianity, all of Judaism, depending upon one's mode of practice, can be seen as a mystical expression.

The most widely recognized symbol or figure from the tradition of Kabbalah is the so-called Tree of Life, which Manly P. Hall depicts in various interpretations. The tree is a diagram devised of ten *sefirot,* which are nodes or spheres; these, in turn, are connected by 22 paths. The sefirot represent the different traits of existence, such as beauty, kindness, discipline, victory, mercy. The paths that connect them traditionally form a zigzagging route up this ten-fold ladder until the point of the Crown, or *Keter,* which is the godhead. This is, in a sense, humanity's union with the divine. Now, the Tree of Life appears in many different permutations in Kabbalistic tradition; there's not one strictly settled upon image or permutation, and Manly depicts four of the most popular interpretations.

The Tree of Life is also associated with the Tree of Knowledge of Good and Evil, as it appears in Genesis 3. Earlier, I noted that when Eve ate the apple—which in itself is a kind of sphere, node, or *sefirah*—she was, in my view, completing human creation. You could see that act as the fall of humanity, as traditionally depicted, but I think there's an esoteric understanding to the drama in which her action represented the liberation of humanity. The result of that liberation is labor. Friction inevitably accompanies illumination. And using the 22 paths to work one's way up the ten sefirot of the Tree of Life is seen as the central task of humanity: to work its way to the highest form of illumination.

Now, the Tree of Life is sometimes associated with the zodiac or various aspects of the cosmos, as it is sometimes associated with the trumps of the Tarot deck. The connection to Tarot was a much later innovation; it did not appear in Kabbalistic practice; nor did it appear in the original uses and practices of the Tarot cards. It is a fairly contemporary innovation that was arrived at by the French occultist, Éliphas Lévi (1810–1875) in his 1854 book, *The Doctrine and Ritual of High Magic* (sometimes translated as *Transcendental Magic*). Lévi made the association between the pathways and the spheres of the Tree of Life and the Tarot deck. It is up to the individual to determine whether you find those correspondences compelling. I do not correlate validity to either the antiquity or the newness of a teaching. But we should know the historical lineage that we're dealing with. Properly understood, the associations between the Tree of Life and Tarot are a modern innovation.

*   *   *

The Kabbalistic masters, as well as the writers and framers of the Talmud, were possessed by a passion to perpetuate Judaism and Jewish learning in an age after the destruction of the Temple. Hence, Jewish tradition post-Temple became a largely liturgical, congregational, and literary tradition. This tradition placed tremendous emphasis on learning, discipleship, and literary and spoken form. The great works that came to be known as Kabbalah or Talmud were, in essence, produced in early book form—and could be carried around, could be circulated, could be transported from place to place, just as the Torah, the great scroll that's composed of the first five books of the Old Testament, could be carried around. It was a transportable religion in a certain sense—in the same way that the Hebrews in the desert carried the tabernacle, or place of worship, with them, moved around, reassembled the tabernacle wherever they encamped before finally reaching Canaan, the so-called Holy Land. Like their ancestors, they were continually on the move. Hence, late ancient and medieval Judaism, in a sense, adapted itself to a life of wandering. It was the faith of a dispersed people.

Not all of the Talmud, even in translation, is necessarily accessible to the everyday person. The questions it addresses can be deeply arcane. There are vast concerns and traditions that feed into Talmudic literature. One branch of Talmudic literature is called the Jerusalem Talmud, completed around 350 A.D., and another is called the Babylonian Talmud, completed around 500 A.D., but further edited in centuries ahead. These terms connoted the different locales in which the books began to be compiled. There is crossover between the two books, though the latter, the Babylonian Talmud, is generally viewed as the most authoritative. The most accessible book of Talmudic tradition, especially if you want to begin your own journey into reading some of this material, is called *Pirkei Avot*, or *Ethics of the Fathers*. *Ethics of the Fathers* is one of the shortest, but, I believe, also one of the most compelling and practical books connected with Talmudic tradition. (It is not strictly a part of the Talmud but quotes from its principal figures.) *Ethics of the Fathers* is basically a series of dialogues between masters and students, most of which hinge upon practical moral questions.

When I was 13 years old, the time at which a boy or girl experiences his bar or bat mitzvah within traditional Judaism, I had an orthodox bar mitzvah. I grew up in a fairly traditional Jewish background, in the borough of Queens in New York City, and I was bar mitzvahed at a small orthodox synagogue called Young Israel of New Hyde Park. It was a very traditional setting in which women and men sat separately, a practice that continues in orthodox and Hasidic Judaism. The Torah was treated as an object of great veneration. There was a tremendous emphasis on learning, including mastery of the Hebrew language itself. My bar mitzvah was a very different kind of event from the type that you may experience today. It was a happy but also solemn occasion.

After I delivered what is called the *haftarah*, which is a weekly reading from the Book of Prophets, I went up onto the altar, or the *bimah*, and the rabbi shook my hand and said to me, "What was your name again?" I laugh whenever I tell this story because today, as some of you reading these words may have experienced, the bar mitzvah ceremony and the party that sometimes follows can almost seem like a coronation. But my little orthodox bar mitzvah was such a low-key affair that the rabbi himself didn't even know my name. And looking back I feel fortunate to have had it that way. We grow from rigor and not pageantry.

Most importantly, in terms of my perspective, was that he handed me two books as gifts from the congregation. The first was called *The Jew and his Duties*, which had some powerful ethical passages. I particularly recall a passage that referenced the one Judaically sanctioned form of revenge. It is to behave so nobly that no one will believe your detractor. And the other was a daily prayer book that contained within it a pretty sturdy English translation of *Pirkei Avot*, or the *Ethics of the Fathers*. And this little book, the *Ethics of the Fathers*, became the lifeline of my existence at that time. There were difficulties at home—including severe financial difficulties and relationship difficulties. My parents divorced when I was 15 and I felt like my world was just coming apart; it was a very scary time. This short book served as a kind of life-boat. I reread it and reread it and reread it. I can still quote from it by heart. In many regards, it marked the beginning of my search and—even though it is not my primary commitment today—it forms a kind of foundation for me and it follows me everywhere, like the tabernacle in the wilderness.

These dialogues get inside you. In one dialogue, a master asks his students, "What are the markings of a good man?" And each student responds differently: one says a good heart; one says a good eye; one says a good name. All give different replies, and all of them display a certain insight. But one student says: "He who borrows and repays." And the master says, "I select your words above those of all the others, because their words are contained within yours." I cited this earlier. Now, you can interpret that statement on a practical scale, which is certainly feasible. Or you can think of it on a vast scale. Isn't debt something that follows you through life? What debts do you hold? What debts do you owe—to your family, to your background, to your teacher, to people who weave in and out of your life, to your dignity as a human being? To *borrow and to repay*—and we're all debtors since nothing is permanently ours, including life itself.

In another section of the book, a young student is wandering in a cavern through which snakes a creek. The student spots a skull floating on the water. He asks the skull, "How did you get here?" The skull responds, "I used my words to drown others. Those words returned to drown me." Within the book there appear warnings, again and again, against smears, gossip, or idle tale-bearing—sometimes called *lashon hara* or "hate talk" within Judaism. I recall vividly a pivotal event in my life when I was about ten years old. I was attending a youth congregation at another synagogue in Queens, and there was a youth rabbi, Larry Ziffer, who lives in Baltimore today, who was delivering a talk to a large congregation of very unruly kids. This youth congregation was typically a noisy affair. It was a warm spring day and everyone wanted to be outside playing and running around; and instead we were stuck inside, with the girls wearing dresses and the boys wearing jackets and ties, and everybody felt very constricted. And these services were no short affair—they could go on for a couple of hours—and so, frequently, there were behavioral problems. I instigated many myself.

But I'll never forget one Saturday where Larry was giving a talk to the kids, and he started to speak about the importance of not engaging in hate speech, rumor mongering, or things like that. And suddenly the room—normally very unruly—grew very, very quiet. And Larry said that in Judaism to speak ill of another person—to smear another person's character, to engage in or listen to gossip or rumor—is superseded in severity only by the sin of murder. Only the sin of *murder* is considered worse than spreading or listening to smears or gossip. (This does not, of course, mean abstaining from calls for justice.) I cannot tell you how *quiet* that room grew. Every child in that room was having his or her own inner experience upon hearing those words. Larry wasn't trying to scare the kids; he was paying them the tribute of providing a message without mincing words. He was pointing out the consequences of assassinating someone's character, even if you think what you're saying is true; and very often it is either not true or it is mitigated by circumstances of which the speaker has no knowledge. Hence, in traditional Judaism, when you assassinate another's character through gossip, rumor, tale-bearing ("true" or not), you are committing a transgression superseded only by taking a life. A reputation is a life. I carried that with me.

I often tell people that if you want to bring an immediate change to your life—if you feel stuck in life, if you feel disrespected, if you feel burdened with a poor self-image—try this experiment: For just 24 hours, desist from participating in any kind of gossip, rumor, or tale-bearing. Don't spread it, don't listen to it. And just *see* if you don't immediately stand taller, if you don't feel a greater sense of nobility, if you don't feel better about yourself—and if you don't also attract greater respect from others. If you want something practical to try, there is something practical.

We tend to think that hallowed ideas must be complex. People look at the Tree of Life and they want to analyze it, figure out the master key to creation, unlock what all the paths mean. How do I progress up these 22 paths? How do I emerge at the apex of these ten sefirot? What does this model tell us about the skeletal work of the universe? What esoteric secrets does it hold for me? Well, it may disclose a great many; but never, never neglect the simple path, which can be the most profound. I wrote an introduction to a book by Obadiah Harris called *The Simple Road*. If you're interested in functioning as a nobler being never neglect what may seem simple. And Larry, a mystic himself in my estimation, was giving us that path on that day. Payment of debt; honor of neighbor; desisting from gossip; forgiving when possible (I do not accept orthodoxy on forgiveness, which I've written about elsewhere); keeping one's word—these are all things, among many more, that populate the works of Kabbalah and the Talmud. Hallowed practices need not seem so *far away*, exotic, or distant. We sometimes use the exotic to avoid the imperative of the moment.

The lives of many orthodox and Hasidic Jews are, in many ways today, still very mystical in nature. That is not my path or individual commitment, but I honor that everything done by the deeply orthodox Jew or the Hasidic Jew is done in a kind of sanctified fashion. Meals are venerated; lovemaking is venerated; human relationships are venerated; the rising and the setting of the sun is venerated; waking in the morning, going to sleep at night—*everything* is done with a sense of repaying one's debt to the Higher. And for that reason, orthodoxy can seem like a slower pace of life, in a sense. The ancient Hebrews and Essenes, and different Gnostic groups that existed around the Mediterranean, often led lives of deep ritual and tradition. They lived by an altered conception of time. Blessings and ritual made everything in life a little slower, perhaps a little more contemplative, because everything was marked by a fealty to the Higher.

Along with the Miraculous Medal, which I talked about in the previous chapter, I also wear around my neck (and it never comes off, day or night) the mezuzah, which is a traditional Jewish talisman for good fortune. Observant Jews fix a mezuzah upon the doorframes of their homes or places of business, on the right hand side, tilted inward, so that it brings good tidings into the home itself. In an observant Jewish household, you will see people kiss their hands and touch the mezuzah as they're crossing over the threshold. Again, this is one of the ways in which Jewish practice brings a kind of mysticism to routine life. And some people wear, as I do, the mezuzah around their necks. The mezuzah contains two prayers from Deuteronomy, one of which is called the *Shema*, which begins, "Hear, O Israel, the Lord our God, the Lord is One." It's the holiest prayer in all of Judaism, and it is encapsulated within the mezuzah, along with another prayer of longevity and prosperity.

Many different people use the mezuzah. I have seen it on the doorposts of Mormon homes. Earlier I considered the African-American magickal tradition of hoodoo. One of the wonderful developments in hoodoo—and something that made it perhaps the first syncretic faith in American life—is that catalogues selling hoodoo goods to practitioners in the early twentieth century began to feature Jewish ritual items, including menorahs and mezuzahs, which were considered items of sacredness and good luck, and which could be used by people of all different backgrounds. Actually, hoodoo catalogues offered a wide range of liturgical items from different faiths. And you can never foresee the impact of something. It was actually my practice of hoodoo that returned me to using the mezuzah, a hallowed item from my youth.

Within Judaism there is an emphasis—somewhat different from what is found within primeval Christianity—on judgment and justice. The Gospels emphasize forgiveness and compassion, and you certainly find that within traditional Judaism; but within the Judaism of the Old Testament, you also do find an emphasis on justice. A core principle is that the individual is ever standing before the judgment of God. "I am a jealous God," says the god of the Old Testament to the Hebrews, "and *you* are a stiff-necked people." So the idea is, again, that one has a debt to pay. One is being watched over—there is a beneficent and life-giving side to God who provides rain in the proper seasons, who responds to petitionary prayer—but there is also a thirst for justice and a deep concern with judgment and balance.

This is understandable, in a way, when one considers the cultural parameters and circumstances of the early Hebrew people. They were a desert-dwelling tribe. On the day that I delivered the lecture that became this chapter I was surprised to find that, without intending, I was wearing a t-shirt that said, "Desert Island," which happens to be a graphic novel and comic book store in Williamsburg, Brooklyn, also home to a large Hasidic community. In any case, this desert-dwelling people existed in a world populated with *hundreds* of different tribes, which sometimes warred with one another for scarce resources—water, livestock, game. Death was a palpable presence. Tribes had their own retinue of gods, their own practices, rites, rituals, orders, and priesthoods. Religion was intimately tied to warfare, agriculture, and survival. It was a brutal world.

So, in response to the need for survival, the early Jewish people erected a series of laws, strictures, boundaries, and a legal system. This later emerged as the Ten Commandments, which provided pillars of our current code of justice: thou shalt not kill; thou shalt not steal; thou shalt not bear false witness against thy neighbor. The Ten Commandments demarcated responsibilities to one another; responsibilities to orphans, widows, strangers, or people in need. It demarcated responsibilities to keep the Sabbath and other ritual observances. Above all, this list of strictures was among the first and most compelling systems of civic law in the Near Eastern world.

Likewise, the early books of the Torah, the so-called Five Books of Moses, also reflected a concern, not only with universal ethics and insight, but with distinguishing the Jewish people from surrounding tribes. That, too, was a matter of survival. Hence, dietary laws were instituted. These things are also very mystical and shrouded in esoterica. I don't mean to suggest that I'm trying to project an exclusively anthropological or sociological reading onto early Judaism—I am not. In religions, as in human nature, there exist a complexity of factors. But I do believe that one factor was the need in this tribal setting—in which there were many different groups competing for limited resources—to set down parameters and demarcations, to foster a sense of structure, lineage, and civil society.

In that vein, practices witnessed in other tribes were often discouraged, banned, or outlawed, such as engraving images onto one's skin, or what we would call tattoos. As you may know, that's not a stricture that I have personally followed. There were different rules about judgment, warfare, diet, family structure, and sexuality. Today people sometimes cite prohibitions against homosexuality found in the Old Testament, and I don't think that translates to our era. I don't think that stands up as legitimate biblical scholarship, for the following reason: It's very difficult—and I'm continually telling this to young people—from our perspective in the twenty-first century to look back upon some of the strictures of the ancient world and make sense of them from our vantage point. We cannot necessarily retrofit our own political or social perceptions onto what ancient people were thinking about. They had a set of concerns to which we cannot necessarily relate. This is why I think it's a mistake not only to project our attitudes backwards, but to project the social attitudes of the ancients forward and attempt to use them to set policy. Yes, the ancients wanted to relate to the Higher. Yes, they believed they owed a debt to God, to the cosmic, to the celestial. But they were concerned with the day-to-day needs of physical survival, which sometimes led them to devise prohibitions that I do not think were universal strictures or dictums, so much as they were *local customs* that separated one tribe from another. Other times their strictures, such as thou shalt not kill, were, in fact, universal. How do we tell the difference? How do we sort out a local dictum from a universal one? To some extent it requires time—in that same way that great works of ethics and wisdom are subject to the juries of the ages. Another factor is that universal precepts are usually echoed and paralleled in other forms of primeval thought, even if the purveyors are separated by vast distances.

Sometimes ancient people would look at what the tribe over the next hill was doing, and they would say, well we define ourselves differently; we don't do that, we're not part of that particular tribe. And—for good or ill, but certainly always for reasons of survival—they would prohibit these practices. We modern people, however, like to cherry-pick from among these strictures—which ones suit our purposes and which ones do we dislike? You'll encounter people of all different political stripes who will cite Scripture, selecting something that they like, discarding something else; and, depending upon one's modern proclivities, sometimes somebody will seize upon a passage that may have been a kind of local ordinance that didn't really have luminescence or universality, yet will insist upon its inerrant nature while simultaneously contradicting themselves by rejecting all kinds of other things.

Some people today who, for example, do not keep kosher dietary laws might seize upon what they perceive as strictures against homosexuality and insist that their beliefs are supported by Scripture. Well there are *lots* of contemporaneous things in Scripture that we don't do—such as stoning to death an adulterer on the doorstep of her father's house. You'll find many things that are *extremely brutal* in the Old Testament, which no thinking person would imagine doing today. So, we must be very careful of this tendency, which we all possess, to selectively pick among the laws of ancient people. What we really must do, in my view, is use the search itself as an act of verification—to distill that which is universal, that which is most transcendent, that which is enduring, that which has attained sound posterity, and to determine, hand in hand with tradition, where the path lies.

There are many deep mysteries in the Jewish faith, and I'm touching on just a few of them. One of the teachings of Kabbalah involves the holy name, the name of God, which is sometimes rendered by the alliterative letters Yod Hey Vav Hey, or YHWH. This is sometimes called the tetragrammaton. I happen to have Yod Hey Vav Hey tattooed in Hebrew on my upper right arm. The design, in which the Hebrew letters surround a luminescent sun with an all-seeing eye at its center, is adapted from a Tarot deck designed by Manly P. Hall and J. Augustus Knapp in 1929, just a year after the *Secret Teachings*.

The pronunciation of Yod Hey Vav Hay, or YHWH, is lost to time; no one actually knows how to pronounce it. The Hebrew language in its earliest form does not possess vowels; it is a language of consonants. In that sense, it reflects an oral tradition—if you do not hear the language, you do not know exactly how it's said. Early Hebrew is also a pictogrammatic language, not entirely different from hieroglyphs. It *does* have phonetic pronunciations, but these phonetics do not necessarily travel from written word to ear; they travel from *mouth* to ear. And, again, because ancient Hebrew did not contain vowels it was not always clear how to pronounce something. The letters themselves were symbols or markers; they didn't come with a strict pronunciation. Within the Hebrew language the letter *Tav* can be pronounced properly as an "s" or a "t" based on dialect. It is often pronounced "s" in Ashkenazi, or East European, Hebrew and "t" in Sephardic, or Mediterranean Hebrew. Earlier I referenced the Talmudic book, *Ethics of the Fathers*—in Hebrew its title can be pronounced *Pirkei Avos* or *Pirkei Avot.*

We do not have a key to all of the pronunciations of the ancient world. Hence, the holy name, the name of God—YHWH—is not pronounceable according to any consensus. It is sometimes enunciated by traditional Jews as *Adonai* or *Elohim.* It is sometimes enunciated by biblical scholars as *Yahweh.* It is sometimes enunciated by Christians as *Jehovah.* But we don't really know how to say it. There is a rabbinic legend that if an individual could come into realization of how to pronounce the holy name, YHWH, all power would come to that person. It's a mystery at the heart of Judaism.

Another oral legend that appears within mystical Judaism is also is found within Islam. This was told to me by the philosopher Jacob Needleman. The legend is that when God pushed Lucifer out of heaven, God whispered, *This way leads to me too.* I'm told by Professor Needleman that that can be found in Islam, as well.

A wide array of mystical stories and lore run through Judaism. One is the story of the Golem, which has become a kind of universal morality tale. It teaches that the 16th century Rabbi Loeb (or Lowe) of Prague (c. between 1512 and 1526–1609) was attempting to protect his people from riots and pogroms. So he created a clay monster and he breathed life into it. And the monster *did* protect the local villagers from rioters; but the monster eventually ran amok and destroyed the same village it was created to protect, which tells us something about the inevitable abuse of power, even by people who were victims. It's a precursor to the Frankenstein story: when the earthly individual creates, there will always and ultimately be a crack in that creation and nothing is complete without the approbation of the divine. We see the same message encrypted on the eye-on-pyramid on the back of the dollar bill; worldly creation, or the pyramid, is incomplete without divine approbation, the all-seeing eye.

Judaism sees men and women as intrinsically flawed, and it is the task of life to work your way up the Tree of Life (or, seen a different way, the Tree of Knowledge of Good and Evil) in order to reunite with illumination. There also appears within Judaism some of the earliest conceptions that came to be associated with Satan or *Shaitaan*, known as the Adversary—which was depicted as a kind of impersonal force, not as something individualized, although this force does appear so in the Book of Job.

In that vein, there is a fascinating and entrancing story within Torah in the Book of Leviticus that gives us the concept of the *scapegoat*. While the Hebrews wandered in the desert, they designated a time of year—today observed as Yom Kippur, the day of atonement—in which to send a goat out into the desert as a sacrifice to Azazel, a demonic being that was said to dwell in the wilderness. In Egyptian esotericism, Set is seen as the god of the desert and the god of storms, in a similarity. This figure of Azazel was said to be placated if you could cast your sins, in effect, upon this scapegoat and send it out in the desert to him.

There's so much richness, so much beauty, so much mysticism, so much insight within the Kabbalistic, rabbinic, and Talmudic traditions within Judaism; and *The Secret Teachings of All Ages* provides a wonderful and broad entry point to these mysteries. And, in a certain sense, to the establishment of Judaism itself—and its endurance—which can be seen as extraordinary, even miraculous, because there were hundreds and hundreds of tribes populating these desert lands in the time of the Hebrews; and the vast number of them—with their gods, their lexicons, their local deities, and their priestly orders—have been forgotten. But this one tiny tribe survived and endured; and from its ranks emerged the figure of Christ, whose teachings literally changed the world.

What are the mysteries that this small group of desert dwelling people knew? I invite you to begin that mystical exploration for yourself.

___ ၈ ၆ ___

The Tarot and Magick

Tarot is a topic of deep personal interest to me. In terms of decks, I have an affinity for the urtext of modern Tarot, the 1910 deck illustrated by Pamela Colman Smith (1878–1951) and designed by the British (though Brooklyn-born) occultist Arthur Edward Waite (1857–1942). Tarot has become an object of increasing interest to me over the past few years; it was always part of my path, but I have delved more deeply into its allegorical and divinatory properties more recently. Tarot is probably the most enduring and popular occult tool on the contemporary scene today. It seems to be a topic of perennial fascination, and Manly P. Hall dedicates a full chapter to an analysis of Tarot in *The Secret Teachings of All Ages*.

I think one of the reasons that Tarot retains such a deep hold on our psyches is that the deck, from its original form in the early Renaissance going forward, is populated by archetypal images—images that are almost at the heart, not only of the Western psyche but, I would say, the psyches of people from all cultures and all civilizations. The cards speak to the most primary figures and pictogrammatic images that form some of humanity's earliest expressions of art and drama: the Juggler or Magician, the King, the Empress, the High Priest (Pope) or High Priestess, Death, the Lovers. Aren't these figures the building blocks of virtually all human stories, of all attempts to characterize ourselves and others?

Once a friend asked me whether the images of the Tarot deck could be understood to speak to humanity universally, and I believe the answer is yes. The image of the Magician, for example, echoes in images that appear in some of humanity's earliest cave drawings from the Paleolithic era, such as the upright antlered being called The Sorcerer dated to around 13,000 B.C. from the Cave of the Trois Frère in southwestern France. The images of Death speak to every psyche, as do the Lovers. A High Priest or High Priestess can, in varied forms, be identified in every civilization.

The deck with which most of us are familiar is the one I previously referenced illustrated by Pamela Colman Smith. Smith is finally getting some of her due as an artist within our own generation. The deck that she co-designed with Arthur Edward Waite in the early twentieth century was previously known as the Rider-Waite deck; Rider was the deck's first publisher. Nowadays it's more commonly known as the Smith-Waite deck. Smith received a fairly nominal fee for illustrating the deck, and when she died in 1951 she was frustrated with the lack of recognition that she had received from art critics and commercial publishers over the course of her career.

And yet, Smith is probably the most influential occult artist of the twentieth and twenty-first centuries, because most Tarot decks that are commercially available today, and there are literally hundreds of variations, to some degree echo her work. Whether it's the vampire deck or the *Star Wars* deck or the gummy bear deck, or what have you—they all use her deck as a kind of urtext. Smith was also the first artist to give full-scale dramatic illustration to the court cards and minor trumps. Although there was precedent—notably the Sola Busca deck from the late 15th century, which was an apparent source of inspiration to Smith—she is the first artist who fully provided dramatic and characterological images throughout the deck.

Hence, Smith made Tarot into the mass, accessible tool that we know it as today. The earliest Tarot decks, which emerged from northern Italy in the early 1400s, were far less expressive in design. We do not possess any complete deck from that era; we have incomplete decks, the oldest of which is the mid-fifteenth century

Sforza-Visconti deck, named for the royal family who possessed it. That deck in its most intact form, containing 74 of 78 cards, is today held by the Pierpont Morgan Library in New York City, on the east side of Manhattan. Ironically the Morgan is across the street, on Madison Avenue, from what used to be a little occult shop owned by writer and actress Eden Gray, who in 1960 self-published the first truly accessible guide to Tarot fortunetelling, *The Tarot Revealed*, which opened the door later that decade to an ongoing vogue in Tarot guides and mass-market occult paperbacks.

The Tarot decks that we derive from the early Renaissance—and those produced generations later in Marseille in southern France, which became the center of Tarot production—are illustrated to a much lesser degree than the decks that we know today. The major trumps themselves are illustrated, but the court cards and the so-called minor trumps are usually illustrated only by symbols—of coins, of wands— not of the characters that have become familiar to us. That was largely Smith's innovation. There were, of course, divinatory decks and images produced centuries earlier, particularly in the late 1700s by the cartomancer Jean-Baptiste Alliette (1738–1791), but no deck or series of images approached the vividness, human texture, and the layers of meaning that Smith brought to her design in the early twentieth century. Hence, Smith's deck has become the template for most of modern Tarot.

*   *   *

Spiritual traditions necessarily undergo changes. Because something is old does not make it valid; because something is new or novel does not make it irrelevant. The story of religion is the story of changes, combinations, and syncretism. We practice all of these things to seek meaning in our world. Now, the history of Tarot is fraught with certain complexities and controversies. There are notions, most of them historically fanciful, that the images of Tarot specifically extend back to Ancient Egypt and represent a hidden primeval book of mystery wisdom; some believe that if you were isolated on a desert island somewhere and possessed only the Tarot deck, somehow all wisdom would become available to you. That general notion got promulgated by occultists of the late 1700s and mid-1800s. Historically speaking, the earliest permutations of Tarot and the earliest uses of Tarot as a card deck was as a game in the early Renaissance era. But I want to be very careful when I'm saying that *because the concept of a game was much weightier and more richly conceived* than what we mean when we use the term "game" today. When we talk about a game today, we're often talking about something that's entertainment or escapism. But for people who lived in the Middle Ages, the Medieval Era, and the Renaissance—when even the wealthy possessed relatively few material objects—everything had a kind of *household sacredness*; every book, every image, every tapestry, and, yes, every game was ceremonial, was rich with symbol and meaning.

And, in fact, the earliest symbols of Tarot, some of which I was referencing before, are images that were drawn not only from the deepest recesses of human imagination, and were influenced not only by some of the primeval archetypes that entered the psyche by way of Hermeticism, but there also existed images, *closest in nature and antecedent to Tarot, that populated the passion plays, carnivals, and stained-glass windows of the Middle Ages.* These images had a *particular* hold on the psyches of men and women of the Middle Ages, to whom carnivals and passion plays were, again, not mere entertainments or diversions, but conveyers of meaning and religious truth.

Hence, to say that something began as a game, or as a *play* (a related term), is not to say that that's *all* it was in our modern colloquial sense. The Tarot also contains a *mystical allegory*, through which we assemble stories about ourselves, our relationships, our inner lives, and the surrounding world. Its images are a kind of archetypal DNA code of human psychology. In that vein, Tarot can be compared with the ancient Chinese oracle the *I Ching*, which itself is a pictogrammatic alphabet of binary code consisting of broken and unbroken lines—not dissimilar to the binary code that computer programmers use today and from which we create vast, multi-dimensional functions, images, and meanings. That's what Tarot is to our psyche.

And there's another dimension to Tarot, as well, which is its *divinatory dimension*. Now, there were certain divinatory uses of Tarot during the Renaissance. Again, everything—every household object, no matter how domestic it seemed—had multiple layers of meaning and possessed a kind of sacredness to the individual. But it was not until the 1780s in France that Tarot began to take on its expressly occult and divinatory quality. In 1781, French nobleman and historian Court de Gébelin (1725–1784) produced an installment of his series of books called *Le Monde primitif, The Primitive World*, or *The Ancient World*, which included an occult retelling of Tarot's history. Court de Gébelin first drew the connection between Tarot and Ancient Egypt. About nine years later, an antiquary and occultist who went by the single name Etteilla (the not-terribly imaginative backward spelling of the surname of Jean-Baptiste Alliette) embraced the Egyptian connection and designed the first Tarot deck used expressly for divination. This effort was expanded on by later writers, including the highly influential Éliphas Lévi, whose 1854 book, *The Doctrine and Ritual of High Magic,* which I referenced in the previous chapter, drew a connection between Tarot and the zodiac, the Hebrew alphabet, and various aspects of Kabbalah, including the *sefirot* or spheres that appear on the Tree of Life.

These were modern innovations. That does not mean that you and I cannot find meaning and validity

within them. But I do believe that any student of esoteric studies, in order to be a real student, must have
some sense of the lineage at our backs. This is vital
to understanding and selecting among ideas. Because
sometimes a widely accepted reference originates
from a fanciful source, like the work of Court de Gébelin, and it gets repeated by rote, as if it's just a matter of
fact. Real history is more complex. But, again, because
we can outline the historicism of Tarot, I do not feel
that does anything to *deny* the mystical allegory of
the cards and the divinatory potentials found within
them. On that note, I have personally performed *hundreds upon hundreds* of card readings—I've done them
on campus at the Philosophical Research Society at
times—and I have found, as many others have found,
that there can appear a powerful symmetry and foresightful quality to the card readings, the question of
which I now consider.

I first want to describe the method of reading that I
personally use and then offer a theory as to what, if
anything, is going on—whether there is any defensibly
foresightful property to the Tarot cards.

Now, the method of reading that I use is very simple. I learned it from an outstanding historian and
artist of Tarot named Robert M. Place. I strongly recommend, as supplemental reading to Manly Hall's
chapter, Place's 2005 book, *The Tarot*. The method that
Robert taught me, and that I have used for years, is

a three-card spread in which I look for a storyline. Hence, if I'm reading for a third party, I will shuffle the deck thoroughly, and I will ask that third party to present a question to me. Or, if he or she doesn't have a specific question, a general reading may be in order. After shuffling, I spread the cards face down in front of me in a half-moon or arc. Then by some process that I cannot rationally describe to you (we'll call it intuition) I select and overturn three cards in a row.

In my style of reading, also influenced by Place, I do not use reversed cards. I treat every card as if it is right-side up; if a card is reversed, I turn it over. My reason is that I think reversed cards are basically a modern artifice. Using Tarot for divinatory purposes is in itself a modern operation—at least as currently practiced in our world—and the notion that you must work with reversed cards is a wrinkle that I don't think is really necessary to gleaning messages from the deck. Given that there are 78 cards in the deck— and given that you can assemble them into what approaches a near-infinite number of variations—I don't think that in order to derive multiple layers of meaning it's necessary to use reversed cards. I also think that reversed cards encourage needless anxiety for the subject, including yourself. If, say, the Lovers card comes up reversed, we're apt to think that that card is some kind of a curse rather than a blessing. I think it's cause for too much needless anxiety. If the cards have a "message" for us, there are certainly

enough images with intriguing meaning—some beneficent, some cautionary, some joyous, some tragic—
that any pertinent point can come through without
necessarily needing to render things more complex or
fraught with fear.

After selecting three cards face up, I then look for
a kind of storyline, almost as if I am reading a comic
strip. I might read from my right to left; I might read
from my left to right; or I might use a method that I
call "wings," in which the cards on the left and right
may be seen to impact or reflect the card in the middle. Based on what I'm able to discern, whether I am
discovering a storyline or if I am finding the images
on the right and the left relate to the card in the middle, I might be able to gain some insight into a certain
situation. For example, let's imagine that I am doing a
reading for you and I pick these three cards from the
Smith-Waite deck: the Knight of Wands; the Seven of
Swords; and the Devil. I might suggest that you, the
present person in the reading, are like the Knight of
Wands, who's rushing bravely into a situation. And
yet there's some kind of deception going on in the situation, as reflected by the Seven of Swords; someone
near you is not behaving in line with your standards
and expectations. The result being that, while there is
union, it's union under the sign of the Devil, as it is
understood by the designers of this deck. And I will
honor their understanding, which may be different
from my own. In this image, the man and woman

at the feet of the Devil are bound together but are bound in some lower form of interaction. Yet if you look closely Smith's illustration—she always included different layers of meaning—the chains around the necks of the man and the woman hang loosely: they can easily be removed.

Now, is there any reason to believe that *any* meaning at all can be derived from this? Is it a Rorschach? Is it randomness? Is it confirmation bias? (One of the most overused concepts in social science—it essentially means prejudice but colloquially it is often used as a rhetorical device to invalidate beliefs, except the user's own.) Well, my personal takeaway is that there is something foresightful in the cards. Which begs the question: *Why*? *Why* should anything be happening at all? Here's one theory: psychologist Carl Jung (1875–1961) and his students worked with the ancient pictogrammatic device known as the *I Ching* or Book of Changes. As alluded earlier, the *I Ching* is a primeval symbolic alphabet which for millennia has been used for divinatory purposes. Each of the 64 symbols or hexagrams of the *I Ching* consists of six lines. The six lines may be variously broken (yin) or unbroken (yang), like a binary code. The querent, using various methods—sometimes a toss of sticks or coins—arrives at a hexagram intended to reveal a given situation. Each hexagram has a particular meaning—like a Tarot card, hieroglyph, or character from Hebrew. Each meaning is also inherently changing and in motion; depending on your throw, your hexagram may have one or more "changing" lines. Each hexagram correlates to an environmental or psychological situation, an animal, or a particular kind of individual; hence, you can decipher a kind of story within it. This is something to which Jung dedicated himself for many years; he and his students conducted thousands of readings and came to feel that there was a certain accuracy there—and that, as a revelatory tool, the *I Ching* itself possessed a kind of personality, a character of its own, including a wry sense of humor.

I've come to feel similarly about Tarot. Now, some of Jung's students theorized the following, and I'm adding some of my own language and interpretation to what they observed: We human beings may be said to occupy an infinitude of events; it can be argued that everything is going on at once; everything is in a state of superposition, to use a term from quantum physics. It can be further argued that linear time itself is illusory—a much bigger topic, which I address in my book, *The Miracle Club*; indeed, I think it's almost impossible for us to justify linear time as anything other than illusory, when Einstein's theories alone demonstrate that time is bendable: if you are on earth and a colleague is on a spaceship traveling at near light speed, time—the actual experience of time—*will move slower* for your spaceship-bound colleague than it will for you. So, we see from the theories of Einstein—as we see from different phenomena within the particle lab, where objects are in superposition, or in an infinitude of positions, until someone takes a measurement—that *we are dealing with a reality of infinite possibilities and of infinitely occurring events.*

It may be that linearity itself is a very necessary illusion that helps us five-sensory beings organize and navigate life—but linearity is not the real story; it's not what's going on. Our sensory existence is coarse and limited. When we can experience something beyond the ordinary senses, something extrasensory, we may be, in a sense, gleaning an experience of actual serial worlds or infinities of events and possibilities within which we live and function, and which we *translate* into linear time through perspective.

All of these fields and theories—time-space relativity; quantum theory; psychical research; experiments into precognition; theories of multiple dimensions or serial worlds—point us toward the suggestion that the conventional reality we perceive through our senses is not actual. We live amid serial events. Hence, it is possible that every moment in perception is like a kind of snapshot, in which everything that's going on can be detected within that single instant. And it's possible that a storytelling or pictogrammatic device, like the *I Ching* or Tarot, could function like a photograph of a moment captured or localized. A "random" throw or selection could reflect or carry the timestamp of whatever is going on, like a measurement. Or the throw itself may be an act of selection—it may produce the events that are now expected or foreseen. As such, this pictogrammatic photograph, with its suggestive imagery, captures a slice of possibility; it conveys a nonlinear composite; we glean a sense of past, present, future. At least based on the trajectory of current events, we could be viewing a snapshot of possibilities.

That may be one reason why methods like Tarot and *I Ching* seem to work. That's just a theory; I also depend upon personal testimony from myself and from others to determine whether there is some revelatory quality to the cards. It has proven a very rich experiment for me; and if this is of any interest to you, it's an experiment that I encourage you to join in. My own deck of choice, as I said, is the Smith-Waite deck, but there are vast numbers of decks that you can choose from. And, at the very least, you'll be delving into a kind of personal adventure and a journey into images that have populated the psyches of men and women from the earliest stages of human expression up through the twenty-first century.

I happen to be wearing a t-shirt at the moment that has the image of Batman. What is Batman, other than a kind of archetypal image—an avenging angel? If you were to show the image of Batman to anybody, anywhere in the world, almost from any time or culture, they probably would have some similar association. They might see the figure as some sort of retributive spirit—not quite good, not quite bad, and very powerful. We're surrounded by and we *think* in terms of archetypal images; so I believe there are wonderful psychological discoveries to be found in Tarot, on whatever terms you view it or however you look at it.

Tarot has proven remarkably enduring. Both Tarot and astrology are probably the two most lasting and popular occult arts in the modern world. There are other magickal arts that have become hugely popular today. In the *Secret Teachings*, Manly writes about the experiments of the alchemists, whose interest was not necessarily in distilling lead or coarse matter into gold, but also in refining the psyche into a kind of gold. Alchemists and magicians were aided by rites and rituals that we sometimes call "ceremonial magick." The spelling of "magick" with a "k," as I often practice in this book, is derived from early modern English; British occultist Aleister Crowley (1875–1947) popularized its use to distinguish occultic magick from stage magic, a practice I honor.

Manly, in *The Secret Teachings of All Ages*, talks about the ceremonial operations of the medieval and Renaissance-era magicians, including the signs, sigils, and spell work that populated the books of figures like Paracelsus (1493/1494–1541), Cornelius Agrippa (1486–1535), Ramon Llull (1232–1316), and many other figures who left behind tantalizing works of occult experimentation. One of the most popular forms of magick practiced in our era is what is called "chaos magick." The ritual at the heart of chaos magick is sigil work, a practice pioneered by the visionary twentieth-century artist Austin Osman Spare (1886–1956).

Spare's formula, which many people experiment with today, involves writing out a simple declarative sentence of what you want; then using a process to eliminate letters (such as crossing out repeating letters); and finally assembling the remaining characters into an abstract symbol or sigil—one that is not recognizable. This symbol comes to *represent* your desire itself. Not thinking of the desire but meditating on the symbol, you bring yourself to sexual climax or some other kind of ecstatic state, as you're focusing on the symbol—thus charging the symbol with some kind of personal or sexual energy. The point is to climax over the symbol and then forget *all* about it, thus allowing the symbol to penetrate the extra-rational and causative faculties of your subconscious. In this way, the symbol is said to manifest into the world.

One of the principles of chaos magick is that you're supposed to use that ceremony to extinguish and thus *satisfy* your own desire for the wished-for thing, so that you're no longer in a state of wanting, you're no longer in a state of hoping, you're no longer in a state of expecting, but you're in a state of *satisfaction*.

The ritual and the sigil itself become a proxy for that which is desired. And the climax or the ecstasy, with which you "charge" the symbol, sends your thought processes or mental energy, so to speak, out into the world and helps establish not that which you want but that which already *is*. The ceremony itself is supposed to instill a sense of receiving and satisfaction so that you're no longer walking around in this unfulfilled state of *wishing*.

This is not entirely dissimilar from the form of magick that sometimes goes under the term New Thought. One of the figures that I greatly admire in that realm is the British-Barbadian mystic Neville Goddard (1905–1972), who I have tattooed on my left arm with the maxim, "Live from the End." Neville's teaching, to a certain degree, comports with chaos magick. He, too, believed that you should not walk around in a state of *hoping* for things, but rather you should try to *feel* as though you've already received that which you desire—"live from the end"—and it will enter your life, and for that specific reason: an assumption, though false, eventually concretizes into fact. This is not only a psychological law, but a metaphysical law.

Neville taught that *your imagination is God.* And that every time you encounter references to God in the Old or New Testament you are encountering a *symbolical representation of your imagination,* which is the Creator clothed in human flesh. The purpose of your existence, Neville taught, is to realize this causative power that exists within you. Desire is sacred, he taught; desire is the voice of God speaking to you, because your imagination *is* God, and that which you desire is prophecy. Your desire is like the burning bush speaking to you—don't turn away from it; go *towards* it.

All that is—all of the world, everything that you experience—is your own emotionalized thoughts and mental pictures pushed out into reality, And he meant that in the most literal sense. When he calls your imagination God, he is not speaking metaphorically; he's speaking literally. And Neville taught that all of Scripture is a psychological blueprint for human development; when Christ goes through the crucifixion, he's actually coming into a full realization of his divine nature—an opening that awaits you and every man and woman.

If you follow the implications of this, the very words that you are reading right now are *your* words; the very ideas that I'm describing are *your* ideas; I am a figment of your imagination—there is no Mitch writing; there's only *you*, God the Creator. I am the figment of *your* thoughts—perhaps because you were ready at just this moment in your development to receive this message.

For many reasons that I won't get into in this writing—there are many other places where I speak and write about Neville—I believe that Neville, who died in 1972, provided the greatest mystical analog to the ideas found in quantum theory. And for that reason, among others, Neville has made deep inroads into popular recognition. His readership is rapidly expanding today. When I first wrote about Neville in

2005 he was considered obscure. Today he is becoming perhaps the best-known figure in New Thought tradition.

I should note that his teaching is not *exactly* the same as chaos magick (or as traditional New Thought for that matter) but it comports with key elements of chaos magick—particularly the principle of feeling *satisfied* that you have already attained what you wish. That satisfaction itself serves as an engine of creation; the world must eventually bend to perception. "As above, so below."

So many magical ideas and philosophies resonate in old and new forms from the foundations of what Manly P. Hall explores in *The Secret Teachings of All Ages*. I've mentioned a wide range of philosophies, practices, figures, and thought systems. And there are still others that we work with today, such as channeling, energy healing, various forms of divination, prayer, and body-mind modalities. All of these things are a kind of offspring, are children of the magnificent family tree of symbols, esoteric teachings, mystical religious encounters, and so much more that Manly writes about in *The Secret Teachings of All Ages*.

As I said earlier in this guide, the presiding deity of our study is Ganesha, the deity who lowers barriers. My deepest wish is that this twelve-part program has lowered barriers for you—has made you feel closer to this magisterial work, *The Secret Teachings of All Ages*;

has helped you find intersections between some of the ideas and traditions written about in Manly's book and practical things that you work with in your own day-to-day experience. And my further wish is that what we have covered across these twelve lessons will return you to the *Secret Teachings* with renewed vigor; and in returning to this book, or picking it up for the first time, you will find within its pages your greatest personal discovery, which is the nature of yourself.

APPENDIX A

─── ⁊ ℮ ───

Bringing the "Secret Teachings" Into the Twenty-First Century

BY MITCH HOROWITZ

The following article appeared in Fall 2003 in Lapis *magazine.*

In the past century, religion and academia have been on uneasy terms—to put it mildly. The philosopher Jacob Needleman once wryly noted that when he was coming up through university, one could study myth, religion, and symbol—but "any possibility that the ideas in religion were true was brushed aside."

Even one of the twentieth century's most influential studies of symbolist religions and tradition, *The Golden Bough*, disparaged the meaning of its own subject matter: "In short, magic is a spurious system of natural law as well as a fallacious guide of conduct; it is a false science as well as an abortive art."

It was in this atmosphere that a young investment banker named Manly P. Hall made a startling departure from the traditional scholarship of his day. In

1928—at the unthinkably young age of 27—Hall privately published one of the most reverent and thorough works ever to catalogue the esoteric wisdom of antiquity: *The Secret Teachings of All Ages*. Hall's *Secret Teachings* became a one-of-a-kind codex to the ancient occult and esoteric traditions of the world. Its hundreds of entries shone a rare light on some of the most fascinating and closely held aspects of myth, religion, and philosophy. Seventy-five years after its initial publication, the book's range of material remains astounding: Pythagorean mathematics; alchemical formulae; Hermetic doctrine; the workings of Kabbalah; the geometry of Ancient Egypt; the Native American myths; the uses of cryptograms; an analysis of the Tarot; the symbols of Rosicrucianism; the esotericism of the Shakespearean dramas—these are just a few of Hall's topics.

Hall wrote in an era immediately preceding the Great Depression. He described the "outstanding event" of his Wall Street career as "witnessing a man depressed over investment losses take his life." One could imagine the young Hall worrying whether the fading Gilded Age-frenzy that gripped our culture would spell ultimate decline for our fluency in myth, symbol, and the love of learning that characterized the voices and figures who populate his volume. Where, the young man wondered, were we headed?

"With very few exceptions," he wrote, "modern authorities downgraded all systems of idealistic philosophy and the deeper aspects of comparative religion. Translations of classical authors could differ greatly, but in most cases the noblest thoughts were eliminated or denigrated ... and scholarship was based largely upon the acceptance of a sterile materialism."

To signal how his approach would differ from the prevailing mood, Hall quoted his philosophic hero, Francis Bacon, early in the book: "A little philosophy inclineth man's mind to atheism; but depth in philosophy bringeth men's minds about to religion."

A CLASSIC, OLD AND NEW

In 1934, Hall founded the Philosophical Research Society in Los Angeles, which has published sumptuous, coffee-table sized editions of his volume ever since. But many readers have also found the book expensive, sometimes cumbersome in size, and often difficult to read on account of small typefaces and occasionally arcane fonts and page design. In an historic first in spiritual publishing, my colleagues and I at Tarcher/Penguin partnered with PRS to produce a new "reader's edition" of *The Secret Teachings of All Ages*. Available in Fall 2003, this reset, reformatted, compact-sized, and affordably priced trade paperback made the *Secret Teachings* available to a large general audience for the first time.

Packaging a new edition of the *Secret Teachings* is like trying to sculpt a rare and precious stone—one serious slip, and its splendor and luminescence are lost. What are the demands of preparing the first mass edition of a work that has previously been the closely held—if deeply influential—treasure of a relative handful among the reading public?

BACK TO THE READING ROOM

While the Canadian-born Hall lived and worked in Los Angeles for much of his adult life, he actually toiled over the *Secret Teachings* in perhaps the greatest citadel to public education our nation has: The beaux-arts Reading Room of the New York Public Library. Entering this magnificent, cavernous space today, it is not difficult to picture the large-framed, young Manly P. Hall surrounded by books of myth and symbol at one of the room's huge oaken tables. Like a monk of the Middle Ages, Hall copiously, almost superhumanly, pored over hundreds of the great works of antiquity, distilling their esoteric lore into his volume. The scale of his bibliography is extraordinary. Its nearly 1,000 entries range from the core works of Plato, Aristotle, and Augustine, to translations of the Gnostic, Nicene, and Hermetic literature, to the writings of Paracelsus, Ptolemy, Bacon, Basil Valentine, and Cornelius Agrippa, to works of every variety on the ancient and esoteric philosophies—religious, mythic, or metaphysical—that have expressed themselves in symbol or ceremony.

In creating his record of the ancient mysteries, Hall also meticulously selected drawings—more than

200 of them—illustrating the meaning and ideas embedded within man's oldest symbols and figures. He worked closely with artist J. Augustus Knapp who created an additional 54 color paintings boldly recreating scenes from the past whose shape we can only speculate upon at the outer reaches of our learning. To publish the new, reader-friendly version of the *Secret Teachings* that we had in mind, it would be necessary to abridge Hall's selected illustrations. Could this be done without detracting from the book's majesty?

This task was too important to be performed without the greatest intimacy with the text. In what seemed akin to reading the Encyclopedia Britannica of the esoteric, I returned to Hall's old haunt: the cathedral-sized Reading Room of the New York Public Library and, seated day upon day in one of its hundreds of wooden chairs, pored over every word, caption, index note, and bibliographic entry in the great work. Which illustrations were imperative and which could be sacrificed? The key was to retain those illustrations—eventually about 125 in all—that worked in concert with—and, hence, were necessary to understanding—the ideas in the text. Making these choices was slightly eased by the knowledge that PRS would continue to publish its own complete edition of the *Secret Teachings*, so that no visual matter would be lost to time.

Above all, however, I set forth the principle that we would not abridge the narrative itself. The full text of the *Secret Teachings* appears in the "reader's edition"—including Hall's original, and extraordinarily detailed, index and bibliography. All that is missing is one of several short prefaces, which remains available in the PRS edition.

BRINGING THE MOUNTAIN TO MOHAMMAD

Perhaps the greatest of challenges was how to reset and reformat the text itself. The original edition is composed of varying columns, captions, and inset text—sometimes as jarring to the Western eye as a page of Babylonian Talmud. In its original trim size, the book's dimensions are unusually large: 12 x 18 inches. It has color plates, foldouts, and an overlay. The small size of its text is sometimes a strain on the eye. Our "Reader's Edition" demanded a typestyle, format, and layout that was, well, readable—yet loyal to the vibration of the original work. This would be no simple task: Until today, none of Hall's 1928 text has been available electronically; PRS, in its many reprints over the years, has used the original plates on which the book is based. In the information age, we are all-too-accustomed to text that can be easily manipulated. The *Secret Teachings* would give itself over with no such ease.

At expenses that ran into many thousands of dollars, we delivered an edition of the book to NK Graphics in New Hampshire, which was capable of scanning text. The book, however, was too large for their scanner beds, requiring the material at the bottom of its pages to be hand-typed. Then the scanned data was submitted to a computer program that—imperfectly—recognizes the symbols of letters and transforms the material into a new manuscript. Alas, such methods are never quite as advanced as we believe them to be, and a professional proofreader had to read the entire text of the *Secret Teachings* against the scanned material to ensure accuracy. Nor could the scanning technology pick up the many Greek and Hebrew characters spread throughout the book; this required us to insert each such character as an original piece of art.

In April 2003, an entirely new manuscript of more than 1,400 pages landed on my desk in a pile about 8-inches high—as though it had newly rolled off of Hall's Edwardian-era typewriter. It was rather shocking to look at a fresh manuscript of a book that has stood largely unaltered for a lifetime. The task, however, was *not* to do something new with it—it was to *keep* something new from being done. We had to reset, reformat, and redesign the text so that it could be published in a standard size, at a standard price—but without "correcting" it. I implored our copyediting and production staff to treat this like an ancient papyrus—arcane spellings, references, and language were to be left absolutely untouched. (For instance, Hall spells Shakespeare as "Shakspere," following the only known signatures in the Bard's own hand.) More than a few times I had to intercede to keep modern forms and styles of usage from disrupting the earlier perfection of Hall's work.

Meanwhile, our design staff set about crafting a page design that would echo the hallowed feel of the original, while framing the text and illustrations within the trim size of a slightly larger-than-normal trade paperback. The words of this article cannot fully capture their success. My colleagues created a page design of classic beauty—one that set the columns in an imposing but inviting way, and that allowed ample space for the crucial illustrations to breathe, yet to be sized in such a manner that the book would be newly wieldy and manageable. When I saw how the text would appear on the printed page, I knew we were very close to success.

An eleventh-hour challenge emerged concerning Hall's extensive index—itself a document of more than 6,700 entries. While we had assumed that a computerized word-search program would be sufficient to recalibrate Hall's index to the newly numbered pages, again we discovered the *Secret Teachings* would not give itself over so easily. In a feature of the book that astounded the professional typesetters, proofreaders, and indexers working on the volume, they discovered that Hall had not necessarily organized his index by terms alone, but often by concept. Hence, the word "sun" in the index might correspond to the term "orb of the day" in the text. So, the indexer herself had to become fully versed in the narrative before the newly formatted index could be complete.

There were other considerations: The original edition uses Roman numerals throughout for page numbers. Also, the chapters themselves were unnumbered. We decided to use easier-to-follow Arabic, or contemporary, numerals to number the pages, while the chapters are newly numbered according to Roman style.

These and other measures drew us closer to publication. We worked tirelessly to hold our price down, so that the "reader's edition" could be widely available. Obadiah Harris, the president of PRS today, pitched in to help, as well—and, with meticulous budgeting and cooperation on royalty rates and other matters, we managed to take a book that had been priced at $54.95 in its least-expensive edition, and make it available at $24.95. This, it seemed, was the final step we needed to make this new edition a reality.

A WORK ENDURING, A WORK REBORN

Readers who discover *The Secret Teachings of All Ages* for the first time today will encounter a book probably unlike any they have seen before. The accomplishment of the *Secret Teachings*, in part, is this: It may be the only such compendium of the last several hundred years that takes the world of myth and symbol on its own terms.

Books such as *The Golden Bough* viewed the ancient past as we would look at items in a museum: interesting and worthy of study, even important, but never broaching the idea that things we read about in the annals of antiquity could be true for us today—true, if not in fact, than, more importantly, in what they whisper about the workings of the cosmos and man's place within it.

We read Thucydides today and marvel at the Greeks' gifts for oration, strategy, historiography, and at the drama of human events that marked the ancient world. How easy it is, though, to simply breeze past those passages in which great statesmen traveled to Delphi to consult the oracle. Contemporary readers rarely pause to notice such events—nor are they encouraged to—as if such episodes can be understood simply as interludes between the true lessons of the work.

For Manly Hall, however, there was no such casual bypassing. One can read his masterly twelfth chapter, "Wonders of Antiquity," and learn something about what was experienced—at least so far as we can venture—in the consultation of an oracle.*

Hall realized, perhaps more deeply than any other scholar of his time, that the ancients possessed extraordinary powers of observation—ways of under-

---

* From my *Occult America*: "Up through the late twentieth century, most classical scholars would have considered Hall's descriptions of oracular rites at Delphi as near fairytale, with their portraits of soldiers and statesmen visiting an intoxicated trance medium seated on a tripodlike throne above a smoky crevice in a cave. Yet Hall's portrayal, based on esoteric source literature, has since been validated by early-twenty-first-century geological and archaeological finds at Delphi."

standing the correspondences between the outer natural world and man's inner state—that were equally potent, and equally worthy of study, as their gifts for calendars, architecture, reason, and agriculture.

Hall would observe the workings of esoteric cultures with the same passion and awe that one finds in historians who were a living part of the history they wrote about. In the darkening night of the decayed Mayan empire, the late-eighteenth century Mayan historian known as Chilam Balam of Chumayel, looked at the culture that had very nearly slipped away—at its calendars, its mathematical skills, its astrology, and lamented:

> *They knew how to count time,*
> *Even within themselves.*
> *The moon, the wind, the year, the day,*
> *They all move, but also pass on.*
> *All blood reaches its place of rest,*
> *As all power reaches its throne . . .*

This, in a sense, is the universal voice that finds its way into each century to tell of the wonders of the past. It found its way to the twentieth—and now the twenty-first—century through Manly P. Hall. His is the voice that runs like a luminescent thread through history telling the stories of those who have passed, not as a distant judge, but as a lover of the knowledge embodied in the ancient ways.

SOURCES QUOTED IN THIS ARTICLE

The Golden Bough by James Frazer; Penguin Twentieth-Century Classics; 1999; original abridgement published 1922.

The Secret Teachings of All Ages: Reader's Edition by Manly P. Hall; Tarcher/Penguin; 2003; Philosophical Research Society; 1928.

The Maya World by Demetrio Sodi Morales; Minutiae Mexicano; 1976.

Jacob Needleman, lecture, Atlantic University, May 31st, 2002.

APPENDIX B

_____ ๑ ๑ _____

Secret Teachings Reborn: *The Mysterious Life of Manly P. Hall*

BY MITCH HOROWITZ

The following article appeared in the May-June 2006 issue of New Dawn *magazine.*

The late-nineteenth and early-twentieth centuries saw an explosion of spiritual teachers and impresarios dealing in "secret wisdom." Their ranks included hacks and frauds—as well as more than a few genuine scholars of esoteric traditions. Most have vanished from memory, their writings a historical footnote.

There exists one distinct figure, though, whose movement and teachings not only survived his passing but are even experiencing a revival in our day. His name is Manly P. Hall. While few academicians will ever know of him, Hall was among the twentieth century's—and perhaps any century's—most commanding and unusual scholars of esoteric and mythological lore. Yet the source of his knowledge and the extent of his virtuosity can justly be called a mystery.

While working as a clerk at a Wall Street banking firm—the "outstanding event" of which involved "witnessing a man depressed over investment losses take his life"—the 27-year-old Hall self-published one of the most complex and thoroughgoing works ever to catalogue the esoteric wisdom of antiquity, *The Secret Teachings of All Ages*. Hall's *Secret Teachings* is almost impossible to classify. Written and compiled on an Alexandrian scale, its hundreds of entries shine a rare light on some of the most fascinating and little-understood aspects of myth, religion, and philosophy.

Today, more than seventy-five years after its initial publication, the book's range of material astonishes: Pythagorean mathematics; alchemical formulae; Hermetic doctrine; the workings of Kabbalah; the geometry of Ancient Egypt; the Native American myths; the uses of cryptograms; an analysis of the Tarot; the symbols of Rosicrucianism; the esotericism of the Shakespearean dramas—these are just a few of Hall's topics. Yet his background betrays little clue to his virtuosity.

A MAN UNKNOWN

Hall was born in Peterborough, Ontario, in 1901 to parents who would shortly divorce, leaving the young Manly in the care of a grandmother who raised him in Sioux Falls, South Dakota. He had little formal schooling. But there was a spark of some indefinable brilliance in the young man, which his grandmother tried to nurture in trips to museums in Chicago and New York.

Tragedy struck early, when his grandmother died when he was 16. Afterward, a self-styled Rosicrucian community in California took him in. At age 19, suspicious of the community's claims to ancient wisdom, Manly moved on his own to Los Angeles where he began a precocious career in public speaking—first giving an address on reincarnation in a small room above a bank in Santa Monica, and soon rising to the rank of minister at a liberal evangelical congregation called the Church of the People.

Word spread of the boy wonder's mastery of arcane and metaphysical subject matter. He attracted benefactors and eventually began traveling the world in search of hidden wisdom. Yet Hall's early letters from Japan, Egypt, China, and India are, in many respects, fairly ordinary: They contain little of the eye-opening detail or wonder of discovery that one finds in the writings of other early twentieth-century seekers encountering the East for the first time. More often they read like prosaic, if somewhat sensitive, linear travelogues of their day.

Like a bolt from the blue, however, one is astounded to discover a short work of immense power from the young Hall—a book that seems to prefigure that which would come. In 1922, at the age of 21, Hall wrote a luminescent gem on the mystery schools of antiquity, *Initiates of the Flame*. Though brief, one sees in it the outline of what would become *The Secret Teachings of All Ages*. On its frontispiece, *Initiates of the Flame* boldly announces: "He who lives the Life shall know the Doctrine."

The short book goes on to expound passionately and in detail on Egyptian rites, Arthurian myths, and the secrets of alchemy, among other subjects. Feeling the power and ease in its pages, the reader can almost sense the seeds of greatness that were beginning to take hold in Hall's grasp of esoteric subjects.

THE SECRET TEACHINGS BORN

Hall soon returned to America, where he tried his hand at banking—though he found his true path in the beaux arts Reading Room of the New York Public Library. Entering this cavernous space today, it is not difficult to picture the large-framed, young Manly P. Hall surrounded by books of myth and symbol at one of the room's huge oaken tables. Like a monk of the Middle Ages, Hall copiously, almost superhumanly, pored over hundreds of the great works of antiquity, distilling their esoteric lore into his volume.

By the age of 27, having pre-sold subscriptions for nearly 1,000 copies (and printing 1,200 more), Hall published what would become known as "The Great Book"—and it has never gone out of print since.

Indeed, Hall is an exception to most of his contemporaries as someone whose work is actually building in influence today. In its day, the *Secret Teachings* was expensive, hefty, and cumbersome. As a result, the book spent much of its existence as an underground classic. In late 2003, however, the *Secret Teachings* found new life in a reset and redesigned "reader's edition," which has sold a remarkable 40,000 copies in less than three years. A little-known 1929 companion volume by Hall, called *Lectures on Ancient Philosophy*, has also been recently reissued.

After publishing his magnum opus, Hall opened a campus in 1934 in the Griffith Park neighborhood of Los Angeles called the Philosophical Research Society (PRS), where he spent the rest of his life teaching, writing, and amassing a remarkable library of esoterica. A self-contained property designed in a pastiche of Mayan, Egyptian, and art deco styles, PRS remains a popular destination for LA's spiritually curious.

Following Hall's death in 1990, PRS barely survived simultaneous legal battles—one with Hall's widow, who claimed the group owed her money, and another with a bizarre father-son team of con artists who, in the estimation of a civil court judge, had befriended an ailing, octogenarian Hall to pilfer his assets. The Los Angeles Police Department considered Hall's death sufficiently suspicious to keep it under investigation for several years.

SECRET WISDOM, PRACTICAL WISDOM

For all his literary output, Hall revealed little about his private life. His most lasting record is a frequently trite, unrevealing childhood memoir called *Growing Up with Grandmother* (in which he refers to his guardian as "Mrs. Arthur Whitney Palmer"). As an adult, Hall's close relations were few. A first marriage ended in his wife's suicide and he remarried well into middle age in a union some surmise was never consummated.

Hence, when Hall disclosed something about his background, it was purposeful. He wrote this in a PRS newsletter in 1959: "As a result of a confused and insecure childhood, it was necessary for me to formulate a personal philosophy with which to handle immediate situations."

Here was someone with a tremendous interest in the arcane philosophies of the world, in the occult and metaphysical philosophies, but he wasn't fixated on immortality, or a will to power, or on discovering keys that unlock the universe. Rather, he was focused on harnessing inner truths in a very practical way. How, he wondered, could such ideas lend clarity to daily life?

We'll take a byroad that steers us in another direction before returning to this point. Our byroad involves one of the most famous novels in history, Mary Shelley's *Frankenstein*. The work has many facets, among them a portrait—not sympathetic, but not as unsympathetic as one might suppose—of the European occult in the Enlightenment era. The portrait comes in the character of a young Victor Frankenstein, a budding scientist torn between the occult teachings that drew him to science as a child and the prevailing rationalism of his teachers. Victor confides his interest in the great alchemists and occult philosophers, such as the Renaissance-era magus Cornelius Agrippa, but his professors dismiss him with complete condescension.

One day in his room, Victor ponders the unbridgeable gap between his magickal visions and the scholasticism of his peers:

> I had a contempt for the uses of modern natural philosophy. It was very different when the masters of science sought immortality and power; such views, although futile, were grand; but now the scene was changed. The ambition of the inquirer seemed to limit itself to the annihilation of those visions on which my interest in science was chiefly founded. I was required to exchange chimeras of boundless grandeur for realities of little worth.

In a sense, Victor spoke for generations of occultists when describing his ideal of boundless grandeur, immortality, power, and visions. (And who wouldn't sympathize with the rebellious young Victor—whose dreams and ambitions, while hopeless, exist on a grand scale—versus the certainties of his crusty professors?)

An occult scholar born at the cusp of the twentieth century, Manly P. Hall signaled a different kind of ideal. Hall told of "a personal philosophy with which to handle immediate situations." After Hall's death, a reporter in the *Los Angeles Times* noted, "Followers say he believed in reincarnation and in a mixture of the Golden Rule and living in moderation."

For Hall, the very act of writing *The Secret Teachings of All Ages* was an attempt at formulating an ethical response to the age he lived in. While the book is at times speculative and some of its sources are limited by the constraints of their era, it is the only codex to esoteric ideas that treats its subject with total seriousness. Contemporaneous works, such as *The Golden Bough*, regarded indigenous religious traditions as superstition—interesting museum pieces worthy of anthropological study but of no direct relevance to our current lives. Hall, on the other hand, felt himself on a mission to re-establish a connection to the mystery traditions at a time when America, as he saw it, had given itself over to the Jazz-Age materialism he witnessed at his banking job.

"After I thought the matter over," he wrote a few years before his death, "it seemed necessary to establish some kind of firm ground upon which personal idealism could mingle its hopes and aspirations with the wisdom of the ages."

In this sense, the prodigious scholar achieved more than a cataloging of esoteric truths. He turned the study of occult ideas into an ethical cause.

INDEX

ABOUT MANLY P. HALL

_⸙ ❧_

A venerated scholar of ancient and esoteric traditions, Manly P. Hall (1901–1990), wrote more than thirty-three books, delivered more than 8,000 lectures around the world, and authored  hundreds of essays and articles. In 1934, Hall founded the Philosophical Research Society (PRS) in Los Angeles, for the study of the world's mythical, philosophical, and spiritual traditions, emphasizing symbolical, esoteric, and ethical philosophy. He worked and studied there for most of his life, assembling an extraordinary library of rare texts and antiquities. Hall's "Great Book," _The Secret Teachings of All Ages_ (1928), remains unparalleled as an encyclopedic codex of mystical traditions and symbols, and has inspired generations of scholars and seekers. Learn more about his work, publications, and ongoing classes and programs based on his ideals at www.prs.org.

ABOUT MITCH HOROWITZ

Mitch Horowitz is a historian of alternative spirituality and one of today's most literate voices of esoterica, mysticism, and the occult. A PEN Award-winning author, Mitch's books include *Occult America; One Simple Idea: How Positive Thinking Reshaped Modern Life;* and *The Miracle Club.* A frequent presence in national media, Mitch is among the only occult figures whose work touches the bases of academic scholarship, national journalism, and subculture cred. Mitch's book *Awakened Mind* is one of the first works of New Thought translated and published in Arabic. Mitch received the Walden Award for Interfaith/Intercultural Understanding. The Chinese government has censored his work. Twitter: @Mitch Horowitz | Instagram: @MitchHorowitz23

Printed in the USA
CPSIA information can be obtained
at www.ICGtesting.com
JSHW011906070824
67747JS00012B/370